文化发展论丛·世界卷（2014）

湖北大学高等人文研究院　中华文化发展协同创新中心◎编

主　编◎强以华
副主编◎李家莲

Culture Development Review: World (2014)

社会科学文献出版社
SOCIAL SCIENCES ACADEMIC PRESS (CHINA)

"经济不平等与世界公正"研究专辑

《文化发展论丛》编辑委员会

顾　问

中国卷　陶德麟　李景源　唐凯麟

世界卷　万俊人　邓晓芒　John Abbarno（阿巴尔诺）
　　　　　Thomas Magnell（麦格勒尔）

湖北卷　冯天瑜　郭齐勇　刘玉堂

总　编　尹汉宁　刘建凡　江　畅

副总编　喻立平　杨鲜兰　戴茂堂

编　委（以姓氏笔划为序）

万明明　王　扬　王忠欣　王泽应　邓晓红
冯　军　刘川鄂　刘文祥　刘建凡　刘　勇
江　畅　孙伟平　李义天　杨鲜兰　吴成国
何元国　余卫东　沈壮海　张庆宗　张建军
陈少峰　陈　俊　陈道德　陈焱光　周海春
姚才刚　秦　宣　徐方平　高乐田　郭康松
郭熙煌　曹荣湘　舒红跃　强以华　靖国平
廖声武　戴木才　戴茂堂

目录

构建经济公正的世界
　　——在第二届"世界文化发展论坛"（2014）上的致辞　　江　畅 / 001
Building a World with Economic Justice
　　—Address at the World Cultural Development Forum (2014)（*Jiang Chang*）

总序：渴望全球正义　　强以华 / 012

推动世界走向经济公正
　　——第二届"世界文化发展论坛"（2014）明尼苏达宣言　　 / 021
Promoting the World Economic Justice
　　—World Cultural Development Forum (2014) Minnesota Declaration

理论前沿

德福平衡原理视角下的经济不平等与社会公正　　周海春 / 031
Economic Inequality and Social Justice from the Perspective of
　　Virtue-Luck Balance（*Zhou Haichun*）

就业：当今世界的巨大挑战　　Hortensia Cuéllar / 048
Employment：Today's Big Challenge（*Hortensia Cuéllar*）

论坛专题

罗尔斯正义论视角下的中国分配公正问题研究　　孙友祥　杨杏蓉 / 069
Distributive Justice in China from the Perspective of
　　Rawls' Theory of Justice（*Sun Youxiang*；*Yang Xingrong*）

经济不平等与世界性的环境正义　　文贤庆　李培超 / 079
Economic Inequality and Globally Environmental Justice（*Wen Xianqing*；*Li Peichao*）

社会公平——中西方共同的社会理想　　昌灏　徐方平 / 091
Social Justice：The Common Social Ideals in China and
　　Western Countries（*Chang Hao*；*Xu Fangping*）

论社会公正与公共善　　Carmen Ramos G. de C. / 100
A Brief Note About Social Justice and Common Good（*Carmen Ramos G. de C.*）

经济不平等与世界正义：自由主义教育　　Corazon T. Toralba / 109
Economic Inequality and World Justice：Liberal Education（*Corazon T. Toralba*）

论中国经济发展不平等中的教育公平　　张庆宗　靖国平 / 121
On China's Equity in Education Against Its Inequality in
　　Economic Development（*Zhang Qingzong*；*Jing Guoping*）

问题探讨

考察正义的两种方法　　彭定光　李桂梅 / 139
Two Ways to Inquire Justice（*Peng Dingguang*；*Li Guimei*）

人类情感与经济正义　　李家莲 / 145
Human Sentiments and Economic Justice（*Li Jialian*）

论语言意识形态与语言秩序
　　——以美国孔子学院风波为例　　郭熙煌 / 158
Language Ideology & Order：A Case Study of the Confucius
　　Institute Incident in U. S.（*Guo Xihuang*）

强"魂"健"体":建设当代中国主流文化的关键　　陈　俊　柳丹飞 / 169
Strengthening the "Soul" and Improving the "Body":
　　Key to Build up Contemporary Chinese Mainstream Culture（*Chen Jun*；*Liu Danfei*）

康德谈两性关系　　　　　　　　　　　　　　　　　徐　瑾 / 180
On Relationship Between Man and Woman by Kant（*Xu Jin*）

哈马克论经济不平等与世界正义　　　　　　　　A. L. Samian / 189
Hamka's Perspective on Economic Inequality and World Justice（*A. L. Samian*）

无灌输的教育:全球公民理想与伦理挑战　　　Paul A. Swift / 201
Education Without Indoctrination: The Ideal and Challenge of
　　Ethical Training for Global Citizenship（*Paul A. Swift*）

学术争鸣

国际经济正义中的几个问题辨析　　　　　　　　　强以华 / 215
Some Issues in International Economic Justice（*Qiang Yihua*）

伟业呼唤公义:经济不平等与世界正义对
　　正义的呼唤　　　　　　　　　　Thomas Menamparampil / 226
When Great Achievements Fail to Combine with Fairness: A Plea for Fairness
　　by Economic Inequality and World Justice（*Thomas Menamparampil*）

全球不平等与正义:遥远的门扉　　　　　　　　Lydia Amir / 264
Inequality and Justice in a Global World: The Distant Poor（*Lydia Amir*）

反思全球正义与道德责任　　　　　　　　　　G. J. M. Abbarno / 293
Re-thinking Global Justice and Moral Responsibility（*G. J. M. Abbarno*）

论当代中国价值观　　　　　　　　　　　　　　　　江　畅 / 305
On Values of Contemporary China（*Jiang Chang*）

构建经济公正的世界

——在第二届"世界文化发展论坛"(2014)上的致辞

江 畅

各位同仁：

我们来自世界七个国家的学者聚集于美国明尼苏达的圣托马斯大学讨论"经济不平等与世界公正"问题，我代表"世界文化发展论坛"(2014)的主办方欢迎大家。这次论坛是由湖北大学高等人文研究院、美国高等教育价值学会、湖南师范大学中国道德文化协同创新中心、国际价值哲学学会、中国伦理学学会联合主办，由美国高等教育价值学会、湖北大学高等人文研究院承办的。这次论坛是继去年9月在湖北大学举办的首届"世界文化发展论坛"(2013)之后的第二届，我们希望本论坛不断地举办下去，而且越办越有影响，通过世界各国学者的共同努力，推动世界主流文化的发展，推进人类的和平、进步和幸福。

大家都承认，今天的世界是一个不公正的世界，这种不公正是世界各国现代化进程起点先后不一的直接后果。由于现实世界极不公正，因而世界公正问题是当代人类普遍关注的重大人类问题。在最一般的意义上，世界公正是指世界各国、世界不同区域、世界人民，以及当代世界的人类与后代世界的人类得其所应得，或者说各得其所。虽然人们对公正及世界公正的具体含义有种种不同看法，却是可以形成一般性共识的。世界公正涉及许多方面，如经济公正、政治公正、文化公正、教育公正、社会保障公正、环境公正，以及代际公正。其中，经济公正是最基本的公正。之所以如此，是因为经济公正是其他一切公正的基础，没有经济公正，就不会有其他的公正。当代世界的不公正体现在经济、政治、文化、教育、社会保障、环境等各个方面，但最明显的在于经济不公正，而且经济不公正是其他所有不公正的主要原因之所在。

当代世界经济不公正主要体现为经济不平等，而这种经济不平等尤其体现为当今世界富人与穷人、富国与穷国、富裕地区与贫穷地区两极分化十分严重。世界银行 2005 年公布了一份根据新标准评出的世界各国财富排行榜。根据这一新标准，世界银行对全球 118 个国家进行了财富评估。其中，瑞士以人均占有财富 64.8241 万美元居排行榜之首，而埃塞俄比亚人均占有财富最少，仅为 1965 美元。非洲撒哈拉沙漠南部的国家几乎囊括十大最贫穷国家，而最富有的十个国家除日本外都分布在欧洲和北美。[①] 有报道称，全球最富的 300 人拥有的财富比全球最穷的 30 亿人（几乎相当于地球上一半的人口）的财富总和还要多。更加糟糕的是，全球最富有的 200 人拥有大约 2.7 万亿美元的财富，远远多于 35 亿最穷人口 2.2 万亿美元的财富总和。有一个报告的数据还更加残酷地说明了世界不平等以及这种不平等将会进一步加剧：最近 20 年，1% 最富者的收入增加了 60%，金融危机不但没有阻止反而加速了他们财富的增加，其中 0.01% 最富者的收入增长最快；与此同时贫富差距在不断扩大，在殖民统治时期，富国与穷国之间的收入差距已从 3∶1 扩大到 35∶1，部分原因在于欧洲列强以自然资源和劳动力形式从南方国家掠夺了大量财富，而现在这个差距已经扩大到将近 80∶1。[②] 另外，根据联合国粮农组织、世界粮食计划署和国际农业发展基金会联合发布的《世界粮食不安全状况》报告，目前处于长期饥饿中的人口已经有所下降，这一数字在 2010 年到 2012 年曾达到 8.68 亿。目前，世界上绝大多数的饥饿人口分布在

---

① 参见《世行新标准下富国排行：瑞士最富埃塞俄比亚最穷》，新华网 2005 年 9 月 19 日，http://news.xinhuanet.com/fortune/2005 - 09/19/content_3509261.htm。
② 参见《外媒：全球贫富差距不断拉大引人忧》，《参考消息》2013 年 8 月 8 日。

发展中国家，只有1570万人分布在发达国家。① 所有这些事实表明，今日的世界在经济上极其不平等，贫富两极分化已成为任何人都不可否认的严峻现实。在这种情况下，我们也许无论在什么意义上都不能说今天的世界在经济上是公正的。

导致今天世界经济不公正的原因很复杂，其中最重要的原因有以下三个方面。第一，富裕国家和地区基本上是现代化先行并已实现的国家，而贫穷的国家主要是没有实现现代化或现代化尚未完成的国家。近代以来的人类现代化是建立在市场经济基础上的，而按亚当·斯密的看法，市场经济是通往富裕和谐的康庄大道。一个国家实现了现代化，就意味着它建立起了完善的市场经济体系，因而走向了富裕，而完全没有实现现代化的国家通常是贫穷落后的。第二，富裕国家和地区都是社会政治稳定的国家和地区，而贫穷的国家和地区大多长期处于动荡和战乱的状态。一个国家或区域的社会政治稳定状况是其富裕还是贫穷的直接原因。许多贫穷的国家之所以贫穷，直接的原因就在于这些国家长期处于战乱中，社会无序，民不聊生。第三，富裕国家对贫穷国家在经济上以及军事上、政治上、文化上不断地掠夺和渗透。有研究表明，富国与穷国之间的收入差距之所以会从殖民统治之前的3∶1扩大到今天的将近80∶1，部分原因在于欧洲列强以自然资源和劳动力形式从殖民地国家掠夺了大量财富。② 近代以来，世界长期存在财富单纯地从贫穷国家流往富有国家的"虹吸现象"。富国政府和跨国机构经常宣传它们向发展中国家提供了多少援助，却从不提它们从贫困国家中掠夺了多少财富。③ 世界银行、国际货币基金组织和世界贸易组织等国际机构最近几十年向发展中国家推行的新自由主义经济政策，虽然是为强制实行市场自由化而设计的，但结果是最终让跨国公司前所未有地获得了廉价的土地、自然资源和劳动力。据马萨诸塞大学经济学家罗伯特·波林统计，贫困国家每年

---

① 《世界饥饿人口下降，但数百万人仍处于长期饥饿中》，联合国世界粮食计划署网站 http://cn.wfp.org/news/news-release/global-hunger-down-millions-still-chronically-hungry。
② 参见《外媒：全球贫富差距不断拉大引人忧》，《参考消息》2013年8月8日。
③ 参见《外媒：全球贫富差距不断拉大引人忧》，《参考消息》2013年8月8日。

因此失去大约5000亿美元的GDP。这也是拉大穷国和富国之间经济差距的重要原因之一。今天世界的经济严重不平等，其根源就主要在于以上三个方面。要消除世界经济的极度不平等，建立经济公正的世界，必须找出世界经济极度不平等的根源，建立经济相对平等的国际秩序。

世界经济公正并不意味着世界各国经济完全平等，而是意味着世界各国经济有差异的平等，或者合理的不平等。那么，世界经济合理的不平等限度何在呢？笔者认为，这种限度主要在于以下三个方面。首先，在市场经济化的当代世界，世界经济合理的不平等首先意味着公平的竞争。在市场经济成为当代各国基本经济形态的情况下，竞争不可避免，但这种竞争必须是公平的。所谓公平的竞争，就是在规则平等的条件下，各国、各地区、各个体（包括个人和企业）凭借实力竞争，而非凭借强力竞争。在公平竞争条件下产生的不平等结果一般来说应该被认为是合理的。其次，在世界各国、各地区和各个体已经形成贫富、强弱的格局的情况下，强者和有关的国际组织必须给处于不利地位的国家、地区和个体的经济自主发展保留空间，使它们主要通过自己的努力摆脱贫弱的状况，逐渐走上富裕强大之路。在这种前提之下，存在的不平等也应看作合理的不平等。最后，联合国、世界银行等国际组织，通过有效的措施给世界最贫困的人口提供起码的生活保障，给最贫穷落后的国家或地区提供经济起飞的必要条件，使它们站在竞争的起跑线上。有了这种起码的生活保障和适当的援助后存在的经济不平等是基本合理的。总之，今天世界经济不平等只能是世界经济主体（国家、地区和个体）在自主发展、公平竞争下形成的不平等，而且这种不平等的前提是它们都有基本的生活保障和竞争的必要条件。这样的不平等是今天人们可以接受的不平等，也可以说这就是当代世界可能达到的经济平等或经济公正。显然，这种经济平等或经济公正还是层次比较低的公正。那种更高层次的经济公正，除了给贫穷者提供生活保障和经济支持之外，还必须给那些最富有者更多的限制，使世界各国、各地区和个人的收入结构趋向最合理的结构模式。

在现阶段，要实现世界经济公正，我们需要做以下工作。第一，消灭战争和动乱。战争和动乱是许多国家贫困的根源，要消灭贫穷，首先必须消灭战争，包括国内的战争和国外的武装干预。在全球化的今天，无论是制止国家战争，还是扼制外国干预，都需要联合国发挥作用。目前联合国的维和部队已在这方面发挥了作用，但作用还很小。对于那些本国无力解决战乱的国家，联合国要实行武力接管，直到其政局完全稳定。第二，消除国家之间直接的以及变相的（如军事的、文化的、意识形态的）经济掠夺和渗透。今天，跨国公司已成为发达国家掠夺发展中国家并向其渗透的主要形式，而控制世界经济的机构仍然由西方国家垄断，所出台的政策有利于跨国公司，于是，跨国公司的权力有时甚至超过了国家主权。要改变日益悬殊的贫富差距，改变现状，就需要改变规则，创建全球民主监督机制来制止贪婪和商业主义。[①] 第三，发达国家特别是有关国际组织要给发展中国家提供经济增长所需的适当的扶植。一些发达国家的发达是与对发展中国家的掠夺相关的，因而发达国家有责任和义务在资金和技术方面支持和援助发展中国家，助其经济起飞。要改变相关国际组织由发达国家控制的现状，使之成为世界走向经济公正的协调组织。第四，联合国要给由于各种原因沦为最贫困国家的人民提供起码的生活保障。联合国要通过改革和改组提高其权威性，确定世界生活贫困线，通过世界税收的形式设立贫困救助基金，对生活在贫穷线下的国家的人民提供起码的生活保障，减少直至完全消灭世界上生活在贫困线下的人口，使我们的世界真正成为人道主义的世界。

最后预祝本次论坛取得圆满成功！谢谢大家！

---

① 《外媒：全球贫富差距不断拉大引人忧》，《参考消息》2013年8月8日。

Building a World with Economic Justice
—Address at the World Cultural Development Forum (2014)

Jiang Chang

Dear Colleagues, Ladies and Gentlemen,

While seven scholars from seven different countries stay together in the University of St. Thomas to discuss the issue of "Economic Inequality and World Justice", please let me extend warmest welcome to you on behalf of the organizing committee of World Culture Development Forum of 2014. Co-hosted by Institute for Advanced Humanistic Studies in Hubei University, the Society for Values in Higher Education, the Collaborative Innovation Center of Chinese Moral Culture, International Society for Value Inquiry, and China National Association for Ethical Studies, the Forum is co-organized by the Society for Values in Higher Education and Institute for Advanced Humanistic Studies in Hubei University. Following the First World Culture Development Forum at Hubei University last September, the Forum is the second one. We hope the Forum will be continuously held with more and more influence, and we hope we could advance the development of the world mainstream culture and promote human peace, progress and happiness with the contribution of scholars from different countries in the world.

We all recognize that we are living in an unjust world, which results from different starting points of modernization in different countries. Such injustice makes world's justice an important human issue, a focus of attention in contemporary world. In the most general sense, world justice means that all the countries, all the regions, and people of the world, as well as contemporary human and our next generations get what they deserve, or what they want. Although people have different views on the specific meaning of the world justice, it is possible for them to reach a general consensus. World justice involves many aspects, such as economic justice, political justice, cultural justice, educational justice, social security justice, and environmental justice, as well as intergenerational justice. Among them, economic justice is the fundamental one, because economic justice is the foundation of other fairness. Without economic justice, there will be no other justice. World injustice is reflected in economy, politics, culture, education, social security, environment, etc., among which economic injustice is the most obvious one and the main reason of all the other injustice.

Contemporary world economic injustice is mainly embodied in economic imbalance. While economic imbalance finds its expression in the increasingly widening gap between the rich and the poor, between rich countries and poor countries, and between affluent regions and poor regions. The World Bank published a new standard to evaluate the world's Top Fortune in 2005. According to this new standard, the World Bank conducts an assessment among 118 countries in the world. Among them, with $648,241 per capita wealth, the Switzerland ranks top, while Ethiopia ranks last, with only $1,965 per capita wealth. The ten impoverished nations are almost in the southern Sahara Desert, while the richest ten countries except Japan are located in North America and Europe. It is reported that the collective wealth of the world's richest 300 people is far more than that of the poorest 3 billion people worldwide (almost half the world population). What is worse, the richest 200 people possess about $2.7 trillion, far more than that of the 3.5 billion poorest people whose aggregate wealth is about $2.2 trillion. A report of the data also illustrates that the world imbalance exists and will be further intensified in a more crucial way: In recent 20 years, the income of the 1% richest people increases 60%; the financial crisis do not hinder their development, but increase their income, among them the 0.01% richest people enjoy the fastest income increasing. Meanwhile, the gap between the rich and the poor is widening. During the colonial period, the income gap between the rich and the poor countries was widened from 3:1 to 35:1, partly because that the European powers plundered the nature resources and labor sources from the southern countries. Now the gap has expanded to nearly 80:1. In addition, according to the "SOFI" which is jointly issued by the FAO, WFP and IFAD, now people in hunger has been declined. During 2010 to 2012, this figure once reached 868 million. Currently, most worlds' hungry people live in developing countries, while only 1.57 million people live in developed countries. All these facts indicate that poverty has become an undeniable reality. In this case, we can not say that today's world economy is justice.

Reasons leading to the world economic injustice are complex, and the major 3 reasons are as follows. First, rich countries and regions start modernization in advance or achieve their modernization, while impoverished nations do not achieve their modernization or do not accomplish their modernization. Since modern times, our modernization is built on the basis of market economy. However, in Adam Smith's view, the market economy is the path to rich and harmonious society. To most countries, achieving modernization means a perfect market economy mechanism has been established. And the countries are on the path to wealthy, while countries which do not realize modernization are usually poor and backward. Second, rich countries and regions enjoy social and political stability, while impoverished nations and regions are mostly in turmoil and long-term wars. Country's social and political stability is the direct cause deciding its wealthy. Why are impoverished nations so poor? The direct cause lies in their long-term war, social disorder, and people in times of hardship. Third, the rich countries plunder and penetrate impoverished nations in military, economy, politics, and culture. Studies have shown that the income gap between the rich and the poor has been expanded from 3∶1 in colonial period to today's 80∶1, partly because that the European powers plunder the nature resources and labor sources from colonies. In modern times, "siphoning" that the world's wealth one-way flows from the impoverished nation the rich countries has long existed. Governments in rich countries and transnational organizations often promote their assistance to developing countries, but never mention how much wealth they plunder from impoverished nations. Over last decades, the World Bank, International Monetary Fund and the World Trade Organization and other international institutions promote neoliberal economic policies towards developing countries. The neoliberal economic policies is designed to enforce the market liberalization. However it finally benefits transnational cooperation, bringing them cheap land, natural resources and labor. According to the statistics collected by Robert Pollin (University of Massachusetts), this makes impoverished countries lose about $500 billion of GDP annually. This is also one of the major reasons why the economic gap between the rich and the poor is expanded. Why today's world economic imbalance is so serious, the major reason lies in the above three aspects. To eliminate the extreme imbalance in the world economy and establish economic justice, we must find the root which leads to such imbalance, and establish a relatively balanced world order.

World economic justice does not mean that the world economy is totally balanced, but means a differentiated balance, or reasonable balance. Well, where the reasonable limit for the world economic inequality lies? I believe that this reasonable limit mainly lies in the following three aspects. First, in today's market economy, the reasonable imbalance means fair competition. As the market economy has become the basic form of economy in most countries, competition is inevitable, but this competition must be fair. The so-called fair competition means that under fair rules, countries, regions, and each individual (including individuals and companies) compete by strength rather than by their power. Under fair competition, the unequal results should be considered as reasonable in general. Secondly, countries, regions and individuals have formed the pattern of rich or poor, strong or weak. The strong one and relevant international organizations must leave some room for disadvantageous countries, regions and individuals to develop their economy, so that they can shake off poverty through their own efforts and gradually embark on a path of prosperity. Under this condition, the existing imbalance should be regarded as reasonable one. Finally, the United Nations, the World Bank and other international organizations, should take effective measures to guarantee the minimum life security for the poorest and provide necessary conditions for backward countries to boost their economy, so that they can have the access to competition. And after guaranteeing the minimum life security and providing appropriate assistance, the economic imbalance is reasonable. In conclusion, today's world economic imbalance can only exist in the self-development of, and fair competition among world economic subjects (national, regional and individual). And the precondition is that they have a basic subsistence. This imbalance is what today's people may accept, or in other words, this is the economic equality or justice which modern world might achieve. Apparently, this economic equity is still at low level. While the higher level economic justice requires more limitation towards the development of the richest, besides provide the minimum life security and economic support, so that the income pattern of the countries, regions, and individuals turns into "olive shape".

At the present stage, to build the world economy, we must accomplish the following tasks. First, we must eliminate wars and turmoil. Wars and turmoil are the origin of poverty in many countries. To eliminate poverty, we must eliminate wars first, including national war and international military intervention. As the globalization deepens, both stopping national conflict and international military intervention requires the help of the United Nations. At present, the peacekeeping troops take effect, but their contribution is quiet limited. For countries failed to solve wars, the United Nations should take over by military force, until it achieves social stability. Second, we should eliminate the directly and other kind of plunder and penetration (e. g. in military, culture, ideology) between nations. Today, multinational companies have become the main form for developing countries plundering and penetrating developed countries. On the other hand, the world economic organizations are monopolized by the developed countries, their policies are beneficial to transnational counties. Therefore, sometimes the power of transnational companies surpasses sovereignty. To narrow the gap between the rich and the poor, and to change the current situation, we need to change the rules and create a democratic international supervision mechanism to stop the greed and commercialism. Third, the developed countries, especially related international organizations, should help developing countries boost their economy. Since many developed countries achieve their economic success by plundering developing countries, therefore developed countries have responsibilities and obligations in offering developing countries financial and technical support as well as economic assistance. We should change the current situation that related international organizations are controlled by developed countries, thus making the world economy coordinated and justice. Fourth, the United Nations should provide the minimum living support for all the people living in the poorest countries regardless of the reasons. The United Nations should improve its authority by reform and reorganization, set the poverty line, establish the poverty relief funds by tax, provide basic life guarantee for countries living under the poverty line, and thus decrease and eventually eliminate hungry and poverty in the world. In this way, our world can be a humanitarian world.

Last but not least, I'd like to extend my best wishes to the Forum.

Thanks.

总序：渴望全球正义

强以华

为了更好地探讨世界文化的发展，以及世界文化的发展与社会正义、经济增长的关系，湖北大学高等人文研究院在 2013 年于武汉举办了第一届"世界文化发展论坛"（2013）的基础上，2014 年 7 月 18～19 日在美国明尼苏达州圣托马斯大学（University of St. Thomas）与该校联合举办了第二届"世界文化发展论坛"（2014），来自印度、菲律宾、马来西亚、以色列、美国、墨西哥、中国等 7 个国家的 23 位学者参与了这一论坛。这一届"世界文化发展论坛"的主题是"经济不平等与世界公正"。在全球化的背景下，不同国家、不同地区之间的世界公正是一个重要并且紧迫的现实问题。在世界公正的问题上，经济的不平等具有最为重要的影响，它不仅影响着当今世界的平等和正义，甚至还进一步影响着当今世界的进一步发展。因此，本届论坛以"经济不平等与世界公正"为主题乃是主办单位精心筹划的结果。与会专家围绕"经济不平等与世界公正"这一主题，就共同关心的问题各抒己见，进行了深入的讨论和广泛的交流，有效地推动了对于经济不平等和世界公正问题的进一步认识，在一些具体问题上达成了广泛的共识。在这些共识的基础上，会议发表了《推动世界走向经济公正——第二届"世界文化发展论坛"（2014）明尼苏达宣言》，并且征集了一批学术质量颇高的学术论文。为了让学界共享本次论坛的学术成果，尤其是为了让本次论坛的成果能够在一定的程度上影响社会，我们遴选了一些优秀论文，并且邀请了国内其他一些有影响的专家学者撰写了相关论文,编辑成这本《文化发展论丛·世界卷(2014)》。

一 理论前沿

在栏目"理论前沿"中,论丛选择了国内学者周海春的论文《德福平衡原理视角下的经济不平等与社会公正》和国外学者 Hortensia Cuéllar 的论文《就业:当今世界的巨大挑战》(Employment: Today's Big Challenge)。这两篇论文或为"经济不平等和世界公正"问题的研究提供了具有重要创新意义的视角,或为"经济不平等和世界公正"问题的研究提供了具有重要创新意义的内容。

其中,周海春教授的论文从一个全新的视角探讨了经济不平等与社会公正的问题,从而为我们探讨当前国际社会"经济不平等与世界公正"的问题提供了非常重要的研究思路。周海春教授认为,经济不平等是一个广泛存在的现象,现代社会会碰到,在古代社会也不会缺席。哪里有不平等,哪里就有公正的呼唤,就有正义的诉求。但是,目前讨论经济不平等与社会公正的思想大多出自西方的经验,较少从中国古代的道德原理出发。他试图从一种新的经验,即中国古代道德原理的德福平衡的价值观出发来为探讨经济不平等和社会公正的问题提供一种新的视角。根据作者的观点,尽管经济不平等是一个广泛存在的现象,但是,在中国古代社会,好像公正的呼声很弱,之所以造成了这种现象,乃是因为中国古代有某种独特的价值观念把社会公正的呼唤给默默地化解了,以至于人们形成了一套观察经济不平等乃至其他形式的不平等的视角,这种独特的价值观念就是德福平衡的价值观念。在周海春教授看来,在中国古代的传统文化特别是《国语》中包含了德福平衡的原理,中国文化传统中的德福平衡原理大略包括如下内容:其一,德和福都包含丰富的内容,具有一定的普遍性;其二,福依存于德,德是福的基础,德可以带来福,德可以转换成福,二者之间具有一定的对应关系;其三,德和福在总量确定的前提下可以互相转换;其四,福德总量的增长和二者比值的调节与人的努力有关，从中也可以体认天命。德福的平衡是天来调节的，也是人来调节的，体现了天人相因；其五，节俭是具有道德完备性的德行，而骄奢是不完备的品行。在这种德福平衡理论的基础上，周海春教授进一步考察了中国传统文化中的基于德福平衡的自利问题。在他看来，在中国传统文化中，自利包括"福利"（福报意义上的福利）的自利和功德的自利。福利包含财富以及对于财富的认知、价值评价、幸福感，还包含人伦情怀，例如为了家庭、朋友、团体、国家、民族而进行经济活动，此外，它还包含了个人的自由、权利、独立和个性。福利的多样化理解是公正的条件之一。更为重要的是，"公正不仅存在于福利多样性之间，还存在于福利和功德之间。那些专注于功德的人能够也乐于接受社会财富方面的损失，而且往往把财富施舍给他人看成美德"。"当人关注心灵的无限性自身的时候，也就是中国传统文化所说的觉悟的时候，对福利的渴望下降了，福利的不平等形成的动机因素也减弱了，这一点是中国文化传统避免社会不公带来社会动荡的重要的经验"。周海春教授认为，根据中国传统文化中的德福一致观点，若把功德和福利的运作看成受到罗尔斯原初状态概念的启发但又有别于罗尔斯原初状态概念的一种基本的原初状态，那么，我们在改造性地借鉴罗尔斯原初状态等理论的情形下，就可以通过另一种路径探讨正义共识与社会公正的问题。我们认为，周海春教授的论文视野独特，值得一读。

二 论坛专题

在栏目《论坛专题》中，论丛选择了一组国内学者的论文和一组国外学者的论文。国内学者的论文包括昌灏和徐方平的《社会公平——中西方共同的社会理想》、孙友祥和杨杏蓉的《罗尔斯正义论视角下的中国分配公正问题研究》、张庆宗的《论中国经济发展不平等中的教育公平》（On China's Equity in Education Against Its Inequality in Economic Development）、文贤庆和李培超的《经济不平等与世界性的环境正义》；国外学者的论文包括菲律宾的托拉巴（Corazon T. Toralba）的《经济不平等与世界正义：自由主义教育》(Economic Inequality and World Justice: Liberal Education)。

孙友祥和杨杏蓉在罗尔斯正义论的视角下探讨了中国的分配公正问题。他们认为，正如分配公正是人类社会永恒的价值追求一样，随着中国经济改革开放以来的突飞猛进，以及随着中国经济突飞猛进而带来的财富的剧增，中国社会也面临着如何让人民群众公正地共享社会财富的问题，也就是说，中国社会也面临着如何实现分配公正的问题。为了解决这一问题，他们借鉴了罗尔斯的分配正义观，指出分配公正作为"社会基本善"，应该像罗尔斯的设想一样以正义的社会制度、正义环境和正义原则为基础。因此，化解当代中国的分配格局失衡、实现分配公正需要秉持"公平的机会平等原则"，以保障公民政治权利平等；并且秉持"有差别的对待原则"，以合理地差别对待。作者的观点具有一定的启发意义。

面对国际经济不平等，建构国际正义不仅需要探讨国际经济不平等的原因，探讨走向国际正义的路径，还需要探讨者以及建构者具有特定的知识背景和实际能力。在这方面，菲律宾马尼拉亚洲太平洋大学的托罗巴（Corazon T. Toralba）博士的论文《经济不平等与世界正义：自由主义教育》做了十分有益的探索。他在论文中重点探讨了通过自由主义教育来解决经济不平等并且走向国际正义的问题。他运用圣托马斯·阿奎那的正义观念并把菲律宾作为一个案例来对经济不平等的原因和结果进行跨学科的研究。在研究中，他指出仅仅用经济的手段来解决经济问题是不够的，还需要通过自由主义教育来解决经济不平等从而走向国际正义。在他看来，"自由主义教育是一种学习增强个体能力和让他们准备处理复杂性、多样性和变动性的方法。它给学生提供广阔的世界性知识以及帮助学生在特殊的兴趣领域进行深入的研究。自由主义教育帮助学生发展社会责任感，并且帮助他们加强智力和实践技巧，例如传播技巧、分析技巧和解决问题的技巧，展示他们把知识和技巧应用与现实世界的能力"。他详细分析了自由主义教育对于建构国际经济正义的具体作用。我们相信，他的论文能给读者以十分有益的启迪。

三 问题探讨

在栏目《问题探讨》中,论丛也选择了一组国内学者的论文和一组国外学者的论文。国内学者的论文包括彭定光和李桂梅的《考察正义的两种方法》、李家莲的《人类情感与经济正义》、郭熙煌的《论语言意识形态与语言秩序》、陈俊的《强"魂"健"体":建设当代中国主流文化的关键》;国外学者的论文包括萨米尔(A. L. Samian)的《哈马克论经济不平等与世界正义》(Hamka's Perspective on Economic Inequality and World Justice)和斯威夫特(Paul A. Swift)的《无灌输的教育:全球公民理想与伦理挑战》(Education without Indoctrination: The Ideal and Challenge of Ethical Training for Global Citizenship)。

湖南师范大学伦理学研究所的彭定光和李桂梅的论文《考察正义的两种方法》探讨了分析正义的"方法论"问题。文章认为,分析正义问题具有两种方法:一种是从个体、差异、局部或者个别现象考察正义的个体论方法;另一种是从整体、全体或者总体考察正义的整体论方法。不同的方法决定着对于正义社会(包括国际正义社会)的不同的理解和不同设计。个体论方法虽然提出了一些具有建设性的观点,但是,从总体上说,它包含了抽象化(抽象出整体的现实生活的某一方面或因素来解释整体现实生活)、还原论(把对于整体社会的正义的考察还原为对于个人或者个体的道德把握)和非历史性(脱离社会的历史过程来考察、理解正义,并且脱离社会固有的整体性质和历史变化来考察、理解正义)三种缺陷。这种方法不可避免地会导致的结果是:在什么是真正的正义问题上争论不休,并难以达成正义共识。整体性方法主要具有三重分析维度。其一,结构,它把人类社会生活的整体看成不同要素组成的层层递进的结构,主张从结构整体的角度来理解社会,同时兼顾"增进社会整体利益和个人利益",认为只有这样的行为才是正义的行为;其二,过程,它把人类社会生活看成有所区别的从过去来到现在再走向未来的整体性和统一性,主张从历史发展的角度来理解社会,同时兼顾差异性和整体性,认为只有超越了以往历史阶段并且体现了社会历史整体的社会才是正义的社会;其三,目标,它把社会整体的最终目标和具体目标统一起来,主张在最终目标的引导下看待具体目标,同时兼顾最终目标和具体目标,认为"真正的正义"总是与最终目标密切关联的正义。文章指出,整体论的方法克服了个体论方法的上述缺陷,它把结构、过程和目标统一起来,是依据社会生活的各个方面来考察正义的正确方法。因此,若要探讨社会正义,我们应该采取整体论的方法。我们认为,探讨社会正义,其中包括从经济不平等和社会正义关系的角度探讨国际社会正义,不仅涉及内容的探讨,也会涉及方法的探讨,采用正确的方法来考察社会正义,进行正确的价值判断和正义设计,是探讨国际正义的必要条件之一。

围绕经济不平等和国际正义问题,除了方法的探讨之外,还有一些论文探讨了其他问题,其中,美国布莱恩特大学(Bryant University)斯威夫特教授的论文《无灌输的教育:全球公民理想与伦理挑战》探讨了全球公民伦理培训的理想和挑战的问题。这篇文章首先介绍了五种已经存在过的伦理教育,包括神正论、实用主义、道义论、义务论、基于美德的伦理和大同主义。文章指出,这五种伦理教育都有自己的缺陷,但是后者都比前者更加进步。在此基础上,这篇文章重点分析了大同主义对于国际政治、经济不平等以及公正问题的启示以及教育公民成为国际公民的意义。在作者看来,不仅前大同主义的几种伦理教育存在缺陷,而且大同主义的伦理教育也同样存在缺陷。但是,尽管如此,大同主义理想对于建立世界公正来说依然十分有意义。为了贯彻大同主义,训练人们像国际公民那样来思考和行动,就必须克服一系列的相关困难。这些困难包括以下几点。其一,知识要求上的严格性。大同主义的方法比其他四种伦理教育的方法更加苛刻。它要求人们学习的不仅仅是自己社团的东西,它还要求人们对人类的历史和文化有高度的敏感度和适应力。其实,正因为大同主义伦理教育与其他伦理教育相比有对知识的这种特殊要求,因此,若要希望每一个人都能成为世界的一员或自认为自己是世界的一员是不现实的。其二,对种族和性别的包容性。为了培养世界公民，需要知道种族和性别的重要性。大同主义应该能够包容他人的不同观点，而不是狭隘地敌对地看待他人。其三，理论可行性检查的艰难性。对于整体来说是合理的但不一定适用于每一个单独的人的理论通常是无法通过检测的不现实的理论。那么，我们究竟经应该如何处理这样的理论呢？文章虽然没有提供明确的答案，但是在结尾处作者指出可以充分发挥联合国这个国际机构的作用。毫无疑问，斯威夫特教授的大同主义理论有助于人们在全球公民伦理培训中接受挑战，并且促进通过伦理培训培养全球公民，也就是说，大同主义观点不是唯一有用的观点，但却是值得借鉴的观点。

四　学术争鸣

在栏目《学术争鸣》中，论丛既选择了国内学者强以华的论文《国际经济正义中的几个问题辨析》，也选择了国外学者麦伦帕拉姆派尔（Thomas Menamparampil）的论文《伟业呼唤正义：经济不平等与世界正义对正义的呼唤》（When Great Achievements Fail to Combine with Fairness: A Plea for Fairness by Economic Inequality and World Justice）、艾米尔（Lydia Amir）的论文《全球不平等与正义：遥远的门扉》（Inequality and Justice in a Global World: The Distant Poor）和阿巴诺（G. J. M. Abbarno）的论文《反思全球正义和道德责任》（Re-thinking Global Justice and Moral Responsibility）

湖北大学高等人文研究院强以华教授的论文《国际经济正义中的几个问题辨析》探讨了国际正义中几个极具争议的问题，包括贫富差距问题、国际分工问题和经济秩序问题。文章认为，这些问题虽然包含了国际经济的不正义，但也无须夸大它所包含的国际经济不正义。例如，就贫富差距而言，在当今世界上，东西方的国家之间特别是南北方的国家之间存在严重的贫富差距，并且这种差距还有扩大化的趋势。贫富差距不等于国际不正义，若要判断国际贫富差距是否包含了国际不正义的现象，就必须深入分析造成国际贫富差距的原因。若这些国家之间的贫富差距是这些国家自身的努力程度不同所致，也就是说，若当今世界中发达国家的富仅仅是由它们自身的努力所致而发展中国家的穷仅仅是由于它们的努力不够所致，那么，它们之间的贫富差距就不包含国际经济的不正义，它们也不构成国际经济正义的研究对象；若是这些国家之间的贫富差距是由"与它们自身努力与否"无关的某些外在的偶然性所致，那么，它们之间的贫富差距就包含了国际经济的不正义，它们也就构成了国际经济正义的研究对象。围绕这样的标准，文章通过分析造成当今世界不同国家贫富的国内原因、国外原因和自然原因后指出，当今世界的贫富差距毫无疑问包含了不正义的现象，但是，一些贫穷国家自身努力不够也或多或少是造成它们贫穷的原因之一，因此，我们也无须过分夸大当今世界贫富差距所包含了的不正义现象。文章认为，"只有持有这样的态度，我们才能在如何消除这种不公正性的问题上采取更为务实的态度，即：发展中国家若要彻底消除自己在国际经济领域中遭遇的不公正性，最终还是应该依赖发展中国家提升自己的内在能力，包括提升经济发展的水平，完善自己的制度，发展自己的科技，等等。这就是说，不要等到有了公正的国际经济环境之后再去发展，更为重要的是，应在发展之中争取更为公正的国际经济环境。为此，发展中国家应在坚持不懈地反对各种不公正性的同时，把主要精力放在提升自己的内在能力方面。"此文的落脚点在于如何才能更为有效地消除各种国际不正义的现象。

面对严重的经济不平等这一国际不正义现象，阿巴诺在《反思全球正义和道德责任》中探讨了如何承担道德责任以便消除这一不正义的现象的问题。根据阿巴诺的观点，尽管世贸组织、国际货币基金组织、世界银行这些组织都提出要消灭贫富差距，指出国家无论贫富都应公平地进行贸易往来，甚至通过贷款帮助贫困国家，但是，由于它们的最终目的还是为了获得更大的利益，所以，最后受益的都是那些发达国家，这样，这些国际机构的措施最终拉大了贫富国家之间的贫富差距。例如，从国际货币基金组织贷款来说，表面看来，这些贷款似在帮助贫困国家增长出口货物，并以此来增加财政收入，但事实上这是一种叫作"不平等交换"的开发利用。这些贫穷的出口国家尽管在用原材料和未被开发利用的资源来获得财政收入，但它们在进口成品（其价格更加昂贵）时就会失去这些收入。这种货物和服务的资金流入就是全球化的显著特征之一，这种方式会加大贫富差距。因此，本文作者提出建立一种新的社会合同来改善欠发达国家和发达国家之间的不平衡。这种社会合同是作为整体的国家之间的行为，而非单个公民的行为（因为公民还是受到国家的政策和行为的影响）。根据本文作者的新的社会合同计划，应该重新建设公正公平的国际组织，并且以是否有利于国家进步为标准来建立新的五年计划，通过鼓励当地居民出国学习深造最后回到自己国家帮助经济发展和振兴等措施来帮助发展中的国家。同时由一个世界组织作为国家间国际公正的裁判人，评定哪些行为违背合同，并在国际法院的裁定下，让违约者对于损失者进行补偿。我们认为，作者在力图消除国际经济不平等的问题上，给了我们新的启迪。

推动世界走向经济公正

——第二届"世界文化发展论坛"（2014）明尼苏达宣言

2014年7月18~19日，来自菲律宾、马来西亚、印度、以色列、墨西哥、美国、中国等7个国家的23位学者，相聚在美国明尼苏达州圣托马斯大学，共同讨论当代世界文化发展，其主题是"经济不平等与世界公正"。参加此次论坛的学者就世界文化发展特别是世界经济不平等和世界公正问题达成了共识，并同意发表以下宣言。

今天的世界是一个不公正的世界，由于现实世界极不公正，因而世界公正问题是当代人类普遍关注的重大人类问题。虽然人们对公正及世界公正的具体含义有种种不同看法，却是可以形成一般性共识的。世界公正涉及许多方面，如经济公正、政治公正、文化公正、教育公正、社会保障公正、环境公正，以及代际公正。其中，经济公正是最基本的公正。之所以如此，是因为经济公正是其他一切公正的基础，没有经济公正，就不会有其他的公正。当代世界的不公正体现在经济、政治、文化、教育、社会保障、环境等各个方面，但最明显的在于经济不公正，而且经济不公正是其他所有不公正的主要原因之所在。

当代世界经济不公正主要体现为经济不平等，而这种经济不平等尤其体现为当今世界富人与穷人、富国与穷国、富裕地区与贫穷地区两极分化十分严重。导致今天世界经济不公正的原因很复杂，其中最重要的原因有：其一，富裕国家和地区基本上是现代化先行并已实现的国家，而贫穷的国家主要是没有实现现代化或现代化尚未完成的国家；其二，富裕国家和地区都是社会政治稳定的国家和地区，而贫穷的国家和地区大多长期处于动荡和战乱的状态；其三，富裕国家对贫穷国家在经济上以及军事上、政治上、文化上不断地掠夺和渗透。今天世界的经济严重不平等，其根源就主要就在于以上三个方面。要消除世界经济的极度不平等，建立经济公正的世界，必须找出世界经济极度不平等的根源，建立经济相对平等的国际秩序。

世界经济公正并不意味着世界各国经济完全平等，而是意味着世界各国经济有差异的平等，或者合理的不平等。这种不平等的合理限度主要在于：公平的竞争条件下，各国、各地区、各个体（包括个人和企业）凭实力竞争所产生的不平等结果；在世界各国、各地区和各个体已经形成贫富、强弱的格局下，处于不利地位的国家、地区和个体在经济自主发展保留空间的前提之下存在的不平等；世界最贫困的人口有起码的生活保障和获得经济起飞必要条件之后尚存在的经济不平等。总之，今天世界经济不平等只能是世界经济主体（国家、地区和个体）在自主发展、公平竞争下形成的不平等，而且这种不平等的前提是他们都有基本的生活保障和竞争的必要条件。这样的不平等是今天人们可以接受的不平等，也可以说这就是当代世界可能达到的经济平等或经济公正。显然，这种经济平等或经济公正还是层次比较低的公正。那种更高层次的经济公正，除了给贫穷者提供生活保障和经济支持之外，还必须给那些最富有者更多的限制，使世界各国、各地区和各个人的收入结构趋向最合理的结构模式。

鉴于当代世界存在严重的经济不公正，各国学者要致力于消灭这种不公正，通过自己的学术研究和实践活动推进世界经济公正的构建。为此，我们特别提出以下主张，并将着重在这些方面做出我们的努力。

第一，消灭战争和动乱。战争和动乱是许多国家贫困的根源，要消灭贫穷，首先必须消灭战争，包括国内的战争和国外的武装干预。我们认为，在全球化的今天，无论是制止国家战争，还是抑制外国干预，都需要联合国发挥作用。目前联合国的维和部队已在这方面发挥了作用，但作用还很小。因此，对于那些本国无力解决战乱的国家，联合国要实行武力接管，直到其政局完全稳定。

第二，消除国家之间直接的以及变相的（如军事的、文化的、意识形态的）经济掠夺和渗透。今天，跨国公司已成为发达国家掠夺发展中国家并向其渗透的主要形式，而控制世界经济的机构仍然由西方国家垄断，所出台的政策有利于跨国公司，于是，跨国公司的权力有时甚至超过了国家主权。要改变日益悬殊的贫富差距，改变现状，就需要改变规则，创建全球民主监督机制来制止贪婪和商业主义。

第三，发达国家特别是有关国际组织要给发展中国家提供经济增长所需的适当的扶植。一些发达国家的发达是与对发展中国家的掠夺相关的，因而发达国家有责任和义务在资金和技术方面支持和援助发展中国家，助其经济起飞。要改变相关国际组织由发达国家控制的现状，使之成为世界走向经济公正的协调组织。

第四，联合国要给由于各种原因沦为最贫困国家的人民提供起码的生活保障。联合国要通过改革和改组提高权威性，确定世界生活贫困线，通过世界税收的形式设立贫困救助基金，对生活在贫穷线下的国家的人民提供起码的生活保障，减少直至完全消灭世界上生活在贫困线下的人口，使我们的世界真正成为人道主义的世界。

参加论坛的各国代表签字：

江畅、Hortensia Cuéllar、孙友祥、文贤庆、李培超、徐方平、Centro Cultural Nayar、Corazon T. Toralba、张庆宗、彭定光、李桂梅、李家莲、A. L. Samian、Paul A. Swift 、Amir Lydia、G. J. M. Abbarno

Promoting the World Economic Justice
—World Cultural Development Forum
(2014) Minnesota Declaration

On July 18 – 19, 2014, twenty-three scholars from Philippine, Malaysia, India, Israel, Mexico, USA, China meet at the University of St. Thomas, Minnesota, to discuss contemporary world culture development with the theme of "Economic Inequality and World Justice". All participants have made consensus concerning the issue of economic inequality and world justice, and agreed to make the following declaration.

We all recognize that we are living in an unjust world, which results from different starting points of modernization in different countries. Such injustice makes world's justice an important human issue, a focus of attention in contemporary world. In the most general sense, world justice means that all the countries, all the regions, and people of the world, as well as contemporary human and our next generations get what they deserve, or what they want. Although people have different views on the specific meaning of the world justice, it is possible for them to reach a general consensus. World justice involves many aspects, such as economic justice, political justice, cultural justice, educational justice, social security justice, and environmental justice, as well as intergenerational justice. Among them, economic justice is the fundamental one, because economic justice is the foundation of other fairness. Without economic justice, there will be no other justice. World injustice is reflected in economy, politics, culture, education, social security, environment, etc. , among which economic injustice is the most obvious one and the main reason of all the other injustice.

Contemporary world economic injustice is mainly embodied in economic imbalance. While economic imbalance finds its expression in the increasingly widening gap between the rich and the poor, between rich countries and poor countries, and between affluent regions and poor regions. Reasons leading to the world economy injustice are complex, and the major reasons are as follows: First, rich countries and regions have been modernized in advance or achieve their modernization, while impoverished nations do not achieve their modernization or do not accomplish their modernization. Second, rich countries and regions enjoy social and political stability, while impoverished nations and regions are mostly in turmoil and long-term wars. Third, the rich countries plunder and penetrate impoverished nations in military, economy, politics, and culture. Why is today's world economic imbalance so serious? The major reason lies in the above three aspects. To eliminate the extreme imbalance in the world economy and to establish economic justice, we must find the root which leads to such imbalance, and establish a relatively balanced world order.

World economic justice does not mean that the world economy are totally balanced, but means that it is a differentiated balance, or reasonable balance. The reasonable limit of imbalance lies in: First, under fair conditions, countries, regions, each individual (including individuals and companies) compete by strength, but the result is unequal. This is acceptable. Second, under the current pattern of rich and poor, strong and weak among regions, countries, and individuals, the less developed countries, regions and individuals still have room for self-development. In this case, inequality is acceptable. Third, if the living security and necessary condition for the poor are guaranteed, the economic injustice is acceptable. In conclusion, today's world economic imbalance can only exist in the self-development of, and fair competition among world economic subjects (national, regional and individual). And the precondition is that they have a basic subsistence. This imbalance is what today's people may accept, or in other words, this is the economic equality or justice which modern world might achieve. Apparently, this economic equity is still at low level. While the higher level economic justice requires more limitation towards the development of the richest, besides, it provides the the minimum life security and economic support, so that the income pattern of the countries, regions, and individuals turns into "olive shape".

In view of today's serious economic injustice, scholars devote themselves to eliminate the unfair, through their own academic researches and practical activities to promote the world economic justice. We would like to put forward and focus our effort as follows: First, we must eliminate wars and turmoil. Wars and turmoil are the origin of poverty in many countries. To eliminate poverty, we must eliminate wars first, including national war and international military intervention. We believe that as the globalization deepens, both stopping national conflict and international military intervention requires the effort of the United Nations. At present, the peacekeeping troops take effect, but their contribution is quiet limited. For countries failing to end wars, the United Nations should take over by military force, until it achieves social stability. Second, we should eliminate the direct and other kind of plunder and penetration (e.g. in military, culture, ideology) between nations. Today, multinational companies have become the main form for developing countries plundering and penetrating developed countries. On the other hand, the world economic organizations are monopolized by the developed countries, their polices are beneficial to transnational counties. Therefore, sometimes the power of transnational companies surpasses sovereignty. To narrow the gap between the rich and the poor, and to change the current situation, we need to change the rules and create a democratic international supervision mechanism to stop the greed and commercialism. Third, the developed countries especially related international organizations should help developing countries boost their economy. Since many developed countries achieve their economic success by plundering developing countries, therefore developed countries have responsibilities and obligations in offering developing countries financial and technical support as well as economic assistance. We should change the current situation that related international organizations are controlled by developed countries, thus making the world economy coordinated and justice. Fourth, the United Nations should provide the minimum living support for all the people living in the poorest countries regardless of the reasons. The United Nations should improve its authority by reform and reorganization, set the poverty line, establish the poverty relief funds by tax, provide basic life guarantee for countries living under the poverty line, and thus decrease and eventually eliminate hungry and poverty in the world. In this way, our world can be a humanitarian world.

Signature from the participants of the Forum:

Jiang Chang、Hortensia Cuéllar、Sun Youxiang、Wen Xianqing、Li Peichao、Xu Fangping、Centro Cultural Nayar、Corazon T. Toralba、Zhang Qingzong、Peng Dingguang、Li Guimei、Li Jialian、A. L. Samian、Paul A. Swift 、Amir Lydia、G. J. M. Abbarno

理论前沿

德福平衡原理视角下的经济不平等与社会公正

周海春[*]

摘　要：价值涉及对不同事物的价值估价，中国文化中的"德"与"福"之间就存在一定的对价关系。德福平衡的思想在中国文化中有悠久的历史，《国语·晋语》明确提出这一思想。"德"和"福"的内容在中国文化思想史上是不断拓展的，"德"是"福"的基础，"德"平衡着"福"，构成了"福"不断增长的基础和动力。在诸多美德中，节俭是具有道德完备性的美德，而过于追求福的享受不具有善的完备性。公正不仅存在于福利多样性之间，还存在于福利和功德之间。当人关注心灵的无限性自身的时候，也就是中国传统文化所说的觉悟的时候。对福利的渴望减弱了，福利的不平等的动机因素也减弱了，这一点是中国文化传统避免社会不公带来社会动荡的重要的经验。

关键词：《国语》　德　福　价值观

---

[*] 周海春，男，湖北大学高等人文研究院暨哲学学院教授、博士生导师，湖北大学中国文化研究中心主任，《文化发展论丛·中国卷》主编，主要研究方向为中国哲学史和伦理学。

Economic Inequality and Social Justice from the Perspective of Virtue-Luck Balance

Zhou Haichun

Abstract: Value involves the judge of different values in different objects. Virtue and Luck in Chinese culture has the relationship of values. The theory of Virtue-Luck balance has been long in China. The content of Virtue and Luck continually develops in Chinese history. Virtue is the foundation of Luck, the balance of Virtue and Luck constitutes the foundation and motivation for the improvement of Luck. Justice exists not only in the diversity of lucky interest, but also in the balance of Virtue and Luck. When the man is concerned with the infinite mind itself, the desire for interest declines, and the consciousness concerning the unbalance of Virtue and Luck has been weakened. This is the most important way in Chinese culture to avoid the social turmoil caused by injustice.

Key words: Guo-Yu; Virtue; Luck; values

目前讨论经济不平等与社会公正的思想大多出自西方的经验，较少从中国古代的道德原理出发。经济不平等是一个广泛存在的现象，现代社会会碰到，在古代社会也不会缺席。哪里有不平等，哪里就有公正的呼唤，就有正义的诉求。但在中国古代，好像公正的呼声很弱，为什么呢？是不是有某种价值观念把社会公正的呼唤默默地化解了，以至于人们形成了一套观察经济不平等乃至其他形式的不平等的视角？是不是人们对这一不平等的问题缺乏一种反思和自觉呢？这两种情况都有可能。不过这里假定，中国人有自觉，而化解了问题得益于德福平衡的价值观。

这里讨论的话题具有假设性，是一种构建的尝试，自然不可以拘泥于思想史的真实来加以评论。

中国古代经济学原理看起来不是很发达，淹没在伦理思考之中。不过这种思考也可以看成是一种伦理经济学的思考。"现代经济学不自然的'无伦理'（non-ethical）特征与现代经济学是作为伦理学的一个分支而发展起来的事实之间存在着矛盾。"① 现代经济学也是作为伦理学的一个分支发展起来的，这给中国古代经济学和现代经济学的连接提供了理论上的可能。把经济学看成伦理学的一个分支有助于张扬中国古代经济思想的价值，并获得一种新的视角，把由于学科分类而支离破碎的中国传统文化还原为一个具有原理性的整体。

以伦理学方法思考经济学问题显然不同于"工程学"的方法，因为伦理经济学关心经济行为的最终目的、价值，尤其是经济行为对人的美德的影响等问题。"'工程学'方法的特点是，只关心最基本的逻辑问题，而不关心人类的最终目的是什么，以及什么东西能够培养'人的美德'或者'一个人应该怎样活着'这类问题。"② 以伦理学的视野看待经济问题，并不意味着会缺乏基本的逻辑，只是相关的问题需要完善和深入。以中国伦理学视野看待中国的经济思想，尤其有很多的工作要做。

一 德福平衡原理

中国传统文化中的"德"概念本来就有平衡力的内涵。德具有平衡力，所平衡的世俗利益就是福。范文子明确提出了德福平衡的思想。"吾闻之，唯厚德者能受多福，无德而服者众，必自伤也。"③《国语》提出德福平衡的思想不是偶然的，而是周文化的典型特征，是周文化的一种高度浓缩和概括，相关思想还见于《国语》的其他篇章。德福平衡的思想深入到中国文化传统之中，到佛教中演变成功德与福报平衡的原理。如禅宗五祖弘忍对门人说："吾向汝说，世人生死事大，汝等门人，终

---

① 〔印度〕阿马蒂亚·森：《伦理学与经济学》，王宇、王文玉译，商务印书馆，2014，第8页。
② 〔印度〕阿马蒂亚·森：《伦理学与经济学》，王宇、王文玉译，商务印书馆，2014，第10～11页。
③ 《国语》，韦昭注，上海古籍出版社，2008，第195页。

日供养，只求福田，不求出离生死苦海。汝等自性若迷，福门何可救汝？"① 这里提出了福田与功德之不同：一个为世间法，一个为出世间法；一为有为、有相法；一为无相、无为法。无为法是解决生死问题的，能够得到出离生死苦海结果的"因"就是功德；否则就是福田。在这里，弘忍已经说明了只有自性的觉悟才能有功德。中国文化传统中的德福平衡原理大略包括如下内容，部分内容加入了现代的阐释，但基本精神不与传统相悖。

其一，德和福都包含丰富的内容，具有一定的普遍性。中国古代文化之所以对很多美德那么推崇，原因之一就是那些美德能够增长功德，违背这些德性功德就会减损。在增长和减损功德方面，道家学说和佛学都有丰富的思想，具有较高的道德实践意义。福的内容也是很丰富的，比如人际关系上的帮助是福报。"众以美物归女，而何德以堪之，王犹不堪，况尔小丑乎？小丑备物，终必亡。"② 在这里，能否享受美人的服务要看自己是否有德来平衡。就国际关系来说，他国的尊重和服从是福报。社会地位和职务是福的范畴，要靠德来平衡。"吾闻之，不厚其栋，不能任重。重莫如国，栋莫如德。"③ "故圣人之施舍也议之，其喜怒取与与亦议之。是以不主宽惠，亦不主猛毅，主德义而已。"④ 财富的分配的基础是德。能否做好事情也与德有密切的关系。"夫敬，德之恪也。恪于德以临事，其何不济！"⑤ 在中国文化传统中，个人健康、智慧、能力等方面，家庭关系和社会地位，社会财富和社会名声等都属于福的范畴。这些幸福的获得需要德来支撑，来平衡。

其二，福依存于德，德是福的基础，德可以带来福，德可以转换成福，二者之间具有一定的对应关系。"夫德，福之基也，无德而福隆，

---

① 郭朋：《坛经校释》，中华书局，1983，第9页。
② 《国语》，韦昭注，上海古籍出版社，2008，第4页。
③ 《国语》，韦昭注，上海古籍出版社，2008，第81页。
④ 《国语》，韦昭注，上海古籍出版社，2008，第36页。
⑤ 《国语》，韦昭注，上海古籍出版社，2008，第182页。

犹无基而厚墉也，其坏也无日矣。"① 德不但是福的基础，德还能带来福。孟子认为，求"天爵"，而"人爵"也会随之而来，就是属于这类思想。中国价值观中的"义利之辨"也包含这一思想，求义因为是"德"方面的事情，虽然没有直接去求利，但是却可以获得利益。而直接去求利属于"福"方面的事情，如果因为求利而丧失了德，求义也不会得到理想的结果。"义以导利，利以阜姓。"② 在范文子看来，"称晋之德，诸侯皆叛，国可以少安"。③ "诸侯皆叛"是福，显然这个"福"从质量上来看，属于负价值。但这个负价值和晋国的德性是相配的，这个负价值反倒有利于晋国的德，这个德就是"国可以少安"。从德的角度来看，不胜才是福，胜利反倒有祸端。"战若不胜，则晋国之福也；战若胜，乱地之秩者也，其产将害大，盍姑无战乎？"④

其三，德福在总量确定的前提下，二者之间可以互相转换。福德总量的确定性可以从"朝三暮四"的故事中得到启发。可以认定功德加上福的总数是"七"，当福是"四"的时候功德就是"三"。当然"七"这个总数可以增长。

总数一致性以及福报和功德的对应性，不意味着福不能出现过度或者不及的情形。如福为"二"，功德则为"五"，福为"六"，功德则为"一"。假设功德为"四"，福为"三"为最平衡的状态，福如果是"八"，则功德为"负一"，这个"八"就是"幸"而非"福"。赵襄子命新稚穆子讨伐狄人并获得胜利，但是他却快乐不起来。他自己的解释是："吾闻之，德不纯而福禄并至，谓之幸。夫幸非福，非德不当雍，雍不为幸，吾是以惧。"⑤ "雍，和也。"⑥ 楚国的军队取得了一定的胜利，范文子的儿子主张逃跑，范文子斥责了自己的儿子。当晋国军队打败楚

---

① 《国语》，韦昭注，上海古籍出版社，2008，第235页。
② 《国语》，韦昭注，上海古籍出版社，2008，第164页。
③ 《国语》，韦昭注，上海古籍出版社，2008，第195页。
④ 《国语》，韦昭注，上海古籍出版社，2008，第195页。
⑤ 《国语》，韦昭注，上海古籍出版社，2008，第235页。
⑥ 《国语》，韦昭注，上海古籍出版社，2008，第235页。

国军队以后，范文子把战胜理解成"福"，"吾何福以及此"。①晋国缺乏必要的"德"来享受此福。如果功德为"八"，而福为"负一"，则出现了功德的溢出，总量上多出一个"一"。前者是福的过度使用，后者是福使用的不足。

如果有两个人恰好是上述情形，那么二者之间的总数依然是平衡的，功德为"八"溢出的功德量足以平衡福报"八"功德的不足，而福报上的"负一"也能平衡福报"八"，总体上保持总量的平衡。这就构成了功德和福的"搭便车"行为。范文子认为晋国取得胜利获得较多的福，恰好是警示楚国修德。"吾庸知天之不授晋且以劝楚乎，君与二三臣其戒之！"②晋国较多的福来源于楚国享有较少的福从而支出较多的功德来支撑世界的功德福的整体平衡。但是如果其中的一方或者双方整体的福的支出超过了整体功德的平衡，福和功德总量的等级就必须下降，相反，如果其中一方或者整体的福的支出减少，同时努力修德，则整体的福和功德的质量等级就会提高，世界就会变得更加有道德，更加文明与和谐。

"搭便车"的情况不仅仅在同代人之间进行，在中国文化传统看来，还发生在代际关系中。祭公谋父认为周先王"时序其德"，"奕世载德"，经常叙说先王的德行，世世代代继承先人的美德，不辱没前人。③"非德不及世。"④没有德惠施于人，就传不到下一代，就不能历世久远。世世代代繁荣是很多人和国家追求的理想，如何才能有这样的福呢？就是要积累功德，这个功德可以给下一代带来福的影响。

其四，福德总量的增长和二者比值的调节与人的努力有关，人也从中可以体认天命。德福的平衡是天来调节的，也是人来调节的，体现了天人相因。"吾闻之，'天道无亲，唯德是授。'"⑤天可以让人失德，进而剥夺了人的福报。"自幽王而天夺之明，使迷乱弃德，而即慆淫，以

---

① 《国语》，韦昭注，上海古籍出版社，2008，第197页。
② 《国语》，韦昭注，上海古籍出版社，2008，第197页。
③ 《国语》，韦昭注，上海古籍出版社，2008，第1页。
④ 《国语》，韦昭注，上海古籍出版社，2008，第118页。
⑤ 《国语》，韦昭注，上海古籍出版社，2008，第197页。

亡其百姓，其坏之也久矣。"① 在这里把幽王的失败理解成上天剥夺了其智慧，从而使其失去了功德，进而无法很好地管理国家，从而给老百姓也带来祸端。但这不意味着功德和福报的增长与人力无关，恰好相反，天调整的依据是人力，并随着人力的调整而调整。"天因人，圣人因天；人自生之，天地形之，圣人因而成之。"② 天道受到人事的影响，人能够创造事物，天地能够顺着人的力量把事情变成现实，圣人根据天道，进而根据天人两个方面成就大事。在中国文化传统看来，诸种美德的意义就在于它能够增长功德进而带来福报的增长。

其五，节俭是具有道德完备性的德行，而骄奢是不完备的品行。节俭是中国文化比较推崇的美德，《道德经》比较推崇的美德是节俭、慈爱和不争。三者之间具有相关性，总的精神是不过分追求福报，而是把福报送给他人享用。儒家和墨家也推崇节俭，在此不一一论述。根据德福平衡的原理，如果一个人以慈爱之心较少消费，奉行节俭、谦卑、不争的美德，那么这个人采用的是最为保险的生活方式。假设自己恰好没有很多的功德来支持福报，较少的福的支出，依然可以获得足够的功德支撑；假设自己有较好的功德支撑，节俭则带来了福的剩余或者功德的增长，这可以有利于他人，方便他人"搭便车"或者功德福总量增长，或者给自己带来持续的福的享受。从各种情形来看，节俭是完备的美德。相反，追求财富的增长或者浪费则具有不完备的善性。财富的增长可以为他人带来利益，这样可以增长功德，并增加世界的福总量，具有善性；但是财富的增长可以使功德减少，从而无法保持福的持续性，并危及自身，这是负价值。因而追求财富的增长从德与福平衡的原理看来，是不完备的。过度消费本身则更加不完备。消费当然有利于生产，能够增加福的量，但是它能较多地消耗功德，从而危及自身的功德。另外，福的使用会带来福总量的减少，或者他人福消费的减少，从而带来不公正，具有较大的负面价值。

---

① 《国语》，韦昭注，上海古籍出版社，2008，第64页。
② 《国语》，韦昭注，上海古籍出版社，2008，第298页。

德福平衡原理是否是真实的，其实很难考论，但它是中国哲人提出的价值观，影响了中国人的价值选择。可以把这个原理当成一种理论的假设，只要这种假设对人类生活的完善是有积极意义的，就有系统化阐释的必要。

二 德福平衡与自利最大化

阿马蒂亚·森批评了"自利理性观"，认为它"意味着对'伦理相关'动机观的断然拒绝"。① 他指出："把所有人都自私看成是现实的可能是一个错误；但把所有人都自私看成是理性的要求则非常愚蠢。"② 依然可以肯定自私或者自利的理性观，不过自利的内涵需要调整。自利包括"福利"（福报意义上的福利）的自利和功德的自利。《道德经》强调不自私反倒能成其私，这一辩证关系的完成恰好说明了自利本身的辩证性质。自私之私属于"福"的领域，不自私成就的"私"属于功德的领域。二者经常性的互换以及互相包含使得自利需要从功德和福两个角度来考虑。对福报性自利的贪着，反映了对功德的某种焦虑不安，是追求功德的另一种表现和形式。

阿马蒂亚·森提出了动机的多元性的问题。"真正的问题应该在于，是否存在着动机的多元性，或者说，自利是否能成为人类行为的唯一动机。"③ 恰如唐君毅先生所言："非人文的经济社会，乃从未存在，不自人文之动机，以改造经济社会之行为，亦从未存在者。"④ 经济行为的动机或者追求的价值大概可以分成如下两个大的层次：功德层次和福利层次。这里所说的福利层次不同于西方经济学讲的福利，西方经济学中的福利主要是指外在的物质财富。

---

① 〔印度〕阿马蒂亚·森：《伦理学与经济学》，王宇、王文玉译，商务印书馆，2014，第21页。
② 〔印度〕阿马蒂亚·森：《伦理学与经济学》，王宇、王文玉译，商务印书馆，2014，第21页。
③ 〔印度〕阿马蒂亚·森：《伦理学与经济学》，王宇、王文玉译，商务印书馆，2014，第24～25页。
④ 唐君毅：《文化意识与道德理性》，中国社会科学出版社，2005，第94页。

福利的第一个内容是西方经济学所说的"福利",即实物财富和货币财富。这一层次是感性欲望层次。人追求实物货币财富是为了满足衣食住行的需要,为了保证人的基本的生存需要。"吾人在日常之经济生活中,恒觉吾人周遭之世界,唯是一财物之世界。吾人生产财物,交换分配财物,消费财物。而财物之用,主要在满足吾人衣食住等本能欲望,以使吾人得生存。"① 获利的欲望、对最大可能数额的金钱的追求,一直存在于所有的人身上,从侍者、车夫、艺术家到贪官,即便是赌徒、乞丐也不例外。可以说,尘世中一切国家、一切时代的所有的人,不管其实现这种欲望的客观可能性如何,全都具有这种欲望。

第二个内容是阿马蒂亚·森所说的"主观能动性",即对上述财富的认知、价值评价、幸福感。"效用虽然通常被解释为福利,但是,把它看成是一个人主观能动的反映或许会更确切一些。"② 对财富的追求有很多层次的主观能动性,或者是不自觉的,或者是理性的,或者是利他的动机,或者是超越的动机,等等。这里主要强调的是"理性",上述二者构成了西方经济学所说的理性自利性。

第三个内容是人伦情怀,也就是为了小家庭、朋友、团体、国家、民族而进行经济活动。自私本身的范围是很难划界的,可以把外在财富排他性的占有叫作自私,也可以把对自我感性利益的执着叫作自私。单纯为了个人的自私在中国文化传统中并不流行,流行的自私是包括小家庭、小团体在内的,也就是人伦情怀的动机。比如赚钱是为了养活父母,是为了让家人高兴,是为了适应社会习俗,是为了有利于别人,是为了担当社会责任,是为了守护诚信,等等。有饭同吃,有衣同穿等都属于此类。这方面的动因以中国古代经济活动最为典型。

第四个层次是为了个人的自由、权利、独立和个性。在齐美尔看来,因为货币根本不与任何特别的目的发生关系,所以它就获得了一种与目的整体性之间的关系。有钱就意味着,钱可以在未来发挥用途;有钱就

---

① 唐君毅:《文化意识与道德理性》,中国社会科学出版社,2005,第58页。
② 〔印度〕阿马蒂亚·森:《伦理学与经济学》,王宇、王文玉译,商务印书馆,2014,第47页。

意味着可以购买想要的东西。一定数量货币的价值就相当于它所要进行交换的对象的价值再加上货币可以在无数其他对象上进行自由选择的价值。货币的价值背后还潜藏着劳动的价值、生命和个性的价值。货币是冰冷无情之物，又是最有个性之物。它的个性就是人的个性，它的价值就是劳动的价值，就是时间的价值，就是身体的价值，就是心灵的价值。财富总是需要人的身心与之相应。财富虽然不说话，它却是大众情人，需要人拿出全面的品质去追求，花费一生的精力去呵护。货币虽然不算美，但它却风情万种。货币不说话，表示它是无情的，不会长久地守护在固定的人那里。货币有利于让人独立，有利于让人表现个性，所以它才那样让人动心，那样触及人心。"可以说，我们应该用一个人所拥有的自由来代表他的利益，而不应该用（至少不能完全用）一个人从这些自由中所得到的东西（福利的或主观能动的）来代表他的利益。"①

　　福利的多样化理解是公正的条件之一。可以假定每个人都有自己的公正性的权衡，并在现实社会生活体系中寻求对自己最优的公正状态。单一的价值观对公正性是不利的。平等与不平等总是在一个特定的尺度上来进行衡量的，如财富占有的平等和不平等。如果从不同的尺度来看，福利是一个多元的系统，财富占有上的弱势可以通过其他尺度上的优势地位得到补偿。比如有的人没有工作，却获得了很多可以自己支配的时间，尽管这些时间的应用会受到财富的限制而不那么自由，但他们可以做财富许可范围内的事情，比如健身、闲谈、看电视、打麻将，而这些对于忙于工作的中国人来说是奢侈的"消费"。当然，这种优势会随着每个人的价值观不同而有不同的价值层次。如对于一个僧人来说，这意味他有时间专注于禅修和诵佛经古卷，他理应较少地占有社会财富。当代中国社会人们痛恨的不公正现象很多属于"通吃"的范畴，即某些人在某个尺度上占据了福利的优势，但不满足于此，还要在其他尺度上占据优势，而后者缺乏实际的付出，缺乏功德的基础。

　　公正不仅存在于福利多样性之间，还存在于福利和功德之间。那些

---

① 〔印度〕阿马蒂亚·森：《伦理学与经济学》，王宇、王文玉译，商务印书馆，2014，第50页。

专注于功德的人能够也乐于接受社会财富方面的损失，而且往往把财富施舍给他人看成美德。如佛教文化即把施舍当成了"六度"之一。在清教伦理看来，财富本是极大的危险。财富的诱惑与上帝之国的无上重要性相比是微不足道的。因而得出的结论是：对财富的追逐毫无意义，而且，它在道德上也是颇成问题的。追逐财富总是给人一种道德上的疑虑，要想回归上帝之国，就要适当约束自己的欲望，当然财富本身也在需要约束之列。唐君毅把福利的追逐看成人追求道德自我的一个表现形式。唐君毅认为有两个原因造成了人生的颠倒。"所谓人生之颠倒相，如人之立于池畔，还望其自身在池中之影。此时人自己看见自己倒立于池中，如一外在客观的物象，而脚在上头在下。此例所喻有二义：一是主体的自己之客观化，或内在的自我之外在物象化，而此外在之物象，则只是一虚影。二是价值高下之易位。此二者，即喻一切人生颠倒相之基本意义。然此基本意义之所涵摄，与表现此意义之人生事相，则几可说无穷无尽。"[1] 颠倒的主体和原因是什么呢？"此颠倒者，即我们上述之主体之自己，或内在的我，或我们之心灵生命存在之自体。"[2] 颠倒的原因就是因为自体是无限的，"如果人们不能就其自体本身，以认识其为一超越的无限者。人们亦可直自人生之一切颠倒相中，认识其深不可测之颠倒性，以反照出其原为一超越的无限者。"[3] 好利有颠倒相。"夫此一区区之一鸡蛋，自其现实而观，固不足以富比王公而甲天下，而自其可能滋生之财富而观，则亦实未尝不可相引而无穷无限量，而人即可以此无限量之可能，为其贪求爱恋之对象，而此无限量之可能，则固唯因人之心灵原具无限性，而后能思维之构想之，以使之宛然呈于此心灵之前者也。然此无限量之可能，又实非真实之可能，而实唯是此心灵之无限性之倒影。"[4] 当人关注心灵的无限性自身的时候，也就是中国传统文化所说的觉悟的时候，对福利的渴望下降了，福利的不平等形成的动机因素

---

[1] 唐君毅:《人生三书》，中国社会科学出版社，2005，第91页。
[2] 唐君毅:《人生三书》，中国社会科学出版社，2005，第93页。
[3] 唐君毅:《人生三书》，中国社会科学出版社，2005，第93页。
[4] 唐君毅:《人生三书》，中国社会科学出版社，2005，第95~96页。

也减弱了，这一点是中国文化传统避免社会不公带来社会动荡的重要的经验。

三 德福一致：原初状态的正义共识与社会公正

罗尔斯以最初状态作为阐发正义的逻辑前提。不过他所规定的最初状态的原则属于福利分配领域的事情，而不涉及对功德分配的考量。从经验的角度来看，在形而上学兴趣缺乏的文化背景下，这一考虑更为现实合理。不过，就中国文化传统而言，现世的福利分配，是上时代功德、福利运作的结果。抛开"承负"或者世代"因果报应"这些被神秘化、迷信化的词语，可以把功德和福利的运作看成基本的原初状态。这一理解的原初状态承认的基本原则与罗尔斯的理解有很大的差别。罗尔斯说："作为替代，我要坚持认为，处在原初状态中的人们将选择两个相当不同的原则：第一个原则要求平等地分配基本的权利和义务；第二个原则认为社会和经济的不平等（例如财富和权力的不平等）只有在其结果能给每一个人，尤其是那些最少受惠的社会成员带来补偿利益时，它们才是正义的。"[①] 德福平衡原理下的原初状态承认人出生所自然带来的不平等是正义的，这个不平等是个体功德和福报平衡的结果和体现，是正义原则调整的必然结果，也是新的社会正义的现实的逻辑起点。人一出生就受到了自己所处的社会关系的限制，这个社会关系已经处在不平等的条件下，初始条件的不平等是每个人进行一生奋斗的背景和基本要素。罗尔斯所说的第一原则在德福平衡原理下可以理解成两点：第一点就自我无限性的功德追求而言，平等地要求分配权利和义务是每个生命基于功德的一种具有创造力的要求；第二点就这一生功德的量可以支配的福报的量而言，可以支配的量需要自己努力奋斗来真正获得，就像银行虽然有存款，但是需要取出来才能够使用一样，每个人对权利和义务的要

---

① 〔美〕约翰·罗尔斯：《正义论》，何怀宏、何包钢、廖申白译，中国社会科学出版社，2009，第12页。

求是其预定的福利，因而是公正的。第二个原则表示一个人在履行新的义务过程中，创造了新的功德和福利或者过度消耗了功德和福利，这个时候，只有新增加了功德和福利并且这些新增加的部分溢出给他人的时候，这个社会才是正义的。罗尔斯所谈论的补偿有特定的对象，也就是"最少受惠的社会成员"，而且内容局限于福利的范围。正义社会的补偿涉及功德和福报的补偿两个方面，其中的原理还有待进一步探讨。

　　罗尔斯所说的第二个原则基本上就是帕累托最优原则。这个原则认为，如果某一种变化有利于每一个人，那么对于这个社会来说它必定是一个好的变化。在这个原则下可以实现不使他人境况变坏的同时可以使自己的情况变得更好。儒家的道德金律与此原则的精神大致相当。关于道德金律笔者曾经给出如下阐释："一个人在参照别人的行为这一事实足以告诫我们，我们自己就是别人的一个可能的价值参照系，一个可能的引导者，我们不得不去考虑这种导引包含着的可能的价值意义和价值事实。倘若每个人都放弃了正面价值的追求，那么社会整体的道德和价值水平自然会下降。所以自己一方面要有所约束，又要有所建设。不对别人施加负面的价值影响，而要给予积极的影响。普适性在于'仁'解释了人生在世的互相影响的现实性，告诉人们在相互影响的过程中如何保持健康向上。普适性在于'己'和'人'的依存性；自己'立'了自然就立了别人；自己不立自然给别人带来麻烦。每个人都追求自己的'立'，自然彼此轻松。普适性不在于其规范性，而在于这一表述包含的人生的基本现实。"① 在狭隘的福利观念的影响下，一些生活原则的价值常常会被遮蔽。比如健康的价值远远要大于所谓"事业"的价值。健康的价值平常难以显示出来，当生病的时候才会显露。健康的价值等于疾病耗费、药物开发、工作成就的价值的总和。道德的价值起码与防范犯罪所花费的努力相当。"无为而治"在当代文化背景下往往被忽视。功德的价值可以参照以上解释来理解，其价值是"百姓日用而不知"的。

　　罗尔斯的第二个原则可以看成对狭隘的福利自利观遇到的难以克服

---

① 周海春：《〈论语〉哲学》，中国社会科学出版社，2013，第194页。

的矛盾的一种理论上的克服。如何增进自己和社会的最大的利益？中西方文化提供了两种基本的思路。一种是自利的最大化追求会产生利他的效用，并增加社会的效用总量，所以是值得肯定的。但在市场交换的社会体系下，其结果必然是带来福利的不平等占有。正因为如此需要有一个正义原则来加以调节。另一种理解是：德福平衡是自利最大化的状态，而这一状态是理想的公正状态。上文已经论述了节俭是完备的德行，而物质财富的创造是不完备的德行，有助于理解这一点。

麦金太尔区分了优秀性正义和优胜性正义，根据上述思路，优秀性的善更为公正。优秀性正义所获得的福利是建立在优秀的付出基础上的。优秀性的正义观也会进一步考虑优秀的功绩与应得的关系。每一个人的实践之善（优秀），也会使得人拥有一些优胜必要的品质，尽管二者有区别，且有时候会互相对立，而优胜必要的品质会让人获得功绩，进而获得优秀的外部奖励的善（应得）。优秀性的正义承认自我完善的追求不同于能够得到相应的外部奖赏。如善考试和努力学习之间的区别。优秀性的正义，以优秀为出发点考虑问题，并努力追求自身的优秀。这种正义观具有一定的宽容性。比如优秀的差异性，有人会唱歌，有人会跳舞，这就要求以不同的尺度和方式来判断。正义就在于对一个人是否是优秀的判断要和其本人优秀的方面相当，以优秀的方面为尺度进行衡量。优秀性的正义从个人角度来看，具有道德的完备性，如 A 为优秀的个体的功德量，如果 A 的量对应的福的量 B，那么 B 可有如下几种获得方式：B1 为当得的；B2 为可得的；B3 为实际得到的。如果 B1 是最高值，当得的和 A 相配合，而 B2 和 B3 则留有余地，可以溢出给他人使用，或者转换成功德。

优秀性的善和有效性的成就是不同的，优胜性的正义着眼点在成功，着眼点在获得善物。优胜的正义要求公平规则保证优秀者成为优胜者。优胜的正义伴随着奖赏，公开的荣耀、权力、财富、地位、声誉奖赏。优胜也有自己的优秀观，但优胜视野下的优秀是有局限的。追求善物获得优胜所要求的品质未必就是优秀的品质。优秀主要是追求这些善物所要求的品质。比如一个人具有赚钱的品质，这个品质可以说优秀。但这个优秀是和钱这种善物相联系的。

如 A 为优胜的个体的功德量，如果 A 的量对应的福的量 B，那么 B 可有如下几种获得方式：B1 为实得的；B2 为当得的；B3 为可得的。当得的和 A 相配合，而 B1 则是福的多占，B3 则留有余地，可以溢出给他人使用，或者转换成功德。优胜性的正义是不完备的正义。马克思在《1844 年经济学哲学手稿》中曾提到货币占有的优胜者能够掩盖自身的不足，包括道德上的不足，丑的可以被说成是美的，缺德的可以被美化成有美德的。货币创造了一个颠倒的世界，一切自然的品质和人的品质的混淆和替换的颠倒的世界。从货币占有者的观点看来，货币能把任何特性和任何对象同其他任何即使与它相矛盾的特性和对象相交换。"货币的特性就是我的——货币占有者的——特性和本质力量……我是丑的，但我能给我买到最美的女人……我是一个邪恶的、不诚实的、没有良心的、没有头脑的人，可是货币是受尊敬的，因此，它的占有者也受尊敬。货币是最高的善，因此，它的占有者也是善的。"① 从德福平衡的原理来看，这些不足就是功德的缺陷。而货币占有的优胜则是福占有过多。

"让我们把这些身体的、精神的和品格的品质叫作有效性的品质；而把那些给这些品质提供其目标和正当性证明的善物叫作有效性的善物。"② 对于优秀性的正义而言，存在着一个潜在的风险，就是有效性的品质可能始终无法获得有效性的善物，也就是所谓的"英雄无用武之地"，"潜龙"不能飞天，没有"伯乐"来认识"千里马"。这种情况要么是功德之不足，要么是福之不足，如果是这种情况，优秀就是一种自我精神或者社会氛围形成的幻象，在这基础上形成的不公平感、受挫折感没有实际意义，不公平的不应当被弄成公平的，不公感反映的是自我对功德和福的亏欠的某种焦虑。如果是功德充足福不足，无

---

① 《马克思恩格斯全集》第 3 卷，人民出版社，2002，第 361~362 页。
② 〔美〕阿拉斯戴尔·麦金太尔：《谁之正义？何种合理性？》，当代中国出版社，1996，第 47 页。

法获得福的原因在于社会机制的运作，而溢出的功德对于自我的提升和社会功德的平衡也是有利益的。从这一意义上说，优秀性的正义总是值得肯定的。

现代生活中（这里指的是中国）经常有不那么优秀的人获得优胜的情况，这造成了社会较为强烈的不公平感。对此也需要详细分析才行。总的来说，优胜也是有功德支撑的，不过这个功德有可能是来自他人的溢出，或者是他人福的溢出。优胜之所以在现代生活中具有强势的地位，就在于它体现了社会整体的功德和福报的运作，尤其是福报的运作。社会机制更多地体现了福报的运作，而个人追求优秀的过程更多地体现了功德的运作。

现代经济生活一直无法克服市场和计划的难题。市场机制和计划机制哪个更公平？因为本文是以中国传统道德思路回答正义问题的初步的尝试，对于这一问题还没有详细的答案，以下初步的思考可以作为参考。

假设10个人创造了20个功德量和20个福德量，二者对应。计划机制由10个人共同创造20个福利的量，但是假设其中有2个人"滥竽充数"，其余的8个人就需要付出更多的功德才能创造20个福利的量。假设20个福利的量的分配由其中的3人按计划分配，如果这3个人中有2个人是"滥竽充数"的人，或者0个人是"滥竽充数"的但是其价值观对2个"滥竽充数"的人很有利，最终比较极端结果是这2个"滥竽充数的人"拿到了最高的福利。

市场机制则不同，市场机制采取10个人单独创造福利的方式，然后进行市场交换，然后创造出20个福利量。在进行市场交换的时候就已经完成了20个福利量的分配。可以看看2个"滥竽充数"的人在市场机制下的命运，他们是不可能获得最高的福利的。

如果这个原理成立的话，公共福利体系运作如果使个人功德福报平衡变得很脆弱，使个人无法按照个人功德和福报平衡运作的逻辑过自利最大化的生活的话，较为普遍的不公正感就会形成。

不是不要社会整体的计划或者调控，而是这个调控不能建立在单一的对福利理解的基础上，权利、时间、道德完善性的需要、人伦交往的需要，都是很重要的福利。自由度的释放、人伦情怀的满足、财富的增长、理性能力的提高都是基本的福利，也是社会公正实现的条件。单一的财富调节并不能实现社会公正。另外，计划需要有利于增进德福的总量并保持德福平衡。佛教"八正道"中有"正命"和"正业"，大概给出了社会行业的功德量的考量。可以把生产创造的额度和水平、个人美德的提升、终极关怀、超越精神等都看成功德领域的事情。另外，可以依据创造的效率、对生命有害或者有利的量、自利和利他的量等因素来划分社会各个生活领域的功德等级。满足基本的生活需要是最公正的，健康、安全、空闲时间、住所和交通这些基本的生活条件是福利的基础内容，同时也是最低限度的功德的体现。"积德"欲望的满足也是很重要的。"积德"的概念出现在《道德经》中，经各家的发展积淀成中国文化的民族心理。"穆斯格拉夫（Musgrave）（1959）以其特殊的理由说明了超越个人偏好的衡量以及赋予'积德的欲望'（merit wants）的满足。"[1] 排斥"良心自由"，并把人们引到财富竞争的道路上，只会加剧社会不公。

---

[1] 〔印度〕阿马蒂亚·森：《伦理学与经济学》，王宇、王文玉译，商务印书馆，2014，第57页。

Employment: Today's Big Challenge

Hortensia Cuéllar[*]

Abstract: This paper is intended to show that one of the effective and best proven ways to fight against financial inequity and against the lack of social justice is putting the issue of unemployment and/or underpaid jobs at the core of the development of nations, which has become a global issue. Why do we have to suffer this scourge? Why governments, in their plans for development and GNP increase, neglect efforts to increase employment for ordinary citizens, which is indispensable for an individual and collective growth and improvement in life quality? ... How can we talk about a poverty-free world if employment sources are required to assure that human beings—men and women—may have at least the minimum required to live with dignity and justice? ... To what extent are we involved? What is our responsibility?

We cannot ignore the fact that human beings, since they first appeared on earth, were born for working, which by no means should be understood as a penalty, but one of the best ways for individual and communitarian fulfilment. Human work sets in motion the development of civilization and culture. Lack of employment threatens human dignity and constitutes an enormous anthropological and social injustice. The case of México is given as a way to illustrate this

---

[*] Hortensia Cuéllar, TEC de Monterrey-Campus Ciudad de México; the Advanced Institute for Humanistic Studies, Hubei University.

analysis.

Key words: work, employment, unemployment, personal and social development, human dignity, life quality.

就业：当今世界的巨大挑战

Hortensia Cuéllar

摘　要：本文认为，失业与低工资目前已成了全球性问题，消除财富上的不平等以及社会不公正需要把这两个问题纳入国家发展的核心问题。为什么我们缺乏这样做的勇气？对普通人而言，就业问题与个人和团体生活质量的提高密切相关，政府在制定发展规划以及 GNP 增长规划的时候，为什么不致力于提高普通人的就业率？如果就业无法在最低限度上确保有尊严的公正生活，何谈消除贫困？何谈我们的责任？我们无法忽视这样一个事实：人来到这个世界就是为了工作，工作和惩罚的观念毫不相干，工作是个人和团体的需要。人类用自己的工作与劳动推动了文明的发展。失业威胁人类尊严，是一个人类学意义上的社会不公正问题。本文给出的墨西哥的例子就是为了论证这种观点。

关键词：工作　就业　失业　个人与社会发展　人类尊严　生活质量

I Introduction

Upon thinking what my contribution to this 2014 World Cultural Development Forum could be, I remembered a reflection made by Martha Nussbaum and Amartya Sen at the Introduction to the book *The Quality of Life* (1993). These authors, in an exercise of distributive realism, quote a Charles Dickens's text from *Hard Times*, published in 1854. This quotation is suitable not only for their book, but also for the subject we are dealing with, "Economic Inequality and World Justice". One of the characters of *Hard Times*—Sissy Jupe—wonders how people could talk about a "flourishing nation", no matter how rich it is, when she—an ordinary citizen—does not know who has the money and whether a part of that money is hers. Why does Sissy wonder? Because, for any ordinary citizen who is told that her country is a flourishing country but she does not have a banknote (be it peso, dollar, yuan, sterling pound or euro) in her pocket, or has too little to live on, such a pompous assertion means nothing at all. It rather makes her wonder why she does not enjoy such wealth, even though she belongs to that "flourishing country".

This is the question. What is the benefit if the treasuries of rich—and not so rich—countries are full of money if that wealth does not reach most of the people? It is not about looking at the State as a paternalistic State (which is almost always the case in dictatorship), which covers (or thinks it covers) almost all the needs of its "children", the citizens, at the expense of a poor management of public wealth and greatly unjust situations and inequities generated by such a paternalistic policy, or else, as a Beneficence State, where—without falling into tyranny—citizens are watched over, trying to solve their problems in a populist way, as it happens in countries in fairy tales, where everything has always a happy ending. For those who dream of such a state, or an ideal society, the hardness of reality—as expressed by Nicolai Hartmann—is expressed in multiple ways: famine, poverty, unemployment, lack of culture, unhealthiness, segregation, violence, war, oppression, all of them forms of injustice and inequity.

Hence the relevance of this World Cultural Development Forum in the 20th Century, where several topics and problems linked to the main subject will be viewed from different standpoints. This will offer the option of focusing on any of their multiple and varied facets. This gives the analytical treatment a high explanatory complexity which will result in expressions of denunciation, surprise and alarm upon what is going on in our planet, where—through today's communication media—it is very easy to learn what is happening on the other side of the world.

But it is not only about critically denounce such situations of injustice and social and governmental poverty, but raising our voice, full of energy and hope, in favor of those who have the least, because *valuing the life and the respect of dignity of any person* is something that cannot be postponed. This should be done through the consideration of issues about a better quality of life, the revision of current economic models and the sustainable development.

This may result in benefits for the common citizen such a real decrease of poverty, an increase of employment without exploitation, better wages and life conditions together with social and political welfare. All this within the framework of respect to human rights, solidary multiculturalism and the responsibility of an integral and entrepreneurial humanism, which is the inspiration source for these reflections where all—particularly the least favored—are included.

II Involved Actors

I am well aware that contributions, recommendations and initiatives to be considered and discussed in this Forum will almost always seem difficult to implement, because they admit more than one answer, involving different protagonists and various institutions, because the responsibility upon the injustice and inequity crisis we suffer is a global one. I briefly mention major actors:

1) In the academic and cultural environment, philosophers, economists, social scientists, managers and educators have a lot to say about this subject, because we represent the *unavoidable intellectual capital* in the debate as that we are working on. Rational, analytical, critical and propositive discussion to be generated must be in the favor of the human being, justice and the search for a better quality of life in this diverse and plural world, with respect to the dignity

of persons.

2) In the political-social field: good resource management and good government are prescriptive issues that should be included in the objectives of rulers of nations. Alternatives that give priority only to an increase in GNP or the role of free market without paying attention to social demands result in an out-of-focus approach (Sen, 2009).

Thus, governments of the various countries should set up, as duties which cannot be evaded, that of working in favor of development and that of setting up public policies that include all persons, particularly those in most need of support: those who are poor, unemployed, rejected, lacking of the minimum goods required for living with dignity and justice, i.e., working *in favor of the common good*, fighting against corruption, pilfering and illicit acquisition of wealth.

3) International financial institutions such as World Bank, IMF and IDB have also the responsibility for the international impact of their policies. Their objective should be set at a global level, and should aim at the implementation of fair monetary policies, including equitable conditions of loans, the correct application of awarded resources, preventing financial greediness and monetary speculation that decreases the sovereignty of over-indebted countries or leads to neo-colonialism.

What could be done? Re-finance the debt of the poorest countries in the planet, or condoning it, at least partially, in order to reduce interests so that favored governments could apply those resources to the benefit of the country's population. This possibility could look like an utter absurdity if viewed from the standpoint of the *idolatrous worship of money*, as the expression of Pope Francis (2013), recalled last April in Washington, D.C., during the "2014 IMF and World Bank Spring Meetings". Christine Lagarde said "Excessive inequality is corrosive to growth; it's corrosive to society". Furthermore, inequality implies a huge anthropological and ethical deficit.

4) Another actor in this problem is the private sector, the entrepreneurial and financial world. Why? Because eventually, in most companies, the creation of employment sources in most of them coexists with exploitation of workers under different guises: illegal working schedules, under-employment, the lack of labor benefits, limited-time contracting, outsourcing, and so on and so forth.

Another type of company channels its resources not only to "carrying out good business and generating wealth", but to productive investment, under the "win-win" principle, so the whole society benefits from the creation of well paid jobs, training and labor benefits for the employees, and service to the community, with direct benefit received by contracted workers. Such a behavior is that of companies certified as "socially responsible" and not only as "utilitarian and pragmatically profitable".

5) Family and school, as basic institutions of society, have a role that cannot be evaded facing the problem of inequity and injustice, because they are the first social institutions where fair or unfair treatment, equity or inequity, poverty or affluence, are experienced, as well as violence and the loss of dignity. This role is not irrelevant or trivial. Integral upbringing of persons, starting at home and school, is essential.

6) Finally, a factor that cannot be ignored in this analysis is the geopolitical position and the natural resources of countries in the world. It is not the same thing talking about Qatar, the United States, China, Canada, Norway, Switzerland, Australia, etc., regarded among the richest countries in the world, as talking about the Democratic Republic of the Congo, Zimbabwe, Burundi, Somalia, Madagascar, Kenya, Ghana, etc., which are among the poorest countries in the world, due to a variety of ancestral and current causes, all of them unfair and inequitable: inhuman colonialism, coups d'état, violence, ignorance, illness, extreme poverty, famine, lack of working opportunities, segregation (due to race, gender, ethnos, religion, origin, as it

happens with most immigrants), etc.

This is why the subject of the World Justice and Economic Inequality Forum is not a simple one, but rather a very complex one, due to the institutions, factors and parameters of different types involved, with multiple explanatory facets and solution proposals. Thus, it is stimulating that the focus of attention brings us together is, as I perceive it, the *promotion of an economy with a human face*, whose aim is a much higher one: *setting up shared work links*, by all of us, with a clear trend towards the *search of alternative development models*, abandoning *State's centralism lacking a positive economic impact of welfare in the population*, which suffocates private initiative, as it happened in the former Soviet Union. Our approach should also reject greedy *Neo-Liberalism*, where big fish eats little fish, as it happens with inhuman capitalism seeking power and money at the expense of anything. There, means are irrelevant. In both cases we, the ordinary people, are the big losers.

This is why I agree with Prof. Jiang Chang, in that we should look for other forms of equity and justice through culture, exchange of experiences, respectful dialogue and attention to what improves human beings. "We believe that, in today's world, where economic globalization and cultural diversity coexist, it is necessary to construct the world's mainstream culture; at least to give priority to it. Mainstream culture is the principle and value which safeguard peace and security of the world" (Wuhan Declaration, 2013).

How? ... Starting with attention to concrete needs and priorities of each locality or nation (*ad casum*), since—at the end of the day—injustice and inequity, even though they may *notionally* be labeled as collective, are *suffered by concrete individuals and societies*. This consideration should not ignore the universal principles, inherited and cultivated by humanity throughout the centuries— which is called classical culture of a transcultural order—since they constitute the spiritual intangible wealth, shared by *human beings, when they wish to be better*, either women or men, either individually or collectively (Cuéllar, 2013).

I resort hereby to perennial values that are welcome at any time and place when the approach is correct, fair and honest. Among these, there are such values as truth, good, justice, laboriousness, solidarity, equity, peace, harmony, love and preoccupation and responsibility for others. These *axiological cores*, at an ethical, anthropological, political and social level, give us *a common framework and a common language with a meaning for everybody*.

I think this is what Prof. Jiang Chang calls "Promoting World Mainstream Culture Construction".

III Work and Unemployment

In this search for new paths as a response to current uncertainty and crisis around economic and social inequity, the subject I chose was that of work and its counterpart, unemployment, as well as underpaid jobs and underemployment.

I will briefly discuss how valuable it is having a work to do, a job, and how "anti-valuable" and unfair it is not having one.

Work, in this essential meaning, is a productive activity, distinctive of free people and not of slaves, as it was believed in several stages of human history. The human being *has been born for working*, as the biblical expression states (*ut operaretur*); *not* as the result of a damnation, but—using Aristotelian nomenclature—as a praxical-poietic activity with a personal and social impact, which *we are naturally called to*, and without which we cannot grow or obtain the means required to live with dignity and justice, individually and collectively (Cuéllar, 2009). Work is a praxical activity because, through its exercise, we grow as persons because of the knowledge, values, habits, attitudes and abilities we acquire; it is poietic because it is almost always directed to the world of the doing, the producing, within the field of performance of such work or job.

Thus, working—and working well, down to the smallest detail—is a demonstration of professionalism, but it is especially *a living testimony of the dignity we have as persons.* No man or woman can neglect working, getting busy in some productive activity, in the immense scope of human work, because work enables him or her to achieve personal growth, to sustain his or her family and to contribute to the development of the community or the country where he or she lives. This is why work is *an essential activity for the human being*, not only from economic and social standpoints, but also from an ethical and ontological, i. e. existential, perspective.

By this I mean that "Any man or woman, generically speaking, can be considered as *workers*, which does not demean their value as persons but, contrariwise, *increases* it, and becomes one of their *distinctive features*, when their task is projected as a multivalent and polysemous activity, always linked with their own being, and with interior freedom that makes human beings their own artificer, as well as artificers of civilization and culture" (Cuéllar, 2009: 110).

An approach like the one we propose is called *a decent job* by International Labor Organization (ILO). This expression was jointly coined by governments, employers and workers, which gives it an international and moral weight. ILO's concept "is based on the understanding that work is a source of personal dignity, family stability, peace in the community, democracies that deliver for people, and economic growth that expands opportunities for productive jobs and enterprise development. Decent Work reflects priorities on the social, economic and political agenda of countries and the international system".

For all these reasons, being unemployed or underemployed hurts human dignity and *causes a decrease in the worker's vital strength* to make the worker, in many cases, an excluded person, segregated from the economic, occupational and social fields.

In such situations, the *human right to have a job*, subscribed at the Universal Declaration of Human Rights in Article 23, is not respected. Or it is snatched from the unemployed person, because of pragmatic or functional reasons, as in the case when somebody is asked to resign his or her job in an unfair way, because "it is convenient to the interest of company's owner", the company being either private or government owned. The question here is: "What about the worker's, the employee's rights?" Little thought is given to this question, because dehumanization, inequity and economic pragmatism have prevailed.

Unemployment, lack of working opportunities, underpaid jobs or underemployment are the opposite of what I mentioned before, whose immediate consequence is "the uncertainty about what will happen tomorrow", because of the lack of income, a lower wage, the lack of a home in property, hunger, insecurity and poverty generated by such condition. And this is only what can be seen. What is *not seen*, in a deeper manner, are the results produced by this kind of situations in the persons who suffer them: a deep dissatisfaction, not only of an economic and political nature, but also psychological and existential, as a social and occupational exclusion. This, according to World Health Organization (2006), can produce dysfunctionalities and/or fragmentation of the family nucleus, a scarce attention to children, depressive conditions, low self-esteem, chronic stress and, in extreme cases, it can lead to suicide

Not having a job, or not having a good job and not earning enough for living with dignity with one's family, causes immediately, as we have said, a variety of problems and crisis conditions (often very severe), both personal and familiar, which collectively added around the planet, adopt a profile of political, economic and social crises with a global character.

In Latin America, for instance, employment is the main source of income for homes, since remunerations coming from work are equivalent, as an average, to over 80% of their income (CEPAL, 2007a). The high poverty indexes prevailing in the region can be partially explained as caused by underemployment and unemployment, the high rates of dependency limiting the participation of women within the working age bracket, the low levels of human capital and the low productivity in many activities (CEPAL 2007b).

CEPAL (2008) explains replication and perpetuation of poverty through time as caused by two major factors: on one side, those who live in poor families have little opportunities to get education and training. Therefore, they have a deficient preparation for work, and they access to precarious jobs. In fact, unemployment occurs more often, and those who succeed in getting a job do it less frequently in a payroll and in formal jobs. On the other side, there is a high rate of demographic dependency in those families, which makes it necessary to distribute income among a larger number of persons. This leads to a situation where poor people not only get lower labor incomes, but they must use those incomes for the survival of a larger number of dependent persons. Therefore, there is no money for the education of children, which leads to a poverty replicating vicious circle.

The lack of working opportunities has caused migration of millions of persons. During 2013, there were 231.5 million international migrants, 81% of them native of developing countries (BBVA Bancomer and CONAPO, 2014: 25).

During the last decade, developed countries have benefited from important migration movements, incorporating migrant workers in low qualification tasks which native population is not always willing to carry out (Cachón 2009). On the other hand, the fact should be pointed out that during latest years, these movements have featured an increase of women's presence in the migration process. Thus, women have gone from a role related to family reunification to one of a major income supplier for their families (Moreno, A. and Marbán R., 2011: 52). At an international level, 48% of migrants are women. However, in regions such as Latin America, migrants are mostly women, amounting to 51.4% (BBVA Bancomer and CONAPO, 2014: 25).

This is why I totally adhere to ILO's Director General Guy Ryder's statement: "It's time to put jobs and growth back at the heart of International policy making". Will it be possible? How long will it take to give back economics and politics a truly human face?

IV Some Data

Guy Ryder, in his latest declaration at 2014 Spring Meetings of IMF and World Bank, pointed out that "A massive global jobs gap that opened at the height of the financial crisis is not closing. In fact, the gap will widen unless the global economy steps up the pace of growth to generate the jobs needed".

This shows that economic growth and investment in most countries is not accelerated, it will be almost impossible *to generate the jobs required* for the people to have a minimum level of welfare without the uncertainty of lack of income and poverty resulting from being unemployed or underemployed.

ILO's General Director points out that "if pre-crisis trends in employment growth had continued, 62 million more women and men would have been working in 2013 when global unemployment reached 202 million. Unless growth picks up, the jobs gap will widen to 75 million by 2018", an information which is dramatic because it would mean that, if there is no improvement in national economies, at a global level in the next four years, there could be 277 million unemployed persons.

This calculation—as foreseeable—is conservative, because if there is a financial turbulence in one region of the world, consequences, with the dominoes effect typical of globalization are unimaginable. We have repeatedly seen it: in 1995, financial crisis in Mexico, and the so-called "tequila effect", caused the volatility of capitals in many parts of the world. In 2008, mortgage and financial crisis in USA had global consequences still being suffered; in Spain, according to official data furnished by Banco de España, unemployment rate for the first quarter of 2014 is 55,4% amongst young people, even though a slight improvement has taken place in job recovery, as per indexes of affiliation at Social Security. Yet, data are alarming.

And what is happening in my country? I will mention three sources, only in the way of illustration. I will not get into the technical details supporting this information. These can be consulted in relevant web pages.

1) As per data furnished by INEGI, in the "Occupation and Employment Survey for the First Quarter of 2014", economically active population in the country was determined as 51.8 million persons, out of a total population of 119 million. This means 58.5% of population aged 14 years and over.

It is shown that 76 out of 100 men, and 42 out of 100 women, are economically active.

Unoccupied (unemployed) population was determined as 2.5 million persons, and the national vacancy rate reached 4.8% of economically active population (EAP), a lower percentage as that recorded for the same quarter of 2013, which was 4.9%.

Under-occupied population (with temporary or part-time jobs), reached 4.1 million persons in the first quarter of 2014, for a rate of 8.3% as compared to the rate for the same quarter of 2013, which was 8.2%.

2) According to OECD (Organization for Economic Cooperation and Development), the rate of unemployment in Mexico during March of this year was 5.1%, the fourth lowest in the 34 countries members of OECD, only below Austria (4.9%), Japan (3.6%) and Korea (3.5%).

This information could seem good news.

It is not so, because this 5.1% unemployment rate affected 2 million Mexicans, meaning an increase of 256,000 additional unemployed persons in only one month, because the unemployment rate in February was 4.9%

3) According to information from CNN Expansión, due to this situation, besides unemployment, there is an increase in underemployment, and an increase in informal jobs.

This shows that the second economy in Latin America has not yet found the way to economic recovery, and the forecast for GNP growth for the second quarter of 2014 in my country is barely 2.7%, as stated by Finance Minister Luis Videgaray, which is too low and insufficient to meet the country's needs and challenges of development, such as productive investment, generation of jobs and prosperity with an effective combat against poverty.

The truth is that, even though macroeconomic data in my country are not as alarming as for other nations in the world, "including the world's largest economies, where wages have lagged behind growth in productivity for over 20 years", as per ILO's information, we Mexicans are not contented with such a situation, because we see how our economy is stagnant—in the best scenario, and grows too slowly, as unemployment, underemployment and informal employment increase, thereby increasing the poverty index.

This generates social discontent, poverty, inequity, increase in crime and corruption, besides mistrust about Government and the suspicion that economic and financial reforms currently being implemented (on taxes, energy, politics and education) haven't yet proved their efficiency.

V Recommendations

What can we do before this panorama of a problem which is not exclusive of Mexico, but a global problem?

The following actions have become unpostponable:

1) **Finding other routes towards clearing and reorientation of current economic and financial models.**

This is why I entirely subscribe Guy Ryder's statement that "it's time to put jobs and growth back at the heart of international policy making", because "the global economy is not yet on a path to strong sustainable and balanced growth". Furthermore, "weak global demand is holding back job creation, wages and recovery even further and one consequence is a slowing of the pace of poverty reduction in the developing world".

2) **Making reforms in the international financial system**, where the excessive indebtedness incurred by governments and at the local level by the common citizen have caused the balance of payment to become unsustainable, income being channeled towards debt payment and *not* towards the productive system of nations for job generation or to family welfare, which is the object of a global clamor.

3) **Revising, critically and audaciously, common problems** linked to the *new hiring trends*, at an international level, where it would seem that *outsourcing* and *underemployment* are the best options in a world in motion.

As to outsourcing, what I think is that the possibility of contracting workers or employees on a temporary basis, in order to respond to temporary needs of labor in companies is beneficial, of course to companies that experience such temporary peaks of labor demand. But it is also beneficial for workers who, through this contractual means, get a job. Outsourcing responds to this demand by having a labor source company (or primary employer) supplying temporary labor to companies needing it. Perhaps a just labor legislation requiring the primary employer to have workers/employees in their payroll on a permanent basis, with all social benefits (social insurance, vacations, severance funds, etc.) granted by law to permanent employees.

As to underemployment, this type of temporary and *rootless* jobs—in many cases—only result in exploitation of workers, because upon scarcity of jobs and the unpostponable need of having a job, they accept whatever the job market offers, almost as "the only option". This shows that job offer market is very deficient, and the prevailing criterion among many employers is protection of their business, greediness, pragmatism and monetary utilitarianism.

Accumulation of capital at the expense of human exploitation is their motto. That type of companies and employers, both at the national and the international levels has become a perfectly lubricated machinery for the exploitation of man by man. Workers who, because of peremptory needs such as survival, join these companies are left unprotected regarding minimum social benefits and stable income.

4) **As related to governments of nations**, implementation of public policies in favor of productive investment promoting the creation of jobs in an environment with equity and justice, peace and solidarity among citizens, is a civic and moral duty for those in power. This means working in favor of the common good, favoring employment in order to fight against poverty, famine and social injustice due to lack of income and contributing to equitable and sustainable development of those nations.

Nation rulers must also allow small and medium-sized companies to grow, facilitating their emergence and development. This will inject dynamism to local economy, generating a natural economic motion inscribed within the framework of "entrepreneurial spirit", which must not be suffocated by obsolete entrepreneurial practices, but rather must be promoted.

We should not overlook the fact that, at an international level, the large job generators have been Small and Medium Enterprises (SMEs). According to a report from ILO, where about 50 surveys are analyzed, the conclusion is that SMEs account for two thirds of all formal jobs in developing countries in Africa, Asia and Latin America, and 80 percent in low income countries, especially in Sub-Saharan Africa.

Even more important than the fact of creating most of the jobs in emerging and low income economies, is the fact that SMEs, particularly the smallest and newest of them, are a fundamental contribution to the net creation of jobs.

There is a widespread opinion that, due to their shorter life cycle, SMEs do not generate many jobs. But, ILO's survey shows that this is not true: 50% of the total creation of jobs comes from companies with fewer than 100 employees.

In Mexico, according to INEGI's 2009 census, there are 5,144,000 economic units, out of which 99.8% are SMEs which, according to Pro-

México, account for 72% of employment in the country, which amounts to about 19.9 million jobs. If 72% of jobs in Mexico are generated by SEMs, this is a sector the Government should heed and support far more than it presently does.

As to national or international macro-companies, governments must watch that their growth serves the growth and development of the countries where they are seated, rather than being only the business for a few people: the large local or foreign investors.

Fight against corruption, wherever it shows up (at a local or national level), with a system of accountability and transparency giving the citizens the certainty that public resources are well managed and are at the service of common good.

5) **Educational institutions** (universities and training centers for work), get linked with employers and with new supply and demand trends of labor, without losing sight of the social and ethical value they should have in order to educate and train young people in the best possible way, so they will not have the terrible experience of not getting a job or having to accept underemployment or sub-contracting (such as outsourcing which, as I understand, is designed for the protection of companies by freeing them of social benefits due to payroll employees).

Institutions should include in the basic curricula of the various careers or training courses the development and promotion of abilities for work and for life, besides a good academic preparation of student. This task becomes unpostponable, and it is a social responsibility indebtedness of universities.

Institutions should favor the mentality of "enterprise hatching" among young people and their families. I must mention here that this an institutional practice in my University, with good results. This is a dynamic and entrepreneurial form of generating "self-employment", as a novel response to the employment crisis we are suffering.

6) **Family and basic level educational institutions** should instill universal ethical-axiological principles that cause persons to become better persons, by enabling them to tell right from wrong, fair from unfair, good from reprehensible. Such a course of action will counterbalance, in daily life, inequitable and unfair situations, not only in the economy and labor fields, but in any other sphere of life as well.

Synthesizing, in the fight against economic inequity, against the lack of employment and in favor of justice and more peaceful and harmonious world, all of us must work, all of us have in a way, a social responsibility.

Acknowledgment: Special thanks goes to my colleagues Atziri Moreno and Laura Pérez Palacios for their comments and suggestions for this paper.

References

ARENDT, H. (1958). *The Origins of Totalitarianism*. Cleveland: Meridian Books. Spanish version: (2006). *Los orígenes del totalitarismo*. Madrid: Alianza Editorial.
ARISTOTLE, (1985). *Methaphysics*. Books 10-14. Cambridge: Harvard University Press.
CACHóN L. (2009). *La España inmigrante: marco discriminatorio, mercado de trabajo y políticas de integración*. Barcelona: Anthropos.
CUéLLAR, H. (2009). *Ser y esencia de los valores. Una axiología para el siglo XXI* (2nd edition). Mexico: Trillas.
CUéLLAR, H. (2014). "Culture and Cultures: Brief Reflections about the Mainstream Cultures in the World". In: *World Culture Development Forum (2013)*. Social Science Academic Press (China).
CHANG, J. (2013). "Making Joint Efforts to Promote the Construction of World Mainstream Culture Construction: Wuhan Declaration of the First World Culture Development Forum (2013)" In: *World Culture Development Forum (2013)*. Social Sciences Academic Press (China).
MORENO, A. y Marbán R. (2011) "Los programas microfinancieros del ICO: un instrumento para la integración de la mujer inmigrante". *Boletín Económico ICE*, 3020 (1 al 30 noviembre).
NUSSBAUM, M. & Amartya Sen (1993). *The Quality of Life*. Oxford University Press. Spanish version: (1996) *La calidad de vida*. Mexico: FCE.

POPE Francis, (2013). *Evangelii Gaudium* (*The Joy of Gospel*). México: Ediciones Paulinas.

RYDER, G. (2003). "La responsabilidad social de las empresas y los derechos de los trabajadores". In: http://labordoc.ilo.org/record/359456? ln = en. Consulted on May 30, 2014.

SEN, A. (2009). *The Idea of Justice*. Penguin Press. Spanish version: (2010) *La idea de la justicia*. México: Taurus (Pensamiento).

论坛专题

罗尔斯正义论视角下的中国分配公正问题研究

孙友祥　杨杏蓉[*]

摘　要：分配公正是人类社会永恒的价值追求，也是实践发展的长久困惑。改革开放和市场经济建设促进了中国经济的突飞猛进，但也助推了分配公正的现实困境，让创造财富的人民群众公正地共享发展成果，成为当务之急。"社会基本善"的分配公正以正义的社会制度、正义环境和正义原则为基础。化解当代中国的分配格局失衡、实现分配公正，需要秉持"公平的机会平等原则"以保障公民政治权利平等，需要秉持"有差别的对待原则"以合理、有差别地对待，同时还要进行积极有效的政府干预。

关键词：分配　公正　机会平等　差别原则

Distributive Justice in China from the Perspective of Rawls' Theory of Justice

Sun Youxiang; Yang Xingrong

Abstract: Distributive justice is the eternal value pursuit of human

---

[*] 孙友祥，湖北大学政法与公共管理学院教授；杨杏蓉，湖北大学政法与公共管理学院研究生。

society, while it is a puzzle in practice in the long term. The reform and opening-up and the construction of market economy has advanced the economy considerably, while bringing about the predicament of distributive justice. It is the primary task for the government to make people creating wealth share the development achievement fairly. The distributive justice of "social primary goods" is based on justice social system, justice environment and justice principle. In order to solve the distributive imbalance and achieve distributive justice, it is necessary to ensure citizens' equal political rights in accordance with "the principle of fair equality of opportunity", make reasonable differential treatment with "the principle of differential treatment" and implement positive and effective government intervention.

Key words: distribution; justice; equality of opportunity; the difference principle

收入差距是一种客观经济现象，尽管一定的收入差距有助于激发劳动者潜能，但对于"超度"的收入分配差距如果不施以合理引导和变革，可能引发社会失序。据调查，目前中国收入最高的10%的家庭与收入最低的10%的家庭的人均收入差距达到65倍，贫富悬殊问题已经成为影响中国社会稳定和经济发展的现实问题。党的十八大提出要"调整收入分配格局，加大再分配调节力度，着力解决收入分配差距较大问题"[①]。罗尔斯关于社会财富平等分配、缩小贫富差距的"公平的机会平等原则"和"有差别的对待原则"的思想对解决当前中国分配不公问题具有重要的启示意义。

一 罗尔斯分配正义观

罗尔斯从正义的主要问题、分配正义环境及分配正义原则等方面阐

---

① 《十八大报告辅导读本》，人民出版社，2012，第15页。

释了"社会基本善"的分配正义。

(一)正义的主要问题是社会基本结构

"正义的主要问题是社会的基本结构,或更准确地说,是社会主要制度分配基本权利和义务,决定由社会合作产生的利益之划分的方式。[①]"也就是说,社会基本结构因为决定着各社会合作者在生活中的最初机会,自始至终决定着人们的不同生活前景而成为正义的主要问题,所以正义价值在社会制度的价值体系中应该是居于首要地位的。罗尔斯视正义为社会制度的首要德性,如真理是思想体系的首要德性一样,任何不符合正义的法律和制度,都必须加以改造或废除。在众多价值取向中,罗尔斯赋予正义以最高位置,主要在于正义是人类社会最起码、最基本的社会规范和标准。只有随着社会发展需要来确定正义原则,并据以制定各种制度,人们才有一个既自由又不损害他人自由的行动空间。罗尔斯视正义为社会制度的首要德性的本义在于:作为建构社会基本秩序和规范社会公共行为的制度体系,社会制度所应追求和可能达到的最高目标,首先且最终是社会制度安排本身的公平正义,依此确定前提,社会制度的运作实践和社会生活秩序的公平正义才是可以期待的[②]。

(二)分配正义的实现环境

罗尔斯认为"公平的正义"的产生和实现需要以一定的环境为依托,即正义环境。就客观环境而言,一是各社会合作者利益的一致性和冲突性并存,利益的一致性在于社会合作是被普遍接受的,利益的冲突性在于社会合作者们不可能不关心合作而产生的较大利益之分配;二是资源存在一定程度的匮乏,罗尔斯认为,一定程度的资源匮乏是正义存在的必要客观物质条件。一定程度的匮乏介于完全充裕和极度匮乏之间,在许多领域正是因为人们的需求和可能得到的供给存在不是特别大的差

---

① 〔美〕罗尔斯:《正义论》,何怀宏、何包钢、廖申白译,中国社会科学出版社,2010,第7页。
② 万俊人:《论正义之为社会制度的第一美德》,《哲学研究》2009年第2期。

距,正义才成为人们必然追求的价值。在主观环境方面,罗尔斯提出"无知之幕"笼罩下的原初状态假设,其相当于社会契约论中的自然状态,存在于思维中:每个自由、平等、有理性的人应该知道的东西很少,少到仅知道所有人类社会的一般事实和自己所处的社会有合作的可能和必需,都关注自己"好"的观念而对别人的利益不感兴趣,至于其他包括所在社会的某些信息,比如每个人的出身、天资、社会地位或者所在社会的状况甚至文明程度,都是不清楚的。"无知之幕"下主体间的互相不感兴趣或者说冷淡便成了理所当然。

按照罗尔斯的观点,社会各合作者一方面在主观上有着相近的利益需求,这样合作才会成为可能;另一方面他们又各自有其生活安排并都对他人保持"无知"状态,正是各自不相同的生活安排才会造成对各种资源利用的冲突,才有适用于正义德性的机会。

(三)分配正义的原则

罗尔斯的分配正义有"一般正义思想"和"特殊正义原则"两个表述。

"一般正义思想"是罗尔斯对其分配正义思想的最初表述,即所有的社会价值——自由、机会、收入、财富和自尊的基础都应该平等地分配,除非对所有这些价值或其中任何一种价值的不平等分配合乎或者说是有利于每一个人[①]。后来经其修正提出这些不平等的分配应该有利于"受惠最小者"。而"特殊正义原则"是罗尔斯后期表述的分配正义思想,包括第一个原则——"最大的自由平等原则":每个人都应平等地享有基本的自由,并且享有基本自由的前提是每个社会合作者不能以侵害他人的自由来扩大自己的自由;第二个原则——"公平的机会均等和有差别的对待原则",即社会和经济的不平等应该这样安排:(1)在与正义的储存原则一致的情况下,适合于受惠最少者的最大利益;(2)依系于公平的机会均等原则,使所有的职务和地位向所有人开放。该原则

---

① 〔美〕罗尔斯:《正义论》,何怀宏、何包钢、廖申白译,中国社会科学出版社,2010,第62页。

的设计目的是保障社会合作产生的有益品的平等分配权,即利益和财富的分配。

总之,罗尔斯的正义理论体现的是一种分配"社会基本善"的正义,是一种分配正义理论:所有的社会价值包括自由(权利)、收入、财富和职务等都应该在平等的条件下进行分配,任何一种不平等的分配只能是对每个社会合作者均有利时才被认为是符合正义的。最理想的状态是对于所有"社会基本善"都平等分配,不平等的分配只能有利于每一个社会合作者或者说有利于社会合作者中的"受惠最少者"。对于"自然基本善"的分配中的"受惠最少者"则应该通过一些制度上的"不平等的分配"给予补偿,以弥补先天不平等分配所造成的后天不平等。即在"基本善"分配上,政府应该积极参与、协调,充分实现"国家干预"而不是采取一种"放任"的态度,完全由"市场"来调节。

二 中国社会分配的现实偏差

改革开放和市场经济建设促进了中国经济的快速增长,但也带来了结构性矛盾,居民收入差距持续扩大,分配格局严重失衡,公平问题凸显。

(一)居民收入差距扩大,分配格局失衡

改革开放以来,中国居民收入总体水平不断提高,但收入差距也在持续扩大。1978 年,中国的基尼系数为 0.1806,2009 年达到 0.49,2013 年为 0.473,大大超过 0.4 的警戒线,财富日益集中。1997 年中国城乡居民收入比为 2.6∶1,2011 年达 3.13∶1,这种"落差"幅度远高于发达国家[①]。地区间居民收入分布呈"东高西低"的态势,差距极大,2009 年城镇居民人均可支配收入最高的地区上海(28838 元)与最低的地区甘肃(11929 元)差距达 16909 元,其收入之比为 2.4∶1。行业间收

---

① 数据来源:中华人民共和国国家统计局 2011 年城乡居民收入增长情况。

入差距不断地扩大，国家统计局统计结果显示，1988年、1992年、1995年和1997年行业间的职工平均工资的变异系数分别是0.1058、0.1384、0.1903和0.2144，并且随着改革的深入以及市场发育的不均衡性的蔓延，行业间职工平均工资的变异系数还在扩大，房地产、电力、通信、能源、医药、烟草等行业职工的平均工资是其他行业职工平均工资的2~3倍。同一企业里，要素所有者之间的收入差距也在扩大，资本所有者分享的收入越来越高，劳动者报酬比重持续下降。中国分配格局严重失衡。

（二）收入分配中劳动报酬比例偏低

大量普通劳动者的工资长期低于劳动力价值。20世纪90年代后期以来，劳动者报酬在国内生产总值中的比重不断下降，从1998年的53.1%降到2000年的51.4%、2003年的49.6%。普通劳动者的工资普遍偏低，尤其是农民工和城镇非正规就业劳动者的工资水平长期低于劳动力价值。许多地方的农民工工资几乎没有过增长，仍停留在几年前的水平。

（三）贫困人口比重大

中国社会科学院发布的2011年城市蓝皮书指出，截至2009年底，全国城镇人口为62186万人，城镇居民人均可支配收入为17175元，按照中国城市合理贫困线人均年收入7500~8500元的标准，全国贫困人口数约为5000万人。此外，收入来源不稳定、一遇疾病等风险即陷入贫困的人数就更多。可见，分配在中国严重失衡，矫正刻不容缓。

三 促进中国分配公正的实现路径

尽管很多学者认为罗尔斯的正义理论主要是服务于资本主义生产关系的，但我们丝毫不能否认该理论对解决中国当前社会公平问题的借鉴意义。

(一)保障政治权利平等是实现分配正义的制度基础

罗尔斯对"最大的自由平等原则"赋予了第一位的优先性。也就是说,一个社会分配正义的实现,首先应当满足"社会中的每个人都应平等地享有基本的自由,并且这些基本自由享有的前提是不能侵害他人的自由"。基于此,保障公民政治权利平等成为分配正义实现的制度基础。

第一,完善基层民主制度,扩大弱势群体的参与权,使各利益群体表达自己利益诉求的平等机会在制度上成为可能,为弱势群体提供表达自己利益的平台,引导他们充分表达自己的诉求和愿望。如2007年对选举法的修改,实现了城乡居民同票同权。

第二,建设信访制度,增加基层群众的利益表达权。在中国,信访作为一种公民表达权利的机制,成为解决公民纠纷一种的途径,完善信访受理、调查、回复、责任追究等制度建设,可以引导基层群众以相对理性、合法的形式向政府表达利益诉求。

第三,公开政府信息,增加弱势群体的知情权。加强社会事务管理信息系统建设,为弱势群体提供所需信息,努力保障社会全体成员的知情权。

第四,加强基层组织建设,集中表达弱势群体的利益诉求。推进工会、行业协会等基层社会组织的民主管理,切实发挥它们在政府与公众之间的桥梁作用,使分散的个体利益得到整体性展现。

(二)合理差别对待是实现分配正义的重要手段

根据罗尔斯的分配正义观,合理的差别包括自然的和社会的差别,法律确认和保护它们,并不是制造不平等,而是遵循比值相等和平等原则安排它们的关系。如果将对弱势群体的合理差别对待作为中国分配制度完善的出发点,那么,教育、就业及公平的市场竞争环境则是实现对弱势群体合理差别对待的基本途径。

1. 对受教育弱势群体的合理差别对待

一是要增加教育支出,并向农村倾斜。早在1993年,《中国教育改革和发展纲要》就提出，2000年要达到财政性教育经费支出占国内生产总值的4%的目标，但直到2011年中国财政性教育经费支出仍仅占国内生产总值的3.41%。因此，各级政府必须增加对教育的投入，并在教育资源配置与教育政策上逐步实现由城市中心取向向"农民工取向"与"农村取向"的转变。二是建立系统化的边远山区、农村地区的教育录取倾斜制度。三是改革、完善与户籍制度相联系的入学制度。公民的受教育权应涵盖正常流动人口子女的受教育权，在无法均衡教育资源的情况下，保障正常的迁移人口的子女特别是流动农民工子女的受教育权成为必需。四是建立系统化的教育救助制度。收入的高低决定了教育资源的获得，而高收费使得收入较低的人群无法享有相应的教育，造成教育资源的分配不公。因此，必须加大教育救助力度并建立系统化的教育资助制度，如完善发达地区对落后地区的定期教育援助机制，使低收入者能够得到应得的教育机会。五是建立完备的教育体系。国家应针对受教育弱势群体中的不同人群的不同需要，积极拓展教育形式，如职业教育、自学教育、成人教育等，创造更适合每一个人的教育条件与选择机会，提高弱势群体中受教育者的数量和范围。

2. 对就业弱势群体的合理差别对待

对就业领域弱势群体应在保障平等就业的基础上合理差别对待。一是以立法引导社会价值观的改变。评价劳动者就业合适程度的标准就是其是否具备承担该项工作的能力和条件，因此，要明确任何人都有通过工作获取相应回报的权利，同时明确就业平等权高于企业用工自主权。二是加强对劳动力市场的监管，赋予执法机构对企业设置不合理就业限制的行为予以监督、纠正的权力。三是完善关于就业歧视的救济途径。可以将求职者与用人单位的纠纷纳入劳动争议解决机制的受案范围，使求职者和在职员工的权利一样得到较好的救济[1]。四是为就业弱势群体无偿提供适合其条件的制度化培训。只有对就业弱势群体接受再教育提供帮助，才能提高其就业竞争力。

---

[1] 宁立成：《禁止就业歧视的人本之维》，《法学论坛》2009年第2期。

3. 对市场竞争弱势群体的合理差别对待

对市场竞争弱势群体的合理差别对待，就是要对中小企业予以特别保护以维护市场竞争的有效性。国家只有通过特别救济法律政策保障中小企业权益，才能实现经济交易状态下的平等[①]。首先，国务院主管部门、各地方政府应当根据自身职责出台政策，建立部门之间、部门和地方政府之间的联动机制，切实加大对中小企业创业、资金、技术和市场等方面的支持力度。其次，减轻中小企业的负担。简化对中小企业有关事项的行政审批手续，减少相关费用，实行差别税率制，使中小企业能够"轻装上阵"。最后，建立完善的中小企业信用担保体系或者创新担保形式等，保证中小企业"有钱可贷"，化解中小企业"融资难"问题。

（三）完善直接干预在实现分配正义中起关键作用

化解分配中的市场失灵、实现分配正义需要对国民收入分配进行直接干预，包括初次分配和再分配。就现实而言，初次分配的关键在于促进居民收入的优先增长，实现藏富于民；再分配应加大对弱势群体的扶助力度，社会保障应当优先满足弱势群体的生存需要。

1. 建立居民收入优先增长机制

居民收入优先增长意味着对国民收入分配的国家、企业、个人三元主体中个人的差别对待。

对于以劳动报酬作为收入的城镇居民，一是要促进最低工资制的实施。关于最低工资标准的确定，要充分考虑物价因素，保证劳动者报酬在扣除价格因素后稳定增长。二是应当推进工会制度改革，让工会作为劳动者的代表直接参与工资集体协商，平衡强势企业与弱势劳动者之间的力量关系，让劳动者得到公平对待。三是考虑各种改革如住房、医疗、教育等对城镇居民实际收入的影响。部分改革已经直接或间接吞噬了劳动报酬的增长，如不断上涨的房价和医疗支出。因此，提升住房保障、医疗保障成为当务之急。

---

① 贾平：《论我国中小企业的法律保护》，《河北法学》2008年第10期。

对于从事个体农务而获得收入的农村居民，一方面各级财政要重视政策优惠和补贴，加强对主要农产品的价格扶持，提高补贴的范围和标准，增加农村居民的收入。另一方面要加强农业制度创新，拓宽农民创收渠道。此外，各级财政要提高用于农村民生的财政支出，增加农村公共产品供给，实施城乡一体化发展战略。

2. 优化、完善低收入群体的社会保障制度

社会保障制度是国民收入分配中的二次分配制度，反映的是一种对不平均"基本善"分配的补偿，也是一种对初次分配中弱势群体的差别对待。目前中国的社会保障制度是对大部分社会群体的基本保障，缺少对"低收入群体"的特别保障。完善的重点是将低收入弱势群体的保障置于优先地位，从低收入弱势群体的基本需要出发，按适度的按需分配原则完善社会保障体制，从根本上解决在市场经济发展过程中不幸陷入恶性循环的社会群体的问题，尽可能满足处于最不利地位群体的基本需求。

目前，资金缺乏是社会保障面临的现实问题。不可否认，社会保障资金的解决是一个渐进的过程，但是对弱势群体基本需要的满足已具备一定的可能性和可实现性。据了解，"中国现在财政收入没有全部纳入预算，2012年全国3万多亿土地出让收入和国有资产经营性收入等都没有纳入，很多财政资金未受到人大监督，造成财政资金分配使用不科学，财政纪律不严肃，超收财政先斩后奏，年底突击花钱，事后补个报告就行"[①]。因此，规范财政收入申报，推进财政资金分配的透明化，使财政收入分配向低收入弱势群体倾斜，是当前迫切需要也完全能够解决的问题。同时，完善社会救助制度体系，建立农民群体等低收入群体的社会保障制度，不但是中国建立和完善社会保障体系的需要，也是对现实存在的不合理分配现象进行有效干预的应有之义。

---

① 陆晨阳：《中纪委原副书记刘锡荣：老百姓再勤劳，也养不起这么多官啊》，《都市快报》2012年3月11日。

经济不平等与世界性的环境正义

文贤庆　李培超[*]

摘　要：现代性发展带来了全球性的环境问题。面对全球性的环境问题，发达国家或地区的人们认为环境问题主要是由于发展中国家或地区急剧膨胀的人口所导致的，这些国家或地区对环境问题负有不可推卸的主要责任；与此相对，发展中国家或地区的人们认为环境问题在根本上源于主要由发达国家或地区设置的不平等社会制度或结构。然而，归责并不能解决问题，面对全球性的环境问题，提出解决问题的实际方案才是第一要务。我们有理由相信，当我们把人类整体的繁荣昌盛作为思考问题的起点时，一种能力方法理论可以为我们提供一种新的突破口。

关键词：环境正义　经济不平等　发展中国家或地区　发达国家或地区　能力方法

Economic Inequality and Globally Environmental Justice

Wen Xianqing; Li Peichao

Abstract：Modern development brings us global environment crisis.

---

[*] 文贤庆，湖南师范大学道德文化研究中心老师，中国特色社会主义道德文化协同创新中心研究成员；李培超，湖南师范大学道德文化研究中心教授，中国特色社会主义道德文化协同创新中心研究成员。

Developed countries believe that the environmental crisis is mainly caused by population expansion in developing countries which must take main responsibility for it. Meanwhile, developing countries believes that environmental crisis originates from the unequal social structure in developed countries. However, blame can not solve the problem. We believe that we can find a new way to solve the problem when we take human prosperity as the starting point of the problem.

Key words: environmental justice; economic inequality; developing countries; developed countries; ability and method

自进入现代社会以来，人类的科技迅猛发展，人类的物质财富极大丰富。与此同时，环境问题成了一个很显著的全球性问题，温室效应、酸雨、淡水危机、水污染、土地荒漠化等就是环境问题普遍化的具体反映。这些全球性的环境问题不断地影响着人类的生活。面对全球性的环境问题，环境伦理学家们主要从传统的哲学伦理学以及生态学中去寻找解决的答案，然而，环境保护的实践表明，上述理论脱离了环境保护的实践，并没有能够为环保运动提供切实可行的指导。正是在这种背景下，很多研究者认为仅仅从一种抽象的哲学观或世界观入手并不能解决环境问题，解决问题的关键在于社会制度或社会结构。很多研究者认为，环境问题的解决在根本上有赖于我们在经济发展和环境保护之间寻得一种正义，我们可以称之为环境正义。① 按照这种观点，环境问题有两个特征。

第一，环境问题具有有限性的特点。因为环境问题在根本上源于人与自然的关系，所以这种有限性就体现为自然环境作为资源对于人类而

---

① 事实上，很多学者反对把正义的观念运用于自然环境，这种思想尤其明显地体现在自由主义理论的坚持者身上，他们认为正义是基于人这样的自由行动者的，比如罗尔斯、巴里等。不过，施罗斯博格通过借鉴一种能力方法理论雄辩地指出正义的观念可以适用于自然。参见 David Schlosberg, *Defining Environmental Justice: Theories, Movements, and Nature*, Oxford: Oxford University Press, 2007.

言的有限性和自然对于人类活动造成污染的承载的有限性。这种有限性使得人与自然处在一种张力之中，在地球这样一个有限的封闭系统中，如果任由人口和经济自由发展，那么总有一天地球的资源会耗尽，人口和经济也会因此陷入衰退状态。① 在面对环境问题时，既然地球的有限性无法改变，那么唯一可能的方法就是改变人类的自由行为活动。因为人类的行为活动体现为关于人类种族延续的生殖活动和人类生活的经济活动，所以环境问题的解决依赖于把人口数量和经济发展活动控制在地球环境能够容纳的范围之内。但在限制何种人的何种行为活动的问题上关乎存在分歧的分配正义问题。

第二，环境问题具有公共性的特点。从资源的角度来看，自然资源作为具有内在价值的东西对于所有人都具有同样的功效，水、大气、土地、矿产等对所有人而言都是具有同等价值的。② 对它们的使用需要一种公共意见。从环境污染的角度来看，温室效应、酸雨、水污染、土地荒漠化等环境问题影响的并不仅仅是个体性的，而是大众化的。对这些环境问题的解决也依赖于人类的公共行动。环境问题的公共性使得我们在处理人类使用资源和承担环境污染的责任时的分配正义问题呈现一种全球性或世界性。从这个意义上而言，有关环境的分配正义必然需要扩展为一种世界正义。

综上所述，环境问题实质上体现的就是一个如何在地球这个公共环境中实现人类发展的分配正义问题，包括对自然资源的分配和对环境污染所承担义务的分配。然而，正是在分配问题上，无论是对资源的占有权利，还是对环境污染所承担的义务，国际社会都存在巨大的分歧。③ 这种分歧尤其集中地表现为发达国家或地区和发展中国家或地区之间的矛盾。我们将分而论之。

---

① 〔美〕丹尼斯·米都斯等《增长的极限——罗马俱乐部关于人类困境的报告》，李宝恒译，吉林人民出版社，1997，第 17 页。
② 这里指出的具有同等价值是从环境对于人类的基本生活而言的，而非从人获取经济利益的角度来说的。
③ 这里直接把视角定位为一个全球性的国际视野，而不谈论一个国家之内的问题。

一 发达国家或地区的视角

从发达国家或地区的视角来看，环境问题的根源在于人口问题，人口问题导致了一系列的资源破坏、环境污染、贫困和不良的经济增长模式等问题。按照这种观点，"世界上的人口太多了，空间没有了，能量用完了，食物将要告罄。虽然有些人已经认识到了，但是我们已经没有时间了"。[1]"全球变暖、酸雨、臭氧层破坏、对流行疾病脆弱的抵抗力、土地和地下水的日益衰竭，全部与人口规模有关，很显然，这些问题对于人类文明的延续产生了现实的威胁，在今后几十年，仅仅由于全球变暖造成的农作物歉收，就将导致近十亿甚至更多的人的提前死亡。数亿人将成为艾滋病蔓延的牺牲品，既然人类自身拒绝制定一个较温和的计划，自然界就把所有这些灾难组织起来编制成一个残酷的'人口计划'"。[2]

从发达国家或地区的视角看来，正是发展中国家或地区急剧的人口增长导致了所谓的人口过剩，结合发达国家或地区主流的个体权利和义务思想，每个人都有同样的义务承担同样的有关环境的义务。现在，环境问题越来越严重，而人口增长又几乎主要发生在发展中国家或地区，所以，毫无疑问，环境问题更多地是由发展中国家或地区带来的，应该由他们埋单。而且，由于环境的公共性，正是发展中国家或地区拖累了发达国家或地区，发展中国家或地区应该对发达国家或地区给予补偿。

按照发达国家或地区的这种理论，非洲、东南亚和南美等地的热带雨林对全球气候和生态系统起着至关重要的调节作用，它们是公共性的，然而，生活在这些国家或地区的人却不断地砍伐这些森林资源，从而在很大程度上导致了全球气候的异常和生态系统的失调，毫无疑问，生活在这些地区的人是破坏热带雨林的直接主体，他们应该为由此导致的环

---

[1] Louis P. Pojman, *Environmental Ethics: Reading in Theory and Application.* Jones and Bartlett Publishers, Inc. 1994, p. 241.
[2] 〔美〕赫尔曼·E. 戴利、〔美〕肯尼斯·N. 汤森:《珍惜地球》，马杰等译，商务印书馆，2001，第69页。

境问题担负更多的责任。同样,发展中国家或地区为了基本的经济发展更多地承担了一些污染严重的工业企业或工业企业的重污染环节,从而导致了更严重的环境问题,并进而影响了发达国家或地区的环境,那么,很显然,发展中国家或地区的人应该为此担负更多的环保责任。按照发达国家或地区的观点,既然个体是权利和义务的主体,那么,很显然,环境问题的破坏在很大程度上就是由发展中国家或地区的人口膨胀和人口过剩所导致的。

正是在这种理论框架下,发达国家或地区认为环境正义的问题首先在于保护现有的良好环境,进而不断地去竭力改善已经破坏的环境。然而,绝非巧合的是,在现代的全球框架下,发达国家或地区拥有比较好的环境,而发展中国家或地区则面临越来越恶劣的环境[①]。考虑环境正义自然首先应该考虑发达国家或地区受伤害的程度,因为发达国家或地区受伤害的程度恰恰意味着人类对于环境破坏的责任。正是如此,发达国家或地区在环境问题上的正义要求被某些学者形象地比喻成"救生艇伦理学"。按照这个理论,环境正义在根本上体现为发达国家或地区对于发展中国家或地区的"人道主义关怀"态度:或者平等对待发展中国家或地区的每一个人,或者有选择地对待其中的一部分人,或者漠视他们;结果就是,平等对待换来彻底的灾难,部分选择伴随着歧视,漠视则带来真正的正义。[②]

如果这就是环境正义,那么正义就是发达国家或地区的正义,就是富人的正义,而这显然是一个令人难以接受的结论。我们还需要看发展中国家或地区的人怎么说,穷人怎么说。

二 发展中国家或地区的视角

从发展中国家或地区的视角来看,环境问题的根源在于社会制度或结

[①] 这里暂不论发展中国家或地区尽管存在但越来越少的、没有遭到破坏的自然环境。
[②] 关于"救生艇理论"的具体细节,参见 Garett Hardin, "Living on a lifeboat", *Bioscience*, 1974, 24 (10).

构。前已提及，在人与环境的关系中，唯一可能的方法就是改变人类的行为活动，或者是人类种族延续的生殖活动，或者是人类生活的经济活动。既然发达国家或地区从人口问题提出的环境正义并不能令人满意，那么从人类经济活动出发就成了另外一个可能的选择。按照这种观点，环境问题从来不是一个孤立的问题，它总是与贫困、种族歧视、城市恶化以及企业活动所导致的生活质量下降等社会不公正问题分不开的，实现环境正义的中心原则就在于对资源、环境利益和社会福利的公平分配，而实现这一点的关键在于一个合理的社会制度或结构的确立。

按照这种观点，每个人都是权利和义务的主体，那么，每一个人至少享有最基本的生存权。基于此，生活在非洲、东南亚和南美等地的人为了基本需求而砍伐热带雨林就是正当的、符合正义的，即使热带雨林对全球气候和生态系统起着至关重要的调节作用，但是生活在这里的人的生存压力要远远大于由于砍伐雨林而给世界带来的环境压力。而且，最为重要的是，这些地区热带雨林急剧下降在很大程度上源自于发达国家或地区的人对于热带雨林的需求。事实上，不仅仅是热带雨林，发展中国家或地区的很多自然资源之所以被开采，自然环境之所以被破坏和污染，在很大程度上都源于发达国家或地区的人对于自然资源的需求。按照每个人是最终权利和义务主体的观点，发生在发展中国家或地区的环境问题有很大一部分责任应该归于发达国家或地区的人。

事实上，按照发展中国家或地区的观点，环境问题在根本上源自于社会制度或结构导致的国际社会存在的巨大贫富差距和经济不平等。正是贫富差距和经济不平等使得发达国家或地区在很多方面区别于发展中国家或地区。就环境问题而言，这主要表现在以下几个方面。

从环境问题的性质来看，能源的消费量尤其是人均消费量反映人从环境获利的程度，还反映人类对资源枯竭和环境污染责任的大小。按照这一指标，发达国家或地区的人在环境上是最大的受益者，而发展中国家或地区的人则较少受益。以 2000 年左右的能耗水平为例，一个美国人每年的能源消费是一个中国人的约 11.5 倍，是一个印度人的约 30 倍。

结合环境能耗和人口数量,按照同一个标准,美国的能耗总量将是印度的 8.1 倍,中国的 2.5 倍。① 按照这种标准,真正人口过剩的就不是发展中国家或地区,而是发达国家或地区。由于资源从根本上来源于自然环境,因此,发达国家或地区无疑是环境上的最大受益者,而大多数发展中国家或地区则较少受益。

从环境负荷来看,资源的消费必然会产生相应的废物,相应的废物会增加环境的负荷,导致严重的环境污染,从而威胁人的健康和生命存续。然而,与发达国家或地区享有更多的环境消耗量不同,由于资源消费所导致的问题却更多地出现在发展中国家或地区。十分明显的一个例子是,导致全球变暖的一个重要因素——二氧化碳的排放——在很大程度上是由发达国家或地区造成的,但由于气候变暖所导致的自然灾害在很大程度上却发生在发展中国家或地区,由此导致的人口伤亡也主要发生在发展中国家或地区。

在环境损失上,由于人们所处的社会地位和生理状况不同,环境破坏的影响给不同的人带来了不同的经济损失和健康损失。一个很明显的现状就是,发展中国家或地区承担了更多的对于环境破坏更大、对身体损害更大的生产行业或生产环节。例如,发达国家或地区工业生产中产生的很多对于人体有害的废弃物的处理工作大多由发展中国家或地区承担,这些废弃物污染着当地的大气、土壤、水,废弃物连同被破坏的环境一起对当地的人的健康造成了极大威害。关于环境污染对人体的伤害,日本的环境经济学家宫本宪一提到三条被广泛接受的原则:(1)"生物学上的弱者"首先受害;(2)"社会上的弱者"首先受害;(3)造成"绝对的不可逆损失"。② 按照这三条原则,由于环境污染所导致的人类

---

① 按照每个人的能源消耗乘以总人口数计算。如果把每个人的能源消耗都换算成石油消耗,一个美国人每年消耗石油 7918 千克,一个中国人消耗 684 千克,一个印度人消耗 270 千克;2000 年美国人口 2.8 亿,中国人口 12.95 亿,印度人口 10.16 亿。
② 转引自韩立新《环境问题上的代内正义原则》,《江汉大学学报》(人文科学版) 2004 年第 5 期。

健康问题（"绝对的不可逆损失"）首先发生在老弱病残（"生物学上的弱者"）和低收入者（"社会上的弱者"）身上。抛开"生物学上的弱者"不谈，"社会上的弱者"主要是因为经济不平等和人为的社会制度或结构安排所导致的。

综上所述，从发展中国家或地区的视角来看，不论是资源消费、环境负荷，还是环境损失，这些环境问题的根源是国家或地区的经济或社会状况。从源头上讲，在全球化的今天，"资本的逻辑"决定了弱势群体（这里主要指"社会上的弱者"）是环境污染最严重的受害者，污染性产业主要集中在贫穷地区和国家；有害的垃圾填埋在地价最低的地方，而地价最低的地方必然是穷人居住的地方……而这样一种结果在根本上源于一种不公平的社会机构或制度。正如博格（Pogge）指出的那样，在现代世界，制度因素才是决定世界正义的最重要因素，对于一个国家而言，"制度因素连同政府的政策工具对经济分配有着重要影响"，"当前的全球秩序基本上是在富国的政府领导人、企业总裁，富国和穷国的政治和军事精英围绕着富国少数人的利益进行长期讨价还价、妥协和合谋的过程中形成的"[①]，"正是这种带有压迫性的社会结构依次产生了强化统治一切的思维方式和生活方式，包括对自然界的统治"[②]。很显然，这样的制度安排首先在于少数人或少数团体的私利，在根本上不利于减小富国和穷国之间的差距，不利于消解民族国家之间的经济不平衡，不利于人类对于全球环境问题的解决。

基于上述分析，从发展中国家或地区的视角来看，环境问题在根本上是经济发展所造成的，而经济发展的问题又主要由符合富国利益的国际经济和政治秩序造成，理所当然地，如果在我们今天生活的时代存在有关人与自然的环境正义的话，那么这种正义首先应该体现为发达国家或地区对于发展中国家或地区的责任，富国对于穷国的穷困，富国对于

---

① 韦森：《极度贫困与人权：从道德关怀到经济分析》，载许纪霖主编《全球正义与文明对话》，江苏人民出版社，2004。
② Joseph R. Desjadins, *Environmental Ethics: An Introduction to Environmental Philosophy*. Wadsworth Group, 2001, p. 236.

人类之于环境破坏所具有的更多责任。①

三 真正的世界性环境正义

前已备述，按照发达国家或地区的观点，导致环境问题的主要原因在于人口的急剧增长，而人口急剧增长主要在于发展中国家或地区；按照发展中国家或地区的观点，导致环境问题的主要原因在于不合理的社会制度或结构，在于经济的不平等。然而，如果说环境问题主要是由于发展中国家或地区的人口问题所导致的，那么这在根本上就是否认生活在发展中国家或地区的人们的生存权利和发展权利。以热带雨林的不断减少为例，热带雨林地区的人砍伐雨林主要是迫于基本的生存和发展压力，是最基本的人权需求。很显然，基本的生存权要大于环境的压力。在这个意义上，即使我们可以指责这是人口问题所导致的，但是既有人口的生存权终归是最先需要得到保障的，而且，对人口问题追根溯源，无论是为了增加劳动力，还是因为没有好的条件进行节育，抑或因为没有好的教育而没有节育意识……这些在根本上都可以归因于经济不平等导致的贫困。当然，如果说环境问题主要是由于发达国家或地区设置的社会制度或结构所导致的，那么这些地区的人同样也会反驳说，我们只是不断地实现人的自由和全面发展，并且我们也在努力帮助发展中国家或地区的人不断地改变贫困的状态，帮助他们保护环境。最重要的是，对于生活在当下的发达国家或地区的人而言，他们很难认可现在的全球秩序是他们的祖先在几十年甚至上百年前的全球化运动中所形成的；即使认可，要他们来承担由此导致的后果也是不公平的。

事实上，不论是从发达国家或地区的视角而言，还是从发展中国家或地区的视角而言，情况的复杂度远高于上面所提及的。然而，问题的关键在于，不论发达国家或地区和发展中国家或地区各自坚持什么样的

---

① 托马斯·博格称之为"消极义务"。Pogge, Thomas, *World Poverty and Human Rights*, Cambridge Polity Press, 2002, p. 130.

观点，认为自己有着什么样的充分理由坚持自己的主张，一个无法改变的事实在于，环境问题已经成为关乎全人类的紧迫问题，人与自然环境之间的问题已经摆在所有人面前。与其追究到底是谁导致了环境问题，谁应该为环境问题负责，不如探讨人类应该如何共同面对环境问题带给我们的挑战。很多有远见的理论家和实践者已经为此做出不懈的努力。罗尔斯在正义论中提出的分配正义原则对于解决环境问题具有重要的参考价值。

按照罗尔斯的理论，社会正义应该这样安排："第一个原则，每个人对与其他人所拥有的最广泛的基本自由体系相容的类似自由体系都应有一种平等的权利。第二个原则，社会和经济的不平等应这样安排，使它们：（1）在与正义的储存原则一致的情况下，适合于最少受惠者的最大利益；（2）依系于在机会公平平等的条件下职务和地位向所有人开放。"① 第一个原则是自由平等的原则，第二个原则包括差异原则和机会均等原则。按照我们前面的分析，人与环境的关系在根本上体现为人类的经济活动，经济活动主要表现为人们对于资源利用和环境污染的分配正义，那么，当罗尔斯独创地将对于每一个人的正义体现为"合乎最少受惠者的最大利益"时，这样的分配正义将真正有利于实现平等。

然而，对于环境正义而言，罗尔斯的正义理论还需要扩展。罗尔斯的正义理论是以理想状态中的个体作为基本出发点的，最终的正义也是为了维护个体的权利和利益，然而，对于环境正义而言，我们最终关注的是人与自然的和谐相处，我们不仅要关注每一个人的权利和利益，也需要关注环境的好坏，或者说，环境的好坏也是我们个人权利和利益不可分割的组成部分。按照这样一种思路，正义理论的终极目的不是单纯地在人类社会结构中实现分配的正义，而是在人与人之间、人与自然之间实现人类的繁荣昌盛。正义不仅是对个人的正义，同时也应该是对环境的正义。这在根本上要求我们不仅把人作为根本的出发点，而且应该

---

① 〔美〕约翰·罗尔斯：《正义论》，何怀宏、何包钢、廖申白译，中国社会科学出版社，1997。

把环境作为我们思考的起点。换而言之，环境和人都应该作为我们思考分配正义的构成要素，这要求一种新的正义理论。由森（Sen）提出，纳斯鲍姆（Naussbaum）和施罗斯伯格（Schlosberg）继承和发展的"能力方法"理论为此提供了借鉴。

按照一种发展了的能力方法理论，人类繁荣是我们关注的道德起点和终极目的，人类繁荣在根本上不仅包含人类的合理性实践，而且包括与我们共同生活在一个自然环境中的非人动物和植物，因此，非人动物和植物的繁荣也构成了人类繁荣的一个要素。既然单个人的生活会直接关联于个人拥有一个真正的机会（能力）按照某种关键的人类方式运行，那么，与我们分享那些能力的非人动物和植物也拥有它们自己的权利。① 因此，当我们面对环境问题时，我们应该依照与人类繁荣相关的不同能力（capabilities）考虑非人动物和植物的参与性（participatory），承认（recognition）它们相对于人与自然和谐相处应该有的地位，为它们分配（distribute）保障它们的生存和发展的基本权利和利益。基于此，实现真正的环境正义要求我们在制度化层面考虑以下几个关注点。

第一，现代化反思。不论是发达国家或地区，还是发展中国家或地区，主流的处理人与自然关系的方式都是基于人的主体性对于客观世界的征服性思想。这在根本上导致了人类与自然环境的对立。如何寻找一种真正的人与自然相和谐的方式是我们改变环境问题的关键。这要求我们对现代化的人类生产方式进行反思。

第二，整全性考虑。环境问题凸显的是地球的整体性问题，是人类

---

① 这里，发展了的能力方法理论指的是施罗斯伯格的理论。就能力方法理论而言，森主要是在人类经济和社会领域进行运用；纳斯鲍姆把它扩展到动物；真正扩展到环境和整个生态系统的，则是施罗斯伯格。限于主题和篇幅，这里没有详细论述。具体可以参见 Amartya Sen, "Capabilitiy and Well-Being", in Martha Nussbaum and Amartya Sen (eds.), *The Quality of Life*. Oxford: Clarendon Press, 1992; Amartya Sen, "Human Rights and Capabilities", *Journal of Human Development*, 2005, Vol.6 (2): 151–66; Martha Nussbaum, *Women and Human Development: The Capabilities Approach*, Oxford: Oxford University Press, 2000; *Frontiers of Justice: Disability, Nationality, Species Membership*, Cambridge: Harvard University Press, 2006; David Schlosberg, *Defining Environmental Justice: Theories, Movements, and Nature*, Oxford: Oxford University Press, 2007.

与自然的关系问题。因此，任何对于人与自然关系问题的思考都应该被纳入，那些从边缘的、遥远的和自然世界出发的观点都应该被考虑，其中尤其重要的是考虑生态的科学观点。

第三，多层次制度。人类活动并不仅仅限于以民族为主体的国家层面。任何工作制度不能仅仅停留在国家层面，而必须是多层次的，包括跨国界的和非官方的。

第四，灵活性处理。现代社会是一个多元化的社会，在一个多元化的社会里，制度化的工作必须保持灵活度。应该基于不同国家或地区的不同情况制定适宜的制度。

第五，持续性发展。只要人存在于地球一天，人与自然的关系就存在一天，人与自然的互动是一种永恒的动态，环境正义是一种与时俱进的不断按照天人合一思想发展的持续状态。

概而言之，环境保护运动的实践应该基于一种多维度、多层次的视角，尤其体现在具有主观能动性的个人、集体、民族、国家以及人类整体对于环境保护和生态保护因为能力的大小而具有的不同责任，不同的环境运动主体应该基于各自的能力具有不同的担当，真正实现环境正义。基于此，我们有理由相信，只有摒弃成见，不再拘泥于个人权利和义务，不再拘泥于民族国家的界限，不再拘泥于以经济发展为第一要务，我们才能真正实现人对于环境的正义。而且，我们有理由相信，这样一种人对于环境的正义才会重新让我们审视人与人之间的正义问题，从而真正实现世界的正义。

社会公平——中西方共同的社会理想

昌　灏　徐方平[*]

摘　要：实现共同富裕，防止两极分化，是社会主义的内在要求。然而，当前中国社会在一定程度、一定范围内出现了贫富分化、社会公平缺失的现象，这必然会引起社会矛盾的激化，其逻辑结果必然是社会危机。如何防止贫富分化，从而实现社会公平，已成为维护我国社会稳定的基本问题之一。对此，以公平正义作为社会理想的欧美发达国家在维护社会公平方面有一些经验值得我们借鉴。

关键词：社会主义　社会公平　贫富分化　社会稳定

Social Justice: The Common Social Ideals in China and Western Countries

Chang Hao; Xu Fangping

Abstract: To achieve common prosperity and avoid polarization is the immanent demands of socialism. However, to a certain degree, the phenomenon

---

[*] 昌灏，男，湖北工业大学经济与政法学院副教授；徐方平，男，湖北大学马克思主义学院院长、博士生导师。

of lack of social justice, the gap between rich and poor appear within a certain range in current Chinese society, which is bound to cause social contradictions, and the logical result inevitably is social crisis. How to avoid the gap between rich and poor so as to realize social justice is the basic problem of maintaining social stability in our country. To this problem, there is some experience worth of reference in western developed countries.

Key words: socialism; social justice; polarization between the rich and the poor; social stability

改革开放是建设中国特色社会主义的历史潮流,势不可挡;然而,改革开放之路是曲折的。我们只能在前进的道路上不断总结经验,不断克服我们前进道路上的种种阻力,不断消除我们思维方式上的种种误区,以克服不公平现象,逐渐有序地实现社会公平,这正是中国特色社会主义事业要实现的目标之一。

(一)防止两极分化是社会主义的内在要求

社会公平是"以人为本"的显著标志,同时也是"以人为本"的具体化。但社会公平与平均主义貌合神离。过去我们囿于"左"倾主义的误导,把社会公平理解为平均主义,结果导致了经济的停滞与倒退,普遍的贫困让社会主义制度蒙羞。平均主义要不得,片面强调平均主义,只能让大家一起受穷,这就是历史留给我们的深刻教训。改革开放,建设有中国特色社会主义,正是针对计划经济、平均主义、"一大二公"的后果提出来的,它解放了生产力,带来了国力的强盛、社会的繁荣和人民生活的改善。2014年5月,北京大学国家发展研究院名誉院长林毅夫指出:"改革开放35年来,中国经济维持年均9.8%的增长,取得了伟大的成就,有望超越美国成为世界第一大经济体"[①]。但同时,我们更应该清晰地认识到,

---

[①] 林毅夫:《中国经济持续增长潜力依然强劲》,《经济参考报》2014年5月5日。

中国经济还有许多市场垄断、价格扭曲问题，特别是不公平竞争等引发的贫富差距、社会震荡问题，亟待改革者的锐意破解。

社会主义建设具有探索性，不可能一劳永逸地解决所有的问题。我们在取得经济飞速发展的同时，也出现了一些负面现象，其中之一是社会不公平在一定程度、一定范围内的逐渐恶化，贫富差距拉大、两极分化日益突出。在社会主义初级阶段，我们不能因为法制不够健全、我们建设社会主义的经验不足、各种利益集团重新组合以及一定意义上的权力滥用问题存在，就认为不公平现象是不可避免的。同样，我们不能因为我们国家出现的不公平现象是暂时的、局部的，就认为无足轻重，就简单地认为它是我们改革发展的必要代价。社会公平是人类的理想，只有实现社会公平，社会主义建设事业才能凝聚人心，才能团结广大人民共同奋斗，才能建设和发展和谐社会。社会不公平，或者听任社会不公平蔓延，势必造成离心倾向，在一定程度上加重部分不公平待遇者对政府的不信任感，加强他们对社会的不满情绪。显然，贫穷不是社会主义，不公平同样不是社会主义。社会主义既要实现共同富裕，又要达到普遍的社会公平。

阶级社会出现以来，社会公平一直是困扰人类社会进步的基本问题之一。社会主义制度的创建，直接原因就是对阶级压迫和社会不公平的反抗。社会主义体现了人的解放，人民从被压迫的桎梏中解放出来，成为自己命运的主宰者。我国宪法明确规定："中华人民共和国的一切权力属于人民"，人民当家做主，是社会主义民主政治的本质。人民当家做主就能最广泛地动员和组织人民依法管理国家和社会事务、经济和文化事业，从而维护和实现人民的根本利益。不能设想，在一个充满等级观念、只为少数人利益最大化的社会中，能够有效地实现社会公平。既然在社会主义制度下人民是国家的主人，那么，贫富悬殊、两极分化就与社会主义制度格格不入，也与社会公平的理念格格不入。由此我们可以得出结论：实现共同富裕，防止两极分化，是社会主义的内在要求。

（二）实现社会公平是保持社会稳定的必要条件

社会公平具有独立的价值，它是社会进步的基本尺度之一。同时，社会公平具有巨大的心理功能，它是社会稳定的充分必要条件。我们知道，社会稳定是人们正常生活与工作的前提，同时也是社会正常运转和不断发展进步的前提。我们需要社会稳定，逻辑上就首先要实现社会公平。在这个意义上，我们不能想要社会稳定就有社会稳定；因为社会稳定作为一个结果，是若干因素构成的，只有满足社会稳定方方面面的要求，才能实现社会稳定。其中，最重要的因素是社会公平。反过来说，满足社会稳定的根本因素缺失，必然会带来社会矛盾，其逻辑结果必然是社会危机。

早在1993年，邓小平同志就富有远见地指出："十二亿人口怎样实现富裕，富裕起来以后财富怎样分配，这都是大问题。题目已经出来了，解决这个问题比解决发展起来的问题还困难。分配的问题大得很。我们讲要防止两极分化，实际上两极分化自然出现。要利用各种手段、各种方法、各种方案来解决这些问题。"[①] 不言而喻，不同的社会成员、不同的社会阶层和阶级、不同的地区、不同的行业之间在社会财富分配方面存在差异是一种正常的现象，但这肯定不意味着，这种差距的不断扩大是正常的。我们之所以要解决困难群体的问题，就是因为社会财富分配在一定程度、一定范围内的不公正，其危险可能导致两极分化，从而妨碍社会公平的实现，妨碍社会稳定。中国目前进入人均GDP 5000~10000美元的转型关键时期。这个关键时期往往是产业结构快速转型、社会利益格局剧烈变化的时期，是既充满新的机遇又面临各种社会风险的时期。就眼下的现实而言，社会转型时期，各种既定利益格局基本被打破，在社会财富不断增加的同时，近年来我国各阶层之间的收入差距不断扩大，城乡之间的收入差距也在持续扩大，贫富悬殊的问题日益突出。相关数据显示，"全国10%最高收入组家庭的实际收入是10%最低收入组收入的9.5倍，20%城镇最富裕的家庭拥有全部城镇金融资产的55.4%"[②]。目前全国城镇享受低保的生活困难人口有2000多万，农村还

---

① 《邓小平文选》第3卷，人民出版社，1993。
② 郑杭生等：《中国人民大学中国社会发展研究报告》，中国人民大学出版社，2012。

有数千万贫困人口，全国还有约 6000 万残疾人口，有近 200 万流动儿童失学或辍学。困难群体一定范围内的存在是我国当前重大的社会问题，其存在本身就是危机，而解决不好这个危机必将孕育更大的危机。另外，贫困人口、困难群体的消极、自卑和不满心理也严重影响社会稳定，其显见和潜在的不公平危机不容忽视。2008 年发生的甘肃陇南群体冲突事件，两千多人围攻市委市政府，打砸抢烧，使较多公共设施和公共财物受损，对社会秩序造成了一定的破坏。其根本原因在于政府征地拆迁后，并没有相对合理、及时地补偿失地农民的损失。① 因此，"建立社会预警机制和'安全阀'机制极为重要，它是预防群体性事件，解决社会矛盾的基础，同时也是社会稳定与发展的晴雨表"②。

阶层差距无限扩大必然导致社会不稳定。如何防止贫富分化，已经成为构建社会公平和社会稳定的基本问题。把不公平化解在萌芽阶段，让危机越来越小而不是越来越大，是整个社会的当务之急。显然，防止两极分化，其前提之一是提高困难群体的社会地位和经济状况。只要我们有效地提升困难群体的社会地位，较好地改善困难群体的经济状况，那么，一定程度上、一定范围内的不公平现象就会得到有效的克服，困难群体的负面心理就有可能逐步消解。目前，就提高困难群体的社会地位和改善他们的经济状况而言，我们已经取得了长足的进步。随着国家财力的增强，国家给无职无业的城市居民和国有企业下岗人员提供的最低生活保障金也在逐步增加。国家已经制定了一系列解决困难群体问题的政策与措施，制定了更加详细的失业下岗人员再就业的措施和办法，对推动全社会的再就业提供了强有力的指导，并在实践中取得了可喜的进步。但我们也要看到，就现实的情况看，就业机会少，就业竞争激烈，是一个客观事实。在可预见的时间里，困难群体生活状况的较大改善不可能一蹴而就。因为，要化解一定程

---

① 杨欢、温志强：《基于利益冲突的群体性泄愤事件研究——以 2008 年甘肃陇南事件为例》，《人民论坛》2012 年第 36 期。
② 〔美〕路易斯·科塞：《社会冲突的功能》，华夏出版社，1989。

度上、一定范围内不公平现象的潜在的和现实的危机,涉及社会的方方面面:增加就业机会、规范社会分配秩序、建立公正合理的收入分配制度、健全社会保障体系、抵制分配不公、建立互助机制、抑制势利倾向、加强对垄断行业收入分配的监督和管理、强化国家税收对收入分配的调节职能、完善个人所得税法、保护合法收入、整顿不合理收入、调节过高收入、有效制止非法收入、倾听民众呼声、弘扬人道主义理想等,这些都是缩小贫富差距、防止两极分化,从而实现社会公平、维护社会稳定的必要条件。

(三)西方国家维护社会公平的措施与经验

1. 英国"公平社会"建设

近年来,英国政府主要的措施有以下几点:(1)增加对儿童特别是贫困家庭儿童的福利。英国儿童的贫穷率下降了10%,成为欧盟主要国家中改善儿童贫困问题效果最为显著的国家。(2)加大对青少年接受教育与培训的支持力度。政府希望到2015年将接受学校教育和技能培训的17岁左右青少年的比例从目前的75%提高到至少90%,有效地改善贫困青少年的发展问题。(3)对老年人与残疾人的照顾。(4)提高公共服务的质量,使全体国民都能享受公平合理的高水平社会服务。(5)改革完善政府的税收制度,使之适应不断变化的社会经济形势,保证所有纳税人之间的公平合理,推动政府宏观社会经济目标的实现。英国政府走出的这么一条总体兼顾经济效率与社会公平的政府执政道路,既符合本国国情,对其现代化发展助力颇多,也为世界其他国家经济、社会的发展提供了宝贵的经验与借鉴。

2. 德国的社会公平和保障政策

德国社会市场经济追求的最高目标是自由、公平、安全和富裕,其思想基础是把市场上的自由与社会平衡结合起来,实现经济效率和社会公平的协调统一,实现个人利益与国民经济总体利益的协调统一。德国的公平和保障政策主要有收入再分配政策、社会保障体系、劳动保护政策、企业职工参与决定政策和劳动市场政策等;通过把税收的一部分以一定形式补贴给失业者、退休者、离休者（退休公务员），调节收入差距。德国法律规定，公民必须参加养老保险、失业保险、工伤保险和医疗保险四大社会保险。以法律的形式来实施强制性的社会保险政策，提高了社会公平实现的可能性。德国的劳动保护政策主要有解雇保护、工资保护、工伤保护、妇女儿童保护等。德国的《企业组织法》保障职工参与涉及雇员权力和利益问题的决策。德国政府采取免费介绍就业、提供寻找职业所需费用、成年人接受教育和专业培训免费等一系列有效措施，实现充分就业。

3. 法国的社会公平调节措施

法国政府通过再分配来调节社会公平，主要有以下手段。第一，通过完善税制增强再分配调节力度，缩小贫富差距。据有关报道，目前法国高级管理人员税前收入是非熟练工人的4倍，而税后可支配收入降到2倍。第二，通过增加社会保障支出、完善社会保障体系来调节社会公平。其社会保障的内容包括工伤、生育、医疗、养老、失业等。第三，通过再分配的重新投入加强公共服务事业建设，让低收入者享受社会福利与公共服务。法国政府将通过税收所得的财政收入的较大部分，重新投到交通、能源、卫生、文化、教育、体育、廉租房等公共服务和社会福利事业中，将此作为国民收入再分配的主要形式，并在制度上尽可能保证低收入者都能享受这些公共服务和社会福利事业，以扩大社会公平。

4. 美国的社会保障制度

1935年8月14日，美国国会通过《社会保险法》，标志着美国社会保障制度的初步建立。《社会保险法》主要内容包括两个部分，一个是老年保险，由联邦政府主办；另一个是失业保险，由联邦政府和州政府合办。近80年来，美国的社会保障制度在不断发展完善，这跟美国政府一直所秉持的理念是分不开的。美国人民判断政府执政效果的好坏，主要是以失业率和自我的生活水平作为参考。在失业率上升的情况下，政府扩大社会保障支出，可以在一定程度上起到稳定社会的作用。从1945年杜鲁门执政开始，美国一直施行扩张性的社会保障政策，这也表达了政府对消除收入分配不公和保障贫困人口最低生活水平的决心。其后，

1946 年的《就业法》、1949 年的《住房法》、1956 年的联邦社保基金（OASDI）更加健全了美国的社会保障制度，社会保障制度覆盖面更加宽广，受益范围不断扩大。

（四）借鉴与思考

1. 加大国家对收入分配的调节力度，缩小贫富差距

我国改革开放 30 多年来，已经取得了巨大的成就。正如邓小平所设计的，"让一部分人先富起来"了，但是没有出现"共同富裕"的局面，而是增长的财富集中在少数人手中，贫富差距越来越大，广大人民群众没有充分享受到改革的成果。法国政府通过再分配来调节社会公平的手段，对于我国缩小当前基尼系数 0.46 的收入差距有借鉴意义。政府作为社会的公共权力，担负维系社会公正的主要责任。因此，政府的职责正是在于通过其必要的行政和法律的手段，来整合社会利益，平抑利益的差别，促成社会的共同富裕。在有效整合利益、抑制贫富差别的基础上，积极地采取各种有效措施，解决为富不仁的问题。

2. 增加公共服务和社会福利事业的投入，完善社会保障体系

当前，在维护和实现公平正义方面，政府还存在一些突出问题：政府提供的社会公共品数量相对较少，不少公共品的质量不高；"公共利益部门化、部门利益合法化"的现象比较严重；少数干部的腐败现象比较严重；政策打架、政令不一、政出多门的现象时有发生；决策科学化和民主化程度有待提高，有些地方、部门的决策失误过多；一些决策多变，缺乏必要的连贯性。所有这些都严重损害了政府维护公平正义的能力，也严重影响了政府的执政能力和公信力。

我国在这些方面也做了不少努力。比如对于房价高涨而低收入群体买不到住房的问题，建设部计划推出更多廉租房和经济适用房，以解决低收入人群的居住问题；通过建立农村新型合作医疗体系来扩大医疗保障的范围；通过免费义务教育政策来促进教育公平。美国、德国以法律的形式来实施强制性的社会保险政策，提高了社会公平实现的可能性，这种做法值得我们借鉴。

3. 落实科学发展观，缩小地区、城乡差距

就我国当前的情况来说，不公正的问题不仅存在，而且在有些方面还相当严重。城乡之间、地区之间、行业之间、部门之间等，都程度不同地存在先天的以及后天的资源分布不均以及分配不均等问题。而深入贯彻落实科学发展观，逐步解决这些问题，是维系社会公正的重要步骤。通过工业反哺农业，增加对社会主义新农村的投入，加快农村基础设施建设，将会有效缩小城乡差距。国家实施西部大开发战略，旨在加快西部地区的发展，加大对西部地区的投资，使西部早日腾飞，缩小东西部地区发展差距。此外，在贫困青少年的发展问题上，可以学习英国的儿童福利政策，促进儿童平等享受发展的权利。

不可否认，公平正义是欧美发达国家的理想追求，它们通过各种立法、政策来实现社会公平。历史上，社会主义之所以有如此强大的号召力，就是因为它承诺要创造切实的经济和政治条件，使社会变得更加公平正义，使全体人民都能享受更加平等的政治经济权利。因此，没有公平正义，就没有社会主义；坚持社会主义，就必须坚持公平正义。今天，我们应该认真贯彻习近平总书记关于社会主义本质的讲话精神，消除贫困、改善民生、实现共同富裕[①]。

[①] 刘永富：《继续向贫困宣战——从三个关键词说起》，求是理论网，2014年3月27日。

A Brief Note About Social Justice and Common Good

Carmen Ramos G. de C. *

Abstract: Social justice is not a theoretical concept, but rather a way of life. It could be identified with the common good of a society, though both concepts are not equivalent. Common good is the good of all who take part in that society, and it is the responsibility of the State to develop it; but the citizens contribute to its growth and viability. When the common good is not achieved, inequity, i. e. social injustice, arises. Justice in a society can be understood in various manners, including distributive justice and commutative justice. But, essentially, its essence is giving to each person what is due him or her in the proportion and extent suited to his or her situation and circumstances. The State is responsible for achieving it. Otherwise, corruption arises, which can be regarded as an aggressive cancer in a healthy society.

Key words: common good, social justice, State, society

---

* Carmen Ramos G. de C. , PhD in Education Section, Ex vice president of Panamerican University in Centro Cultural Nayar, México City.

论社会公正与公共善

Carmen Ramos G. de C.

摘 要：社会公正不是一个理论概念，而是一种生活方式。社会公正可以用社会公共善来定义，尽管这两个概念不可以彼此等同。公共善是社会全体成员的善，推进公共善不仅是国家的责任，也是公民的责任。当公共善无法实现时，就会发生不平等问题或社会不公正问题。社会领域内的正义可以从不同角度来理解，既包括分配正义，也包括交换正义。然而，就本质而言，它指的是提供给每个人与其地位和处境相称的东西。若非如此，就会发生腐败，对社会而言，腐败是腐蚀社会肌体的癌症。

关键词：共同善　社会公正　国家　社会

SOCIAL JUSTICE AND COMMON GOOD

The concept of social justice coined by ILO is as follows:

"Social Justice is based on equality of rights for all peoples and the possibility for all human beings without discrimination, to benefit from economic and social progress everywhere. Promoting social justice is about more than increasing income and creating jobs. It is also about rights, dignity and voice for working women and men as well as economic, social and political empowerment".[①]

This notion of "social justice" involves in its essence basic concept on which it is supported: human person, dignity, common good, legal justice, economics, employment, work, etc., all of which are related with the general concept of common good. According to Antonio Millán Puelles, a Spanish

---

① ILO, Justicia social. In: http://www.ilo.org/wcmsp5/groups/public/@dgreports/@dcomm/documents/publication/wcms_151881.pdf. Retrieved on May 25, 2014.

philosopher of the 20th century, common good lies, in the first place, in the struggle for installing and maintaining peace[1]. If there is no peace in the community where you live, you might have to think that there is a lack of friendly relationships in that community. And if there are no friendly relationships, it is difficult to think that there could be something in common. This leads us to say that, in order that social justice as understood by ILO, it is necessary that common good is favored, whose immediate goal is peace among citizens of the world, leading to the conclusions reached by Kant in *Perpetual Peace* (1797) or, from another just as relevant, by Michael Walzer, in his important book *Spheres of Justice* (1983), where he also discusses several questions on distributive justice.

Generally, we think that the common good is produced when, within a society, political interests converge with citizens' interests, and all help each other so that a just and suitable distribution of wealth prevails, including employment and, in general, opportunities for development. And this is true: common good and social justice require a convergence of wills and a joint effort by all persons dwelling in this planet, today and at all times.

Common good is achieved, as we have said, by a convergence of wills and a good relationship of interests. Rafael Alvira, professor at the University of Navarra (Spain), points out to a relationship between common good and the human person, in his article "*Common Good and Social Justice in the Different Spheres of Society*[2]. He asserts that being a person goes far beyond mere individuality. Being a human person implies putting at society's service the person's inherent capabilities specific to human nature, particularly, the person's freedom. Certainly, society is meant for the person and not the person for

---

[1] Millán Puelles, Antonio. *Persona humana y justicia social*, Madrid: Editorial Rialp, 1962.
[2] Alvira, R., *Bien común y justicia social en las diferentes esferas de la sociedad*, Pamplona: Editorial UDEN, 2009.

society. But society is composed by persons having particular interests, which quite often must be subordinated to the good of society. This is where the difficulty lies for achieving a social justice or common good which, among other requirements, will be common good because of whatever *good* it has, and not for whatever *common* it has.

When stating that society is for the person, I suppose a subordination of society to the person, difficult to practice because, very often, it demands that "several persons" are submitted to "one", or that because of "one", "several persons" are not benefited. It is then when debate about "social justice" arises.

Quite often, when there is in political life a reference to the concept of common good, this is referred to a given population, and to external aspects of life. If common good is limited to a sector of population, to some concrete current circumstances, and to aspects that are merely material and perishable, the effort to achieve it weakens in a short time. The desire of living in peace is watered down and it even reverts itself and, what pretended being good for everybody ends up being good for *some few*. When the human person, individually, is regarded as superior to society and is considered with the dignity inherent to its nature, the country's organization, the focusing of budgets and the political activity will be directed towards the human person's defense and protection so that its capabilities can be developed and put at the community's service, thus contributing to the equitable growth of countries and, of course, to the achievement of common good.

But, since the society is constituted by individuals, a question arises, difficult to answer to: which ones, out of those individuals, should be given attention in the first place? Here is where the difficulty lies for making laws that will benefit all members of society and strengthen their particular capabilities. There is an additional difficulty that dims the shine of a society at the service of persons: that modern world has placed individual freedom as absolutely fundamental, to the extent that individualistic will is the ultimate criterion. By pointing out to this fact, it is not meant that freedom is something dangerous. What is harmful is the false notion of freedom that has set on: that everybody may do whatever he or she wants, just because he or she wants it, without taking into account persons around him or her.

This is illustrated, for instance, in the Western world, where there is a misunderstood "respect" for young people's will out of fear of disturbing them. Does this happen also in the East? What is well known, at least in China, is respect for elders—parents and teachers.

On the other hand, in many companies and institutions, there are slogans aiming to emphasize that their activity is based on the recognition of the person's primacy: "we are a company at the service of the customer", "for us, you are what matters", "serving you as you deserve: this is what we look for". All these slogans, intended to impact and entice customers, often indulge in an exacerbation of individualism. Even solidarity—a human virtue that should be present in any peace-promoting relationship—is looked upon as what is usually called "the cherry in the cake": once everybody has taken care of what is his or her own, it becomes excellent being solidary towards the others. There is a Spanish proverb loosely translated as "when you finish your task you should help your colleague"①. Would it not be better if you tried to help your colleague even before finishing your task? True solidarity—a demand of common good—lies in fulfilling human duties regarding other people (Cuéllar, 2009). By this we mean that being truly social implies forsaking "what is mine" to serve the others; being individualistic means a deep disregard of almost everything about other persons: common activities, service, etc. What matters is only "I and my circumstance", as expressed by Ortega y Gasset.②

---

① "El que acaba primero ayuda a su compañero".
② Ortega y Gasset, *Meditaciones del Quijote*.

RESPONSIBILITY AND SOCIAL JUSTICE

We start from an apparently obvious principle: an individual person is not strong enough to create what is common, because "common" means from all people and for all people, i. e. above what is individual. A common will cannot either talk about a common will... How hard it is to wish what all wish, in the same way and with the same strength! Thus, an "organ" is required, i. e. a group of persons with sufficiently knowledgeable and prudent to propose what should be regarded as a common good, and how to apply it as a reference to practice equity and social justice in the society they rule. This group is constituted by the *political sector* of the various countries. Politicians should carry out the arduous task of working in favor of the common good: they should respect and promote the demands of human nature regarding both the particular individual and the group of persons living in the community they rule. They should watch over such group and also for each of its members, with total respect to their fundamental rights.

People responsible for State's tasks often get confused about what is public and what is common. Caution must be exerted on this, because such confusion could go against social justice principles. "Common" is something in which all take part.

In a country, common good is constituted, for instance, by supplies and services indispensable for life: water supply, electric power, street cleaning, traffic control, etc.

"Public", on the other hand, means something that is expressed or something that is made available to a group of person. Maybe it is not a good where not everybody takes part, but rather something that is set up under concrete circumstances and tending to disappear when such circumstances cease to exist. For instance, suspending, for solid reasons, the publication in local newspapers of news about a crime that could seriously shock citizens.

This decision could be based on public good sense, and although it was made precisely for the sake of common good, it cannot be regarded as a decision made for everybody. It is understood that social justice favors common good, but it does not entirely identify with this concept. As we have said, there are differences and various nuances between them. Justice proper is a social virtue, i. e. , its practice implies the equitable distribution of goods, which considers everyone as everyone. Aristotle, in his *Nichomachean Ethics* (Book V), refers to justice as proportional equality: give to each what is his or her, what is owed to him or her. He says that what is owed to each citizen must be proportional to his or her contribution to society, to his or her needs and to his or her personal merits. This is why justice is not only distributive—give to each what is owed to him or her; it is also commutative, referring to the personal commitment between each other. It sets up the obligation of recognizing the other inasmuch as he or she is the other, without the need for him or her to give anything in exchange. We could say that, in a way, when our personal commitment for justice is real, we are not doing anything else but what we ought to do. It is not an act of generosity. We are giving personal and social reality the value it deserves.

In terms of distributive and commutative justice, what is public and what is private are mutually required and complemented, so that the better private affairs are, the better public affairs will be. As an example, there are religious associations that set up private teaching or sanitary centers which are open to public; that is to say, they "use" what is private for public good.

If, on the other hand, public institutions are used for the major benefit of private persons or groups, such as political parties, corruption takes place, essentially being the use of what is public for a private good. Or else, a private good can be used for the benefit of a reduced public sector (Sampere, 2004). Here is where inequity starts its development: social justice is missing, since this favors some people but not all people. It provides for the suitable development of what is "convenient" for a few, at the expense of majority. Deterioration caused in society by a social injustice situation can have unsuspected consequences that, if materialized, will become impossible to cancel; on the contrary, they will grow and harm the majority of citizens.

However, the State is an institution and, as such, it has some objectives to fulfill. Its function is proposing that best conditions occur in a community, so that citizens might contribute as much as possible to the common good. But the State is incapable, by itself, to fully fulfill such objective. To this purpose, it must have the contribution of other institutions. That is to say, a two-way subsidiarity must be set up: the State supporting private institutions, and conversely: the enterprises pay taxes that give economic support to initiatives proposed by the State, and the State, in turn, supplies the indispensable means for the life of citizens, which is what the common good is. Social justice determines what and how much corresponds to each side.

CONCLUSIONS

1) Social justice is closely related to common good.

2) Common good is not only the responsibility of leading groups. It is also the responsibility of individually considered persons. The society, in its different spheres, is responsible for contributing to the achievement of the welfare of a country. Assigning this task just to one part would impair the behavior of the parts that constitute a community.

3) It could be said that social justice pertains to all members of a society willing to be productive and free and to reach a full development in favor of the common citizen and the community in general.

References

Alvira, R. , *Bien común y justicia social en las diferentes esferas de la sociedad*. Pamplona: Editorial llDEN, 2009.

Aristotle, *Nichomachean Ethics* (Spanish version), Mexico: Editorial Porrúa.

Cuellar, H. , *Ser y esencia de los valores, Una axiología para el siglo XXI*, Mexico: Editorial Trillas, 2011.

Kant, I. , *La paz perpetua* (trad. De F. Rivera Pastor), Alicante: Biblioteca Virtual Miguel de Cervantes. En: http://www. cervantes-virtual. com/obra/la-paz-perpetua-0/, 1999.

Millán Puelles, A. *Persona humana y justicia social*. México: Editorial MINOS, 1994.

Sampere, F. , "Corrupción: fraude a la confianza". México: Revista Istmo, 2004.

Walzer, M. , *Spheres of Justice*, New York, 1983.

Economic Inequality and World Justice: Liberal Education

Corazon T. Toralba*

Abstract: This is an interdisciplinary study on the causes and effects of economic inequality. Using St. Thomas Aquinas' notion of justice and with the Philippines as a case, it will point out that economic solutions to economic problems are not enough. It will emphasize the need for liberal education in solving the unwelcome effects of economic inequality. The essay will start with the examination of the phenomenon of economic inequality and the notion of justice, followed by the need for liberal education to address the issue.

Key words: economic inequality; liberal; education

经济不平等与世界正义：自由主义教育

Corazon T. Toralba

摘 要：本文从跨学科的视角研究了经济不平等的原因与后果。通过运用圣·托马斯·阿奎纳的公正概念并以菲律宾为例，本文指出，对

---

* Corazon T. Toralba, Ph D at the University of Asia and the Pacific, Philippines.

经济问题采取经济的解决方法是不够的。本文强调，消除经济不平等问题所引起的不良后果时，需要自由主义教育。本文首先分析经济不平等现象和社会公正概念，然后分析解决这个问题的自由主义教育。

关键词： 经济不平等　自由主义　教育

I

Economic inequality is usually defined by economists as the difference in the measurement of wealth across households. It is a relative comparison of the gap in household incomes across a given region, country or the world. The world's 1,210 current billionaires, *Forbes* reported in March 2011, hold a combined wealth that equals over half the total wealth of the 3.01 billion adults around the world who, according to Credit Suisse, hold under $10,000 in net worth. Pervasive presence of economic inequality is inimical not only to those who are economically disadvantaged—the poor, but also to the well-being of society. It hinders economic growth, poverty reduction efforts, social and economic stability, and lastly, socially sustainable development.

Thorbeke and Charumilind reviewed available literature on the socio-economic impact and economic inequality and co-related the effects of economic inequality with economic growth. They noted that social conflicts, political instability, health issues, crises in education, and crimes are among its effects. Based on the empirical studies conducted in both developing and developed countries, they noted the following: first, less inequality is conducive to economic growth; second, high inequality could lead to a lower level of democracy, high rent-seeking policies, and a higher probability of revolution; third, under investment in human capital translates into lower economic growth; fourth, income directly affects health because it influences individuals' consumption of commodities; and fifth, income inequality has also been found to affect such behavioral outcomes as higher rates of homicide and violent crimes. It could also affect social cohesion. Such effects are undesirable; hence, studies suggest that policy makers address the issue.

The *Report on the World Social Situation* 2013, building on the 2005 report, emphasized that addressing inequalities is not only a moral imperative but is also necessary in order to unleash the human and productive potential of each country's population and to bring development towards a socially sustainable path. To adequately respond to this issue, one needs to know the causes and solutions that are in place and evaluate its effectiveness. The perceived causes of world inequality are government policies; lack of quality and equitable access to education; corruption and illicit financial flows; gender, ethnic, and religious discriminations; and market failures, deregulated markets, institutional failures, and public expenses cuts. The proposed policy responses to combat economic inequality in the world are the following: increase access to quality education; reduce school fees and build more schools especially in rural areas; correct power imbalances in the labor market through implementation of International Labour Standards; where possible, encourage a set of interventions to improve or protect human capital, such as labor market interventions (labor law and wage setting), social insurance (pension, unemployment support, family benefits, sick-pay) and social assistance (cash transfer and subsidies, disability insurance or specific support to marginalized groups) with the aim of assisting individuals and families to better manage risks during an economic crisis; and for the governments to actively engage individuals and groups, particularly those living in poverty, in policy design and implementation.

Zeroing in on the Philippine scenario, the National Anti-Poverty Commission (NAPC) reports that inequality in the Philippines, measured by the Gini index, has been almost constant for more than 20 years (1985 – 2009). Moreover, the causes of poverty in the world are echoed by the said report. NAPC Report mentions weak economic growth and employment generation; political, social and environmental shocks; and lack of participation in political decision making. An Asian Development Bank study reports that the causes of poverty in the Philippines are "low to moderate economic growth for the past 40 years; low growth elasticity of poverty reduction; weakness in employment generation and the quality of jobs generated; failure to fully develop the agriculture sector; high inflation during crisis periods; high levels of population growth; high and persistent levels of inequality (incomes and assets), which dampen the positive impacts of economic expansion; and recurrent shocks and exposure to risks such as economic crisis, conflicts, natural disasters, and 'environmental poverty'". An earlier study lists the trends and factors affecting household income inequality, namely, rising proportion of urban household, age distribution changes, an increasing number of highly educated, and wage rate inequality. An International Monetary Fund study mentions that the low economic growth in the Philippines compared to its ASEAN neighbors could be traced to unhealthy economic policies. Moreover, the level of educational attainment and labor mismatch also had their roles to play.

The Philippine government addressed the problem and noted the reasons for the failure of the poverty reduction program. NAPC reported the following: decline in government expenditure on basic services from 1996 to 2006; weak and fragmented social programs; poor targeting, monitoring, and evaluation of anti-poverty programs; corruption and weak institutional capacity, including that of local governments; and lack of effective participation of the poor in government bodies. Hence, the present administration focuses on expanding access of the poor in the poorest regions and provinces to basic social services so that those who are especially in need of public support can be provided with the mechanisms to improve their lives; people's participation and empowerment; rationalization of anti-poverty reduction programs; strength-ening targeting and monitoring mechanisms for poverty reduction; addressing institutional aspects of poverty reduction; the participation of the poor in policy making; supporting local government initiatives; extending anti-corruption reform to promote innovation and entrepreneurship, discourage rent seeking, and minimize political intervention in business; and instituting political reforms, to name a few.

Towards this end, the Philippine government adopted the Conditional Cash Transfer Program funded by World Bank and dubbed it *Pantawid Pamilyang Pilipino Program* (4P), targeting the poorest of the poor. Initial reports hail its success, citing among others the following: increased enrollment and improve-ment in school attendance for the targeted age group; improved nutritional status of children, and easier access of women to pre-natal and post-natal cares; changed spending patterns of poor households, with beneficiary households spending more on health and education and less on adult goods such as alcohol. Moreover, the program has improved the effectiveness of other govern-ment programs for the poor, as evidenced by the increased reported coverage of PhilHealth. However, the study was unable to identify a program impact on aggregate consumption/expenditures, even though expenditures on education and health increased, and results from some areas suggest an increase in savings. The Department of Social Welfare and Development first quarter report states that as of March 31, 2013, close to 4 million households have enrolled. The monitoring of program conditionalities for the months of January and February reported compliance rate in education at 96.28%, health at 95.81%, and FDS at 96.18%. The strong compliance performance shows that poor households are maintaining their co-responsibilities as beneficiaries such that children are in school and healthy, while parents are increasing their knowledge and skills in parenting.

While the adopted program (4P) seemed to meet its developmental goals, the World Bank report lists the challenges that need to be addressed. First, while there is an increase in enrollment for the targeted age group, enrollment among the older age group did not, and the challenge of continuing secondary education still exists. A need to extend the age group to 18 to enable these youths to finish high school and be gainfully employed is being proposed. Second, the continuity and expansion of maternal and child care needs to be improved. Third, the beneficiaries must be assured of receiving the full grant amounts they are entitled to receive. Last, program implementation issues that should address local situations.

II

Reviewing the causes and the proposed and adopted solutions with the accomplishment reports both on the global and local scene, one would notice that the adopted solutions that contributed greatly to reducing income inequality are those investments, specifically in education and health programs, that benefited directly the marginalized sector, while those that hinder the success of the program refer to policy defects and corruption. Again, the person is at the center and root of development as has been argued elsewhere. Persons are both the benefactors and beneficiaries of development. They, simultaneously, are the ones who solve the problem or are part of the problem, provide a solution or part of the solution, and being challenged to be different or make a difference in one's or another person's life. However, the lens by which the people see a problem or propose a solution is the understanding of what a person is and how that person should be dealt with.

The person is a complex reality, a being both spiritual and material, whose mode of being in the material world is that of reflective relational co-existence. The person lives with other beings whose existence he/she affects. Living with others demands living harmoniously with them and anticipating their needs and probable course of action in relation to a single or collective concern whether he/she is the one responsible to answer or provide that need. How does one ascertain the needs and foresee the actions of others? This will require accepting that all human beings are essentially the same but existentially different. All human beings share the same nature, but each express that nature differently. They have common needs to be alive and to live one's life in the best way one could using a standard one has set for him or based on a model one could emulate. To maintain that life, one's basic needs have to be met. Depending on one's stage in the developmental process, meeting such need is always a concerted effort of many individuals. No one is capable of providing for oneself all the basic needs of life. One is dependent on the others who have the resources and ability to provide such using one's competitive advantage. Whether one has the right or the duty to meet that need is the concern of justice.

What is justice? For Thomas Aquinas, justice is a moral virtue. St. Thomas follows Aristotle's definition of virtue as that which makes a person and his actions good. Justice is fittingly defined as "the perpetual and constant will to render to each one his right". This definition prompts one to ask "Whose right and whose duty?" In the world concern on economic inequality, who has the duty to overcome inequality or mitigate its unintended consequences? Are the "victims" of some people or nations getting richer entitled to the help others should provide?

Actual practices point to international organizations aiding less economically prosperous nations to pull people out of miserable situations they find themselves in. Aids come to the victims either through governmental agencies or non-governmental organizations. Governments are compelled, by virtue of its mandate, to attain the common good, the raison d'être of society, understood as the needed societal conditions for each member of society to develop holistically. Attainment of these conditions will require that all members of society cooperate in their personal capacity, with the governing body co-ordinating everybody's efforts. That cooperation is necessary because what is at stake is each one's interest, which is achieved, sustained, and furthered if the needed societal conditions are in place. It may sound self-serving, but unless one thinks of promoting the concern of the rest of the members of society, then one's interest could be threatened. Formerly, the reasons that prompted the more affluent societies to help those that are less privileged are the unwanted threat to one's pacific and comfortable existence. Recent literatures emphasize on the sus-tainability, placing development of persons as a moral imperative; thus making it a duty for everyone to alleviate poverty. As aforementioned, the victims become part of the solution; their input in the developmental process is taken into account. To one's duty to help someone is a corresponding right of that someone to be helped. What is the basis of such right?

Right, according to Aquinas, is the proper object of justice that is expressed through a law. Further, political justice is both natural and legal. It is natural when something ought to be done in an exchange of favors, whereas it is legal if it is a result of an agreement between interested parties or decreed by someone in authority that something must be done to attain a sort of equality or balance. Right and duty reclaim each other. To a right that someone claims for is a corresponding of another to render that right. As mentioned above, in a community, the governors have the duty to promote the common good and all members—including the governors—to create those needed societal conditions; hence, the right to those conditions. However, to claim that right to the needed societal condition is a corresponding duty to take part in creating those conditions.

Justice, though, is not enough. Economic justice or equality will be an elusive dream because of individuals' different existential conditions; there will be no equal one-one-one correspondence of economic benefits. Persons differ in the use of their talents and relating to others as well as meeting the challenges of their particular milieu. Inequality is part of life, but enormous inequality which deprives the majority of the needed means for survival while the fortunate minority lives in a lap of luxury is a phenomenon one cannot allow to perpetuate. One might argue that what the affluent members of society enjoy are legitimate fruits of one's work. Such is a legitimate claim.

Justice, then, must be coupled with charity, as proclaimed by Pope Emeritus Benedict XVI. Justice without charity is philanthropy whereas charity without justice falls short of addressing the needs of the other. "*Charity goes beyond justice*, because to love is to give, to offer what is 'mine' to the other; but it never lacks justice, which prompts us to give the other what is 'his', what is due to him by reason of his being or his acting. I cannot 'give' what is mine to the other without first giving him what pertains to him in justice. If we love others with charity, then first of all we are just towards them. Not only is justice not extraneous to charity, not only is it not an alternative or parallel path to charity: justice is inseparable from charity."

Moreover, technical expertise is not enough in solving the challenges that economic inequality brings with it. "True development does not consist primarily in 'doing'. The key to development is a mind capable of thinking in technological terms and grasping the fully human meaning of human activities, within the context of the holistic meaning of the individual's being." As Alasdair McIntyre notes, the major disorders of the 20th century and the first decade of the 21st were results of the actions of distinguished graduates of distinguished schools who have forgotten Newman's idea of an educated mind because the universities where they come from have overspecialized, forgetting the unity of knowledge, unity of understanding, and academic division of labor. A holistic approach to development demands a mind that is capable of integrating the various involved disciplines and the hierarchy that reigns among these disciplines. The type of education that trains the mind of the person towards that end is liberal education.

III

Liberal Education is an approach to learning that empowers individuals and prepares them to deal with complexity, diversity, and change. It provides students with broad knowledge of the wider world (e. g., science, culture, and society) as well as in-depth study in a specific area of interest. A liberal education helps students develop a sense of social responsibility as well as strong and transferable intellectual and practical skills such as communication, analytical and problem-solving skills, and a demonstrated ability to apply knowledge and skills in real-world settings.

Liberal Education is a philosophy of education characterized by challenging encounters with important issues, and more a way of studying than specific content, liberal education can occur at all types of colleges and universities. By drawing on a broad range of knowledge, it asks students to grapple with complicated, important issues, and usually expects them to learn at least one subject in greater depth and at an advanced level. Graduates with this kind of liberal education will have gained high-level abilities, transferable from discipline to discipline and from one environment to another. By knowing the lessons of the past, possessing the ability to hear others in their own languages, and demonstrating an impressive toolbox of skills, graduates will look toward the future prepared for whatever arises. They will be flexible employees, as fields not yet imagined emerge.

Liberal education differs from the liberal arts in that the former is an approach to college learning while the latter originally referred to the education proper of a free man that includes the *trivium* (grammar, logic, and rhetoric) and the *quadrivium* (arithmetic, geometry, astronomy, and music). It is a skills-based education that challenges and forms the intellect not to be content with simplistic approach to problems but wrestle with the complexities that one encounters in real world. "The liberal arts are dedicated to the individual—to the education of the whole person (intellectually, socially, morally, emotionally, physically [and spiritually at church-affiliated liberal arts institutions]), with studies undertaken across the range of human experience. Students learn about the past and possibilities for the future, become involved in self-discovery, and understand the importance of being a caring, effective, and responsible citizen. "

Since this type of education looks at the person in his totality and not simply as a number, a consumer, or a function, then professionals who have received a good dose of liberal education are, in principle, more apt to study the complexities involved in developmental efforts. Faced with the challenges of the effects of economic inequality, the graduates of liberal education are not simply focused on the problem at hand but looks at the past, projects the solution to the future, and are committed to help others to help themselves. They will not be content with quick-fix solutions but will dedicate time to reflect on the problem and come up with an integrative evaluation to the solutions proposed and implemented because the ultimate aim of liberal education is for the educated person armed with knowledge and virtue to improve the world.

Economic inequality is not a result of chance but of purposive actions of persons who were motivated by strongly motivated interests that may or may not foresee the unintended consequences of intended actions. The critical thinking skills honed by liberal education encourage persons to refine their capacity for analytic thinking; ask difficult questions and formulate responses; evaluate, interpret, and synthesize evidence; make clear, well-reasoned arguments; and develop their intellectual agility. Above all, the reflective modes by which persons examine their life and actions that lead to self-knowledge is what makes them better persons, who acknowledges that with their freedom to pursue a certain mode of conduct comes a sense of responsibility to answer the consequences of those actions. To be an educated person is "learning how to be a human being capable of something more. It means learning how to be a human being capable of love and imagination" .

Unfortunately, this type of education has been eclipsed by the trend to specialize or be more responsive to the demands of the industry. Idealism has given way to pragmatic concerns, but still we need the liberating effect of the liberal education from simply being immersed in the humdrum of everyday existence. There is a need to go back to the transcendent dimension of education, that is, step out of the narrow confines of what works here and now but be more concerned of the morrow. Thus, solutions to challenges that economic inequality brings with it will not be limited to the measurable and tangible criteria but must take into account the creativity present in man when he tries to lift himself up from the banality of quick-fix solutions.

On China's Equity in Education Against Its Inequality in Economic Development

Zhang Qingzong; Jing Guoping[*]

Abstract: In the past three decades, there has emerged prominent inequality and imbalance during the process of China's rapid growth in economy, which, to a great extent, triggered inequality and imbalance in the development of society and education: unreasonable phenomena still exist in the structure and layout of education; an imbalance in the development of education can be found between urban and rural areas; development of education lags behind in rural, poor and ethnic minority areas, just to name a few. Consequently, it was proposed in China's *National Medium and Long-term Plan for Educational Reform and Development* (2010 – 2020) that to promote equity is a basic national policy of education with its fundamental measures in the proper allocation of educational resources, and in the priority given to rural areas, remote and poor areas and ethnic minority areas for the acceleration of narrowing the gap in education.

Key words: China; inequality in economy; urban-rural disparity; equity in education

---

[*] Zhang Qingzong, Professor, Dean of the School of Foreign Languages, Hubei University; Jing Guoping, Professor, Dean of the Education College, Hubei University.

论中国经济发展不平等中的教育公平

张庆宗　靖国平

摘　要：30多年以来，中国经济高速发展过程中出现了明显的不平等和不平衡现象，这在某种程度上引发了社会和教育领域内的不平等与不平衡：教育体系中依然存在不合理的现象，城市和乡村教育发展不平衡，农村、贫困地区和少数民族地区教育落后，等等。《国家中长期教育改革和发展规划纲要（2010-2020）》指出，推进教育公平是国家的基本教育政策，需要制定基本措施合理分配教育资源；为了缩小教育差距，需要对边远和贫困的农村地区以及少数民族地区给予教育的优先权。

关键词：中国　经济不平等　城市—农村不平等　教育公平

Introduction

Inequity in economic development is a global issue mainly manifested in the gap of income among individuals and different regions, as well as in the discrepancy in social welfare, opportunities, rights and interests. The inequity and imbalance in its economic development may become more prominent when a nation is standing at the critical stage of economic boom, which in turn will trigger the inequity and imbalance in the educational development. Consequently, government at all levels need to formulate fair and just policies in education and to introduce effective measures and interventions for scientific allocation of educational resources so as to ensure the basic right of education for all citizens and the practical benefit by educational resources.

As the largest developing country in the world, China, also the most populous nation on this planet, has witnessed spectacular achievements in educational development as a result of its booming economic and social development in the past few decades. By the end of 2011, the nine-year compulsory education has been universalized throughout 2856 counties (cities, county towns and municipal districts included) from 31 provinces (autonomous regions and municipalities included). In addition, the net enrollment rate of primary schools has amounted to 99.79%; the gross enrollment rate of junior middle schools, senior middle schools, colleges and universities have amounted to 100.1%, 84.0% and 26.9% respectively. [1]

Since the beginning of 21st century, the Chinese government has actively been advocating the principles of "equity", "non-profit" and "benefit for all" in education to ensure the legal rights of minors and other adult citizens to receive good education. Accordingly, the Chinese government spared no effort in running all schools, offering all students good education, ensuring no students from poor families dropping out from schools due to financial difficulties, guaranteeing children of migrant workers to have an equal access to education and securing the right of handicapped people to receive education. The Chinese government also saw to it that school-age children and teenagers can attend school and enjoy high-quality education good for the students' growth and to people's satisfaction. As a result, a basic educational service system covering both urban and rural areas has been established in an effort to provide the public with equal educational services and to bridge the gap among different regions.

1. On China's Equity in Education against Its Inequality in Economic Development

Generally speaking, the inequity and imbalance of economic development is an immediate cause and a crucial factor to that of educational development. Acco-

---

[1] Yang Yinfu, "Considerations on Making Great Efforts to Run Education to the Satisfaction of the People", *Educational Research*, 2013, (01): 4.

rding to the indexes to educational development (including such indexes as opportunity of access to education, investment in education and equity in education) in 31 provinces from a research conducted by Chinese scholars Wang Shanmai et al., in 2009, the economically developed provinces and municipalities like Shanghai, Beijing, Zhejiang, Tianjing and Jiangsu enjoyed higher educational level, while economically undeveloped provinces like Guizhou, Yunnan and Tibet stood at lower educational level.

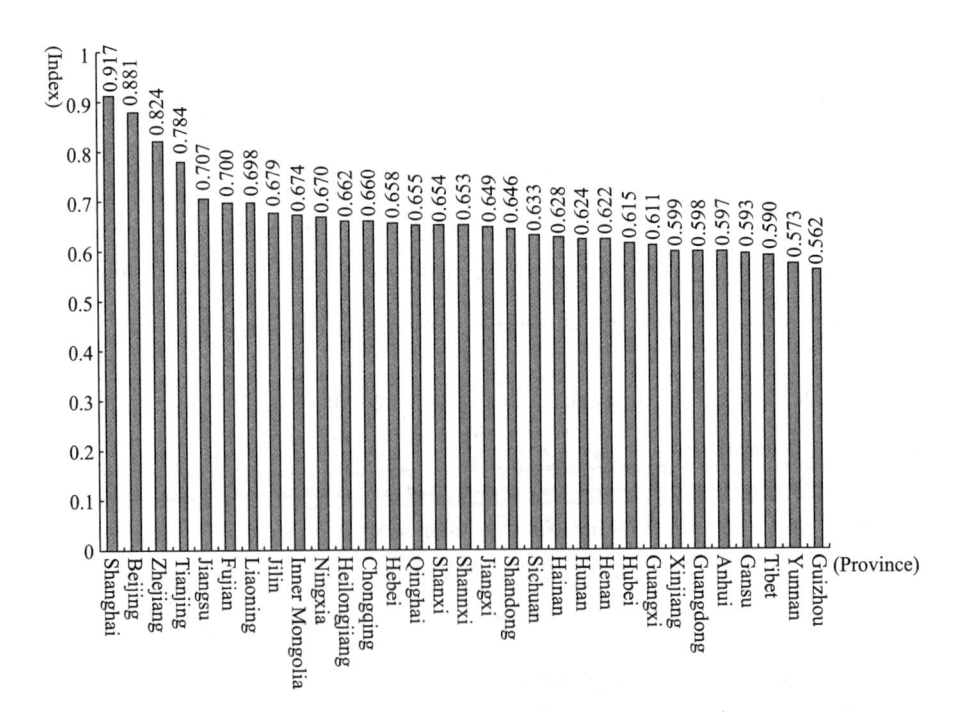

By and large, there lies a close correlation between educational development and economic development. However, an exception can be found in Guangdong, an economically developed province, where the level of educational development only ranks the sixth from the bottom owing to its lowest rank in the level of equity in education and a fairly low level in educational investment. The phenomenon above proves that economic development does not necessarily bring about educational development as there are other factors which may influence educational development level like population, educational cost sharing, provincial division of fiscal powers, etc. ①

1.1 Inequity in the Allocation of Educational Resources

Over the past two decades, rural education in China has been confronted with unprecedented crisis with the accelerating urbanization, the frequent migration of rural residents and the increasingly integrated industry structure between urban and rural areas. With the disintegration of traditional system, rural education in its initial natural state has lost its integrity, stability and sustainability. For instance, spurred by the comprehensive development of market economy and acceleration of urbanization, lots of rural students flooded to large cities with their parents who migrated to work there. As a result, a number of rural primary schools, middle schools and education stations had to be closed, terminated, merged or transferred for other purposes due to the students drain. Meanwhile, the situation was worsened by the move from a bulk of outstanding rural teachers who gave out their current post to seek better development in cities, resulting in the decline of education quality in rural schools for rural students to have slimmer chance landing on top universities.

A primary cause attributing to the above-mentioned phenomenon lies in the inequity and imbalance of allocation of educational resources. Since the 1980s, in light of social and economic condition and traditional cultural beliefs, we have been attaching great importance to test-oriented selection in China's educational system as "scores of tests" played a decisive role in educational and social stratification. Under such circumstances, a great number of key primary and secondary schools have been established in large cities and county towns, thus educational resources of high quality were preferred to allocate to key areas

---

① Wang Shanmai, Yuan Liansheng, etc., "The Comparative Research on the Level of Regional Development of Education in China", *Educational Research*, 2013, (06): 29.

and key schools. Accordingly, the nine-year compulsory education was popularized in three regional tiers by stages and in groups, manifesting the imbalance of policy objective, schedule target and specific measures.

1.2 Inequality in Opportunities of Access to Education

Equity in education can be generalized into three levels: the first is to ensure that everyone has equal rights and obligations for education; the second is to provide relatively equal educational opportunities and conditions; the third is to offer comparatively equal opportunities for educational success and educational effect, namely, each student can attain the basic standard after receiving education at the same level, including substantive equity in academic performance, in education quality and equality in objectives. Among them, it is precondition and foundation "to ensure that everyone has an opportunity of access to education", followed by a further requirement "to provide relatively equal educational opportunities and conditions" which is also the precondition for "comparatively equal opportunities for educational success and educational effect". Normally, those three levels are summarized as the equity in education access, education process and education result.

Inequity in allocation of educational resources is an immediate cause leading to unequal educational opportunities, and vice versa. American scholar James Coleman once defined equal educational opportunities in the way that "the concept of equal opportunity means equal efficiency of opportunity; in other words, equality is contained in the basic factors that influence study". Professor Lao Kaisheng, a Chinese scholar, holds that "equality of educational opportunity seeks to eliminate unequal treatment of education to individual development, commits to bring everyone's potential to full play, and provides members of society with an environment for fair competition". "Equality of educational opportunity includes connotation in four aspects: equal opportunity to access educational system; equal opportunity to enjoy educational conditions; equal educational results; equal possibilities to influence prospects of life by *education"*.[1]

In accordance with the study on unequal opportunity and its changes in China's elementary education from 1976 to 2000, Professor Liu Jingming, another Chinese scholar, distinguished two different factors with the degree of impact upon the equality of educational opportunity as the criteria: "internal family resources" and "external family resources". Currently, the main influencing factors to the inequality of educational opportunity in China are external ones which may be easily affected by external conditions and social process.

1.3 Inequality in the Participation of Social Competition for the Educated

A consequence of unequal educational opportunity caused by the "external family resources" is inequality in the participation of social competition for the educated. For example, during the past decade, influenced by such factors as family financial conditions, allocation of educational resources, social values and ethics etc., the proportion of senior middle school students from rural areas enrolled in China's key universities like Peking University and Tsinghua University etc. has suffered a drastic fall to the present proportion of between 20% and 30%, compared with over 50% in the 1980s. The phenomenon above is bound to decrease the opportunities for the whole group of students from rural families to strive upward, hence universal beliefs like "knowledge is wealth" and "knowledge upgrades life" upheld by Chinese have encountered unprecedented challenges.

By contrast, affected by multi-factors like family conditions, social mobility, external temptations, market orientation and the new edition of "education-is-useless" philosophy, many students from primary and secondary schools in rural areas have accelerated their "downward process". They were

---

[1] Lao Kaisheng, "Opportunity Equality of Education: Introspection from Practice and Value Pursuit", *XinHua Digest*, 2013, (06): 119.

obliged to abandon their opportunities to further develop and cultivate themselves by receiving general education and vocational education at higher levels; instead, they have become "rural migrant workers" engaged in simple manual labour lacking technical support with low income, which affect the quality of workers and the entire population to a large extent.

2. Causes for How Inequality in Economic Development Leads to Inequity in Education

There is a direct, inherent relevance between inequality in economic development and inequity in education. To be specific, inequality in economic development is manifested in several aspects: different structures, policies, patterns of economic development and social changes as its consequence, to name few; all those will lead to the formation of inequity in education. In a word, there are three major causes for China's inequity in education triggered by the inequality in economic development in recent years. Those causes are shown as follows.

2.1 The Gap between Urban and Rural Education Widened by Dual Structure in Urban and Rural Economy

With a vast territory and a large population, China has an imbalanced economic and social development in the eastern, centre, and western regions. The polarization of economy and society between urban and rural areas becomes quite prominent due to longstanding dual structure in urban and rural economy, production mode and benefits patterns. Since the 1980s, China's reform of market economy has spurred the major development and prosperity of cities whereas it has widened the gap between urban and rural education.

During this process, the total size of schools in rural area has shrunk. Professor Wu Zhihui, a Chinese scholar, pointed out that schools in rural area of China have undergone a profound layout adjustment since the beginning of 21st century. In 1949, there used to be 346,800 primary schools with

24,391,000 primary students in China. Yet in 2010, the number of primary students increased to 99,407,000 which was 4.08 times as large as that in 1949 while the amount of primary schools reduced to 257,400, accounting for only 74.22% of the number in 1949. From the layout adjustment of schools since the reform and opening up, the recent ten years saw the most significant adjustment with the primary schools in rural areas as its major target, accounting for 73.62% of the total number of reduction in primary and secondary schools (including towns and villages) nationwide. [1]

In addition to differences of education between urban and rural areas, regional differences and gender differences can never be overlooked. The former includes regional differences in people's literacy and education level, educational appropriations, school facilities, faculty qualities and enrollment rate of higher education; and the latter embraces gender differences in education level as well as in educational achievements. [2]

2.2 Inequity in Education Caused by SEZ and Metropolis Orientation in Economic Development

During the past three decades, there emerged a tendency of SEZ (Special Economic Zone) and metropolis orientation in the economic development with the restriction from multiple factors, especially the imbalanced economic development. Before the comprehensive implementation of reform in market economy, there has established a series of economic reform pilot cities like Shanghai, Shenzhen, Xiamen and Zhuhai etc. in the eastern coastal areas. With the deepening economic reform, China has been shaping a pattern of economic development oriented by large and medium-sized cities, which led to the gap among regional differences in economy and sped up the swarm of IT

---

[1] Wu Zhihui, "Discussion on the Core Problems of Integrated Development in Urban and Rural Compulsory Education in China", *XinHua Digest*, 2013, (02): 112, 114, 113.

[2] Yang Xiaowei, "Evaluation Indicators for Compulsory Education: A Study Based on the Orientation of Equity", *XinHua Digest*, 2013, (20): 110.

personnel and social labour forces to the developed regions especially the above-mentioned cities. Meanwhile, educational resources of high quality tended to be allocated to economically developed regions centred by those large and medium-sized cities, which, as a result, quickened the inequity in education to form "the Matthew effect" in imbalanced development of education.

Also, the tendency of SEZ and metropolis orientation in the economic development led to the significant difference in comprehensive development of education in different regions. According to the research report issued by Chinese scholars Fang Xiaodong et al., despite an increasing trend in the comprehensive development of education in recent years, the development level in eastern, central, and western China has significant differences and features. To be concrete, the development level in eastern China is comparatively higher while that of western China is lower. Moreover, the comprehensive development of education has a huge difference in different provinces. From the comparison between comprehensive development of education and per capita GDP, it is shown that per capita GDP has an obvious influence on the comprehensive development of education, the level of which is in pace with the economic development. [①]

2.3 Inequity in Education Caused by Economic Development and Unequal Social Mobility

Economic development and social mobility is crucial lever to educational development. As education has become an important means for social stratification which influences one's prospective social and economic status, the inequality in economic development will inevitably intensify social inequality and imbalance of social mobility, which will compound unfair competition in education. Under the current circumstances, it is an urgency to form and

---

① Fang Xiaodong, Gao Bingcheng. "A Research on the Comprehensive Development Level of Education in China", *Educational Research*, 2013, (12): 32, 38.

implement a rather rigid policy for the allocation of education opportunities and a fairly balanced development pattern of education so as to ensure equal allocation of educational opportunity and relatively equal social mobility.

According to American scholar John Rolls, if the social resources cannot be allocated equally, the allocation of social resources must be subject to the maximum benefit of those receiving the least benefits, known as "principle of difference", in which the formulation and implementation of education policy should benefit the lower class and the female, making those people may enjoy an opportunity for education of higher degree and high-quality when they fail to meet the unified enrollment standards.

3. Policies and Ways for Equity in Education against Inequality in Economic Development

At present, China's economic aggregate ranks the second in the world, nevertheless, inequality in economic development will exist for a long time to come. The gap in economic development in eastern, central and western China will not be eliminated in a short period. In light of the status quo, it is an arduous and pressing task for governments at all levels in China to implement institutional reform and to adjust policy at macro, meso, and micro levels in order to take feasible measures to restrain the inequity and imbalance of education.

3.1 At Macro-level: Accelerating the Modernization of Economic and Social Development and Urbanization

It is a strategic task advanced by Chinese government to achieve holistic economic and social development in urban and rural areas and to establish the mechanism for the development. According to statistical analysis, the modernization of social development, informationalization and urbanization are conducive to the comprehensive development of education. Currently, though

China's per capita GDP has just exceeded 6000 dollars and its input of fiscal funds to education has accounted for 4% of the overall GDP, the conflict between the inadequate educational sources and growing demands still stands prominent; besides, China is, as before, plagued by the low security level and imbalanced, unsustainable economic and social development, which will hinder China's efforts to ensure the equity in educational development for a long period. Fundamentally, only through accelerating the modernization of economic and social development, informationalization and urbanization can the equity in education be guaranteed and be realized.

It was proposed in China's *National Medium and Long-term Plan for Educational Reform and Development* (2010 - 2020) that to promote equity shall be a basic national policy of education for it is a vital foundation for social equity. To guarantee the equity in education, it is a key step to provide equal opportunities by ensuring the legal rights of all citizens to receive education as its basic requirement with the promotion in balanced development of compulsory education and in assistance to the people with financial difficulties as the focus and with proper allocation of educational resources, and in the priority given to rural areas, remote and impoverished areas and ethnic minority areas for the acceleration of narrowing the gap in education as the fundamental measures. Undoubtedly, the main responsibility for equity in education falls on the shoulder of the government; still, the joint efforts from the whole society are indispensable.

It is important to establish a mechanism of the holistic compulsory educational development of urban and rural areas, and give a priority to rural areas in terms of financial appropriation, school construction and faculty allocation. We should aim to achieve the balanced compulsory educational development of urban and rural areas in counties (districts) and then extend to a wider scope. We should step up the transfer payment in compulsory education in old revolutionary base, ethnic groups, borders and poverty-stricken areas, and encourage developed regions to provide assistance for undeveloped ones.

The central government, through increasing transfer payment, will expend more in the educational development of rural, remote and impoverished and ethnic minority areas, and consolidate key areas and strengthen weak links to resolve acute problems. By 2020, the educational informationalization system covering all kinds of urban and rural schools at all levels shall be basically established so as to foster the modernization of curricula, teaching methods and approaches with greater importance attached to the information infrastructure in rural schools to narrow the digital gap between the urban and rural areas.

3.2 At Meso-level: Establishing a System to Promote Holistic Educational Development in Urban and Rural Areas

Great progress has been made in China's rural education with China's realization of popularizing the nine-year compulsory education in the late 20th century, the establishment of a new mechanism of guaranteeing funds to rural compulsory education in 21st century, the implementation of a plan to make nine-year compulsory education generally available and basically eliminate illiteracy among young and middle-aged adults, the "Specially Contracted Teachers Plan" (a plan to hire university students to take part in rural compulsory education), free compulsory education both in urban and rural areas and free normal education policy. In 1989, China established 116 state-level pilot counties and 30 regional (city level) liaison points for all-round reform of rural education, and the total number of pilot counties (cities) amounted to almost a thousand together with those at provincial level. All those pilot counties (cities) and liaison points serve as good examples to promote an all-round reform in rural education.

Since the beginning of 21st century, China has gradually intensified efforts to carry out comprehensive educational reform in urban and rural areas in a holistic way by setting up "pilot areas for comprehensive educational reform" with the cooperation between the Ministry of Education and Chongqing municipality, Chengdu city, Hubei and Hunan provinces. It was stipulated in the *Opinions of the Ministry of Education to Further Promote the Balanced Development of Compulsory Education* issued in 2005 and the newly promulgated *Compulsory Education Law* in 2006 that "the State Council and governments above county-level should properly allocate educational resources and promote the balanced development of compulsory education". In January, 2009, then Premier Wen Jiabao pointed out that "rural education shall be of great importance by taking holistic measures to develop urban and rural education". "The key" to address current problems facing rural education, according to Wen, "is to narrow the gap between urban and rural areas, and to boost the balanced development between them". Besides, it was stipulated in the *National Medium and Long-term Plan for Educational Reform and Development* (2010 - 2020) "to establish a mechanism of holistic compulsory educational development of urban and rural areas, and give a priority to rural areas in terms of financial appropriation, school construction and faculty allocation".

It is a long-term and arduous task to establish a system of promoting holistic development of education in urban and rural areas. Professor Wu Zhihui, a Chinese scholar, pointed out that "there are three indexes to assess whether the holistic development of compulsory education in urban and rural areas has achieved: first, whether the allocation of compulsory educational resources have achieved equalization; second, whether the compulsory education in rural areas enjoys the same appeal as that in urban areas does; third, whether students from rural areas have equal access to further education of high-quality after compulsory education as those from urban areas do". He also stated that "to attain the goal of holistic development of compulsory education in urban and rural areas, it is necessary to set up a system in which the system designers and executors can fulfill mutual encouragement and smooth cooperation, exercise self-constraint and take measure of safeguard". [1]

---

[1] Wu Zhihui, "Discussion on the Core Problems of Integrated Development in Urban and Rural Compulsory Education in China", *XinHua Digest*, 2013, (02): 112, 114, 113.

3.3 At Micro-level: Reconstructing the "Embedded" Educational Ecology in Rural Areas

"Consolidating the foundation" is an important guarantee for the holistic development of education in urban and rural areas. Namely, if rural education has no relative independence, or it just acts as an affiliation to urban education, there is no easy way out to achieve the balanced holistic development of education in urban and rural areas. Furthermore, school construction needs to be integrated with development of rural communities in rural areas. Currently, reconstruction of the "embedded" educational ecology in rural areas becomes an important and urgent task for Chinese educational reform and development.

In accordance with a study from a Chinese scholar, Professor Wu Zhihui, the development of rural education must be the precondition of the integration of urban and rural compulsory education. In other words, the absence of rural education results in impossibility of urban-rural integration. Presently, in many areas of China, diversification and embedded rural educational patterns are in progress mainly in four ways. [1]

The first pattern is "Hop Village and Habitat". In China, towns like Dezhou (in Shandong province), Pujiang (in Sichuan province) and other places carried out reforms of "Hop Village and Habitat" through "village merger and rural community establishment". Thanks to the reforms, there established a centralized residency and modernized community for villagers, thus it helped to make it possible to retain students and outstanding teachers in rural schools and to implement high-standard construction and configuration; it also laid further foundations for the development of the integration of rural compulsory education.

The second pattern is school busing. Given the situation that there exist many terrace areas in China with small per capita area of cultivated

---

[1] Wu Zhihui, "Discussion on the Core Problems of Integrated Development in Urban and Rural Compulsory Education in China", *XinHua Digest*, 2013, (02): 112, 114, 113.

farmland and poor transportation, it is not suitable to set up centralized rural communities; instead, it is feasible to run centralized schools in densely-populated towns and to promote the holistic development of urban and rural compulsory education through improving local transportation and equipping school buses to facilitate the link between schools and communities.

The third pattern is boarding. It is not only of great significance but also a practical approach for the improvement of rural education by establishing the designated boarding schools. The latest tendency shows that the amount of school boarders under compulsory education has expanded year after year in Tibet, Inner Mongolia, Yunnan, Qinghai, Hubei and other provinces (autonomous regions). Although boarding schools in rural areas have experienced rapid development, their backwardness in standardization and culture impact the quality and standard of boarding life.

The last pattern is education station. There are some remote mountainous areas in China with severe natural conditions in which the three patterns mentioned above are not applicable, thus the education station mode becomes the only choice to implement compulsory education. The "education station" is usually equipped with only dozens of students and a few teachers and even merely one teacher in some places. From the 1980s to the 1990s, China's rural education stations witnessed rapid development from the number of 162,600 in 1989 to 193,600 in 1995; but they have been declining till only 65,400 in 2010, a decrease of nearly two-thirds (a reduction of 66.2%). In the past few decades, education stations played an important role in China's rural education. Even in the United States, the most developed country in the world, there still retains more than 20,000 education stations. In order to ensure the education quality in rural education stations, first and foremost, we need to enhance the training of teachers and to explore complementary teaching methods; next, we must improve the facilities to enhance distance education and network-based teaching resources; finally, we have to increase the expenditure in the education stations.

问题探讨

考察正义的两种方法

彭定光　李桂梅[*]

摘　要：正义的国际社会应该如何设计、应该遵守哪些正义原则，这与人们考察正义的方法有着直接关系。迄今为止，人们考察正义的方法主要有两种：一种是从个体、差异、局部或者个别现象考察正义的个体论方法；另一种是从整体、全体或者总体考察正义的整体论方法，它将人类社会作为一个整体，将社会整体的各个结构因素、发展过程和目标结合起来以寻求正义的方法。前者是难以达成正义共识的有缺陷的方法，后者是依据社会生活的各个方面来考察正义的正确方法。

关键词：正义　考察方法　个体论方法　整体论方法

Two Ways to Inquire Justice

Peng Dingguang；Li Guimei

Abstract：How to design a justice international society? What rules should we follow? The questions are directly connected to the way for us to inquire

---

[*] 彭定光（1963~），男，湖南师范大学伦理学研究所教授，主要研究方向是伦理学基础理论、政治伦理学及道德理论；李桂梅（1964~），女，湖南师范大学道德文化研究中心教授，主要研究伦理学原理、家庭伦理和思想政治教育理论。

justice. Up to now, there are two ways for us to inquire justice, one is from the holistic perspective which takes human society as a unity and inquires justice form the unity of different social constituent, development process and goals, another is the individual perspective which inquires justice from different aspects of social life.

Key words: Justice; the way of inquirement; individual method; holistic method

某一国家内部乃至整个国际社会应该遵守哪些正义原则，这是与人们的正义观或者正义理论直接相关的。自有文明以来，人们提出了各种各样的正义理论。尽管这些正义理论之间存在着区别，然而，其考察正义的方法主要都有两种：一种是从个体、差异、局部或者个别现象考察正义的方法，即考察正义的个体论方法；另一种是从整体、全体或者总体考察正义的方法，即考察正义的整体论方法，同个体论方法一样，这种方法又有多种表现形式。方法上的这种区别，决定着它们对正义社会（包括国际社会）有着不同的理解和设计。

一 考察正义的个体论方法

在西方近代以前，人们考察正义的占统治地位的方法是整体论方法。自近代起，个体论方法取代了整体论方法，成了人们考察正义的占统治地位的方法。这种方法之所以能够占统治地位，是由当时社会的商品经济、政治生活、个人自我意识（在当时的社会生活条件下往往会被强化为个人权利意识）的发达及自然科学研究范式所决定的。

考察正义的个体论方法虽然提出了一些不容忽视的观点，但在总体上是有缺陷的。其缺陷主要表现在以下三个方面。

第一，抽象化。它指的是人们从现实生活整体中抽取某一方面、某一因素，并以此来解释整个现实生活的思维方法。这种思维方法是近代以来的学者在考察正义时普遍运用的方法，他们从不同的角度来阐释各自的正义观，以为各自所强调的东西正是整个社会生活的根本价值甚至唯一价值，并以此作为整个社会生活的组织原则、判断标准和价值目标；同时他们又强调，他们用来构建社会秩序的东西正是根源于人性的。理论需要抽象。然而，作为人们考察正义的个体论方法中的"抽象"，它只是一种人们随心所欲的"抽象化"，是对丰富多样的社会生活的任意片面化，既不反映整个社会生活的本质和规律，又割断它与其他事物和整体的有机联系，因此，它不能把握整体的全貌，抓住事物的根本。

第二，还原论。在持个体论方法的人们看来，社会是虚构的，是所有个人的总和，或者是所有个人的合作体系，个人或者个体才是真正的、唯一的实体。于是，在他们那里，对整个社会的正义的考察就可以归结为对个人或者个体的道德把握。然而，人们对个人或者个体完全可以做出不同的甚至截然相反的理解。如果说，在亚里士多德那里，个人或者个体是体现和包含社会性的存在物的话，那么，在现代自由主义者那里，个人不会含有社会性，个人只是孤立的、互不关涉（或者互不偏涉）的个人，社会在根本上也只是个人。因此，在自由主义那里，正义不应从社会中去寻找，相反，要从个人中去寻找，并依赖互不关涉的个人之间的社会契约而确立。

第三，非历史性。它指的是这样两种情形，第一种情形是脱离社会的历史过程来考察、理解正义。这种考察方法由于坚持还原论立场，把所有社会现象还原为个人，并从个人视角来考察社会现象，因而，一方面，它割断个人与整个社会的联系，不仅割断个人与社会之间的横向的、空间上的联系，而且割断个人与社会之间的纵向的、时间上的联系，这样，它就既看不到社会是一个不断发展的统一的历史过程，又看不到个人是随着这一社会历史过程而不断改变的过程；另一方面，它否定社会固有的整体性质，否定社会本质的历史性变化，认为正义根本不涉及社会的本质、与生产资料所有制所决定的社会制度无关。与第一种情形密切关联的第二种情形是，它认为个人生而有自由、平等等神圣不可侵犯的权利，任何社会历史时期的个人都有这种权利，这种权利是固定的、永恒的，否定个人具有由变化着的社会所决定、所规定的历史性权利。

考察正义的个体论方法，由于只关心孤立的事物，只重视个人，否定社会的整体联系和社会发展，而且由于持这种方法的人总是从各自的价值立场出发理解个人权利，因而，它就必定会导致这样的结果：他们在什么是真正的正义问题上争论不休，难以达成正义共识。他们之间的争论不是为了得到实质性的结论，而只是为了坚持自己的立场。这种情况反映在西方国家的制度设计、政府行为上就是缺乏定规，摇摆不定；就是以合法性取代合理性。它所导致的第二个结果是，否定社会发展，否定不同社会形态之间在正义的内容和性质方面存在根本区别，否定个人对社会的责任。

二 考察正义的整体论方法

整体论方法则克服了个体论方法的上述缺陷，是依据社会生活的各个方面来考察正义的正确方法。这一方法就是以事物整体为考察对象而揭示正义的方法，它是建立在对"整体"予以正确理解的基础上的。由于它所理解的这种"整体"并非就是人们所强调的整体大于部分之和这一抽象规定，而是由多个方面所构成的，因此，它在考察正义时就同时具有多个分析维度。具体来说，它主要有三重分析维度。

其一是结构。按照系统论的观点，整体或者系统是具有一定的结构的，它不仅在空间上既包括垂向的、各层次的部分，又包括横向的各个要素，而且包括时间性的、动态性的各种不断变化着的东西。就人类社会生活的整体而言，它包括自然、社会和人三大基本要素，每种基本要素又包含相当多的各个部分、各种因素。我们不能孤立地理解这些要素或者部分，而应该作为整体来把握，应该将各个要素与社会整体结合起来理解。如对个人与社会整体之间关系的理解就是如此，既从社会整体角度理解个人，又从个人角度理解社会整体，强调社会整体的同时不忽视个人，着眼于个人又不忘却社会整体。这实际上是说，从整体的结构意义上看，兼顾和同时增进社会整体利益和个人利益的行为就是正义的。

其二是过程。过程是一个时间概念，它指的是事物发展从过去来到现在再走向未来的持续性。然而，作为整体意义上的过程范畴，并非一个纯粹的时间概念,它既指事物发展从过去来到现在再走向未来的整体性和统一性,又指事物发展的这三个阶段的相互区别,还指事物发展的过去阶段和现在阶段的局限性和不完善性,以及这两个阶段为走向不断完善的未来阶段所做的准备和所付出的代价的合理性。就社会整体而言,它的各个发展阶段或者各种具体的社会形态都是局部性的东西,只是统一的社会历史过程的部分与环节。虽然它们共同构成了统一的具有过程性的社会历史整体,但它们之间又是存在性质上的区别的,这些区别不是由它们各自的独特性所决定的,不是表明它们具有相对于其他部分而言的特殊性质,而是显示它们各自相对于社会历史的整体性和一般性而言的独特性质。正因为如此,社会整体的各个发展阶段或者各种具体社会形态之间的真正区别,只有在各个阶段与整个社会的关系的历史总过程中才能真正辨明。从正义的意义上看,既然社会整体的各个发展阶段或者各种具体社会形态并非孤立的现象,它们必须从社会发展的总过程角度来理解,那么,当某一社会发展阶段或者具体社会形态被人们抽取出来单独考察时,它的正义性是不能从自身得到彻底说明的,而只能从社会历史总过程的意义上才能得到最终解释。这种解释,一是从这一社会历史阶段相对于以往社会历史阶段而言的进步性和合理性来解释,此社会历史阶段在这种意义上的正义,只是相对性的正义或者有局限性的正义;二是从这一社会历史阶段相对于社会历史总过程而言是否体现了社会历史整体的真正性质来解释,此社会历史阶段在这种意义上的正义,是绝对性的正义,是马克思所说的"真正的正义"。如果人们把某一社会历史阶段或者社会形态当作孤立的事实来考察,那么,他们就会犯"存在即正义"的理论错误,就没有哪一个社会不认为它所宣扬的正义是绝对的正义,而这实际上等于取消了人们对社会历史的根本性质的探求和对社会发展的责任。

其三是目标。这里所说的"目标",并不是指某一社会历史阶段的人们所追求的目标,而是社会整体意义上的目标,因此,它又可以称为"最终目标"。这两种目标虽然存在着区别,但它们又是联系在一起的。正因为这样,每一个社会历史阶段都可以也需要提出自己的目标。由于这一目标是在人们揭露和批判前一个社会历史阶段的弊病和不合理性中逐渐明确并确立起来的，因而，它只是意味着这一社会历史阶段相对于以往社会而言的进步性，并非就是整体社会的完善性，也不是社会历史整体的根本性质的真实体现。可是，最终目标毕竟具有对于具体目标而言的根本性和优先性。正是最终目标所具有的这种根本性和优先性，使人们移开凝视社会现实的目光，审视现实，超越现实，彻悟社会历史的真谛；也使人们欲像新自由主义要求的那样在正义问题上保持价值中立成为不可能，因为"真正的正义"总是与最终目标密切关联的；同时它使人们在正义问题上抛弃自我的立场。而且，社会历史整体所内含的这种最终目标，决定了正义并非"底线伦理"，并非米尔恩所指的基于人权的"普遍的最低限度的道德标准"。

综上所论，考察正义的整体论方法，就是将人类社会作为一个整体，将社会整体的各个结构因素、发展过程和目标结合起来以寻求正义的方法。如果将这三者割裂，或者只注意到其中的某一方面，它就会变成片面的甚至错误的方法，就会难以寻求到真正的正义。

人类情感与经济正义

李家莲[*]

摘　要：经济不平等问题，实际上就是经济正义问题。经济世界是人类从事经济活动而产生的世界，是一个与人类经验世界密切相关的世界。人类在经验世界内的一切活动，都是人受到情感推动的结果，离开了人类情感，就不会有人类活动。然而，人类在经验世界内的情感必然具有功利性特征，人类情感的功利性特征决定了人类经济活动中必然产生经济不平等现象。要从根本上消除经济不平等，不能寄希望于在现实经验世界实现人人平等的大同世界，而需要人类向内调整情感方向，通过发掘情感自身具有的超经验和超功利元素，并从中感受到超功利快乐，这是人类获取经济正义的情感之路。

关键词：经验世界　情感　功利　超功利

Human Sentiments and Economic Justice

Li Jialian

Abstract：The issue of economic inequality, is the issue connected with

---

[*] 李家莲，女，浙江大学博士后，湖北大学哲学学院副教授，高等人文研究院院长助理，主要研究西方伦理思想史。

economic justice. Economic world is created from human economic activities closely connected with human experience. All kinds of human activities in this world are excited by human sentiments. Without human sentiments, there will be no human action at all. However, the human actions in the experience world much have the characteristic of utilitarianism which determines human economic activities to be unequal. If economic inequality is to be removed fundamentally, the perspective must be turned from the outside world to the inner world, and we must find the ways to transcend utilitarian quality of human sentiments.

Key words: the world of experience; sentiments; utility; the transcendence of utility

  我们生活的世界,是一个经验的世界,也是一个科学的世界,各种各样的科技成果正在逐步把我们的世界以图画的方式呈现给我们。科技成果给我们提供了各种各样的图画,我们的生活中到处充斥着图画,我们的时代真正变成了一个读图时代和视觉时代。从早到晚,我们总在不断受到图画的侵袭。在手机闹铃的催促下,早上起床时,我们首先会看一看手机上用作屏保的图画,那些图画都是我们精心挑选过的,要么代表了我们的心境,要么体现了我们的价值诉求。吃早餐的时候,我们会看见碗盘上的图画以及牛奶盒或饼干盒上的图画。乘交通工具上班,我们会看见各种各样的广告,有的是美丽的旅游景点的照片,它们在吸引我们利用闲暇时间出去度假;有的是浪漫的婚纱照,它们在提醒我们,如果自己或朋友结婚,选择该公司不仅是一件浪漫的事情,而且是一件有价值的事情。上班之后,我们需要处理很多与图片有关的信息,比如照片的编辑与发送、图书目录的编制与修订、PDF 文档的阅读与处理、地图的查询、蓝图的设计或图表的修订等。上班之余,在片刻的休憩中,我们打开互联网,映入眼帘的是各种丰富多彩的图片,既有帅哥靓女的美照,也有可亲可爱的动植物照片,还有各类新闻照片以及搞怪类照片,每点击一张照片,我们就会由这张照片进入一个世界。晚上回家,我们会打开电视机,看着一幅幅不断闪烁的图片,我们既获取了有关世界的信息,也使自己疲惫的身体得到了放松。上床睡觉的时候,我们甚至还不忘打开手机看看微信,微信上的每一幅图片,不仅给我们传递了诸多生活的信息,而且使我们借此可以与朋友交流价值观,看见心有灵犀之处,我们不禁互相点赞,然后带着疲惫和满足安静地进入梦乡。然而,即使在睡梦里,我们也还是会遇见一个由图片组成的梦幻世界。

不过,尽管我们身处科学世界和经验世界的包围,我们却常常对这个世界感到不满,我们常常渴望能够超越这个世界,得到一种全新的人生体验。为了超越这个按部就班的图画世界和科学世界,我们希望能够在宗教中直接与神对话,使我们的精神与至高的宇宙相通,并由此得到救赎,获得永恒的自由,因此,我们常常觉得需要放弃图片,直面生命的永恒。为了做到这点,我们选择了旅行。我们会试图通过长途旅行把自己放逐到陌生的世界、一个没有图片的世界。在大自然的优美景色中,我们压抑已久的心灵得到了释放,我们被放逐的灵魂找到了回家的方向,我们隐隐约约地发现,那个由美所主宰的世界,而非这个由科学主宰的世界,才是我们人生的真正的故乡。为此,在科学成果的推广与应用中,我们总不会忘记给它添加一些审美的元素,例如,给计算机装上风景优美的桌面文件,或给最新的电子产品绘上可爱的卡通图画,等等。我们之所以这样做,其原因在于,我们虽然离不开图画世界和科学世界,但我们却不甘心被它们俘虏,因为我们的灵魂渴望纯真的自由。

面对科学世界和经验世界,我们内心充满矛盾。一方面,我们享受科技带给我们的便利和舒适,另一方面,我们却渴望超越科学,追逐自由。这种矛盾直接源于人性结构中的深层矛盾,是我们自身永远需要面对的永恒矛盾的最直接体现。这种矛盾决定了人总是行走在两个世界,总要从两个世界获取生存的养料。如果说人生是一场演出,那么,一个人注定要在二元性的生存结构中演绎人生。就人原本源于自然、是自然的一个普通物种而言,自然世界中的人类情感必然体现出物性。就人有别于自然、是自然的精灵而言,超越自然的人类情感必然展现人类情感对物性的超越。自然给人创建了一种物质的生活,使人脚踩大地,头顶天空，傲然屹立于天地之间，繁衍不止，生生不息。然而，人类在地球上的绵延不绝绝非是因为人能吃能喝，或懂得如何向自然索取生存之物，而是因为人具有有别于这种物质生活之外的某种东西。看到人与自然之间的区别，就可以看到独立于其他物种的独特性和神圣性，以及由此展现的精神性。就此而言，人总是生活在两个空间，即物质和精神，或者说，自然和自由。人性的这种二元生存结构决定了人的地位，它既不是纯粹的物质，也不是纯粹的精神，在它的身上，既有着物的卑贱，也蕴含着神的光辉。人性的二元结构决定了"人与自然界的特殊关联使人永远也变不成神，人与神的特殊关联使人永远不会成为动物……人的存在是精神的，但人又不具有绝对的精神，因为他不能彻底拒绝物质世界的诱惑"①。

当人在两个世界生存的时候，人的一切行为，如果不受到情感的推动，根本就不会产生，就此而言，人总是在用情感来表达自己的全部生存境遇。夏夫兹博里认为，"若非通过适合动物的感情或激情，没有哪种动物能恰当地行事"，"由动物所做的如此这般的一切事情或行为，仅仅只出自某种感情或激情的推动，如恐惧、爱或恨"②。离开了情感的推动，我们的一切行为，无论是物质性的还是精神性的，都将成为不可能。所以，夏夫兹博里认为，人的情感是所有哲学话题中最有价值的话题，研究哲学就是研究人的情感，研究人类生活，也即研究人类情感。在曼德维尔看来，人的一切行为，包括理性行为，都只听从情感的命令，它们仅仅只受情感的推动而产生，因为人是一个由激情组成的复合体，"我相信，人（除了皮肤、肌肉、骨骼等眼目所及之处）是一个由各种激情组成的复合体，所有这些激情，一旦它们被激发并表现出来，就会不管人的意愿而轮流支配人"③。激情是"人与生俱来的，属于我们的本性，在我们尚未觉察到的时候，其中一些就已经存在于我们心中，至少它们的种子已经存在于我们心中了"④，在这些激情面前，理性是无足轻

---

① 戴茂堂：《人性的结构与伦理学的诞生》，载《哲学研究》2004 年第 3 期。
② Shaftesbury, *Characteristics of Men, Manners, Opinions, Times*, Kessinger Publishing Co., 2004.
③ Bernard Mandeville, *The Fable of the Bees*, Penguin Group, 1970, p. 77.
④ Bernard Mandeville, *The Fable of the Bees*, Penguin Group, 1970, p. 323.

重的，处于被支配的地位，只是按照激情的指导而发生作用，"我们总是按照我们所感受到的激情所指引的方向运用理性"①。哈奇森也持有类似的观点。在他看来，人的一切行为都只会受到情感的推动，不会受到除情感之外的任何其他东西的推动。对于推动人的行为的理由，哈奇森称之为"推动性理由"。在我们所做的平静而理性的每一种行为中，我们会预先假定某种目的，而我们所有的目的都必须以我们的感情或欲望为前提，人的所有目的都包含在情感之内，"没有哪种目的能先于感情全体，因此不存在先于感情的推动性理由"②。按照通常的逻辑推理，对于人的行为而言，在所有推动性理由的终结之处，必定存在着某种终极性的目的。是什么样的推动性理由推动了终极性目的的产生？对此，哈奇森引用亚里士多德的话，认为"存在着不带任何他物之意图的终极性目的"③。如果我们为终极性目的假定推动性理由的话，这就意味着，不存在终极性目的，否则，我们就会在一个又一个的无限序列中欲求一个又一个事物，在这种无穷无尽的序列中，我们找不到终极性目的。既然终极性目的不受推动性理由的推动，相反，一切推动性理由都指向这种终极性目的，那么，这种终极性目的是什么呢？在哈奇森看来，它就是人性中存在的本能、欲望或情感。正是这种本能或情感自身推动了人的一切行为。这种情感或本能，作为终极性目的，不需要任何推动性理由就可以存在。在这个意义上，人的一切行为都因推动性理由而产生。休谟认为，除了快乐和痛苦的情感之外，我们的生活不会受任何其他东西的推动，"人类心灵的主要动力或驱动原理是快乐或痛苦，当这些感觉从我们的思想和感受中被清除以后，不管是在思想上，还是在感觉上，我们在很大程度上都无法产生情感、行为、欲望或意志"④。斯密也认

---

① Bernard Mandeville, *The Fable of the Bees*, Penguin Group, 1970, p. 337.
② 哈奇森：《论激情和感情的本性与表现，以及对道德感官的阐明》，浙江大学出版社，2009，第156页。
③ 哈奇森：《论激情和感情的本性与表现，以及对道德感官的阐明》，浙江大学出版社，2009，第157页。
④ 休谟：《人性论》，九州出版社，2007，第1172页。

为，情感不仅是推动主体行为的第一动力，而且是判断主体行为是否合宜的终极标准。

生存于二元世界中的人，一切活动的展开，都离不开情感这个引擎。人所面对的二元性，不仅展现在自身之内，而且展现于人类的一切情感活动中。自然科学视域的人类情感以外在自然事物为对象，外物对人的有用性决定了情感的产生与情感的效果，因此，处于外在经验世界中的情感，就其结果来衡量这是一种具有功利性特征的情感。在超越科学的自由世界中，人类情感以自由为对象，自由是自由情感的特征与本质，由于这种情感所指向的对象直接超越自然世界与科学世界，这种情感没有"结果"，无法像经验世界中的情感那样，用"结果"来衡量，因此，这种情感本身也体现了对人类功利的超越，从而展现出超功利的特征。经济活动是与人类生活息息相关的人类活动，这种社会活动直接受人类情感推动而产生，以最直观的方式展示了人类情感的功利性特征，并因财富的多少、经济不平等的现状而决定了人的经济地位的高低。虽然经济不平等是不可改变的现实，但人总在欲求改变这种现状，从而谋取人与人之间的绝对平等。经济不平等极容易导致贫富差距，并威胁社会稳定，因此，人类总在寻找解决经济不平等以及贫富差距的有效方法。事实上，若不超越自然科学的世界，就永远难以实现经济平等，唯有超越自然科学世界，到达自由世界，我们才能找到超越经济不平等的有效路径，这时候，即使身处经济不平等的社会，我们每个人却可以不被这种不平等所束缚，从而找到真正的平等之道。

一

自然科学培育了自然主义的眼光，自然主义眼光中的自然科学注重定量研究。自然科学研究之所以重视定量研究，其原因在于，自然科学以自然为研究对象，探索自然的一般规律。面对自然，科学家所从事的科学活动具有两个典型特征。其一，在与自然打交道的过程中，科学家总会求助于仪器、实验室等科学研究的工具，并在这些工具的指导下对自然展开定量研究，从而使研究对象呈现定量性的特征；其二，科学家与自然（物）是一种彼此外在、主客二分的关系，自然在科学家面前是被分析、被征服的对象。自然科学视域中的人类情感也必然具有定量性与分离性这两个特征。

在自然科学世界中，人的情感总是以某种自然物为对象，正如自然对象在科学家的眼中总可以进行定量研究，以自然为对象的情感也必定会表现类似定量研究的可计算性特征。夏夫兹博里认为，以人类这个生物物种的整体善为目标的情感之所以是善的情感，是因为它可以促进幸福，这种感情，作为道德的感情，是可以得到计算的，就像数学计算法一样。"幸福和美德之善，源自一种感情，即与自然相符、与物种或种属的治理相符的效果……在这些具体情形中，我们就可以像做加减法一样计算出幸福总量的增减，假如这个道德算术（moral arithmetic）的过程不存在可以反驳的步骤，我们的研究就具有了重要的证据，如同数字或数学中的证据一样重要。"[1] 哈奇森认为，人对人的情感以及人对神的情感，都可以用数学公式予以精确计算。计算可以推动我们提升被造物的幸福，提升神的善性。在哈奇森看来，对于我们所有各种类型的爱来说，其道德程度都是可以得到计算的，计算的原则是，"指向任何人的爱的量都处于他身上为人所理解的爱的缘由和观察者身上性情的善性的复合比例中"[2]。如果用 L 表示 quantity of love，即爱的量，用 C 表示 cause of love，即爱的缘由，用 G 表示 goodness of temper，即性情的善性，那么，爱的量就可以用公式表示为"$L = C \times G$"。在这个公式中，哈奇森认为，"由于我们无法理解拥有超出其缘由比例的爱的程度的某种善性，最高尚的性情就是爱等同于其缘由的性情，它因此可以用统一性予以表达"[3]，也就是"$G = L/C$"中的"L"与"C"相等。这个公式可

---

[1] Shaftesbury, *Characteristics of Men, Manners, Opinions, Times*, Kessinger Publishing Co., 2004.
[2] 哈奇森：《论激情和感情的本性与表现，以及对道德感官的阐明》，浙江大学出版社，2009，第 220 页。
[3] 哈奇森：《论激情和感情的本性与表现，以及对道德感官的阐明》，浙江大学出版社，2009，第 220 页。

以应用于我们指向神的爱。哈奇森认为,"两个人对神圣善性具有同样公正的理解时,两人身上对神的爱会与性情的善性成比例"①,也就是说,当"C"相等时,"L"就随"G"而改变。

科学的研究视域决定了人类必然会在主客二分视野下从事科学活动,从而在研究对象和研究主体之间划定明确的界线,当人类情感在自然科学视域中展开时,必然也会展现由主客二分的思维方式所导致的"分离性"特征。首先,这种"分离性"体现为"主体"与"他人"之间的分离,在情感上体现为自爱与仁爱之间的对立。近代英国情感主义在自然主义和科学主义的视域中研究人类情感,以自爱和仁爱为核心,可以划分为以莎夫兹伯里、哈奇森、巴特勒为代表的阵营,以及由曼德维尔、休谟和斯密为代表的阵营,前者强调仁爱,后者强调自爱,它们之间针锋相对的论辩,充分体现了主体与他人之间的对立。其次,这种"分离性"体现为人的内在自然性与自由性的对立。近代英国情感主义带着浓厚的科学思维方式研究人的情感,他们把人视为纯自然的存在,他们重视世俗的功利,并发明了"道德算术"对情感的道德性进行有效的计算,这样做的直接后果就是忽视了人性内部的自由性。在自然与自由的对抗中,天平的平衡彻底偏向了自然的一边,人性深处的超越性和自由性消解殆尽。夏夫兹博里就把自然感情之乐等同于精神性的快乐,认为精神快乐要么来自自然感情自身的直接运作,要么来自自然感情所产生的结果,"由理性被造物适当产生的自然感情,是使他产生一系列精神快乐的唯一方式,也是使他产生确切与稳定幸福的唯一方式"②,因此,"精神性快乐实际上就是自然感情自身"③。哈奇森一方面认为,由美的感官和道德感官而来的美的快乐和道德快乐都具有超越功利的特征,另一方面又认为,"理性主体之最大以及最广泛的幸福"不过就是经验

---

① 哈奇森:《论激情和感情的本性与表现,以及对道德感官的阐明》,浙江大学出版社,2009,第223页。
② Shaftesbury, *Characteristics of Men, Manners, Opinions, Times*, Kessinger Publishing Co., 2004.
③ Shaftesbury, *Characteristics of Men, Manners, Opinions, Times*, Kessinger Publishing Co., 2004.

性的世俗利益。在早期版本的《论美与德性观念的根源》以及《论激情和感情的本性与表现，以及对道德感官的阐明》中，哈奇森非常细致地用数学的方式列出了有关德性计算的各种公式，并由此得出结论说，"为最大多数人获得最大幸福的那种行为就是最好的行为，以同样的方式引起苦难的行为就是最坏的行为"[①]。对人的情感进行计算的过程直接导致人失去了精神的自由家园，近代英国情感主义从讨论超越性的人类情感开始，最终却走入了极具自然主义特色的功利主义结局。

事实上，在自然科学视域下，人类情感必定是功利的，人类经济活动就是这种功利性的最直接体现。经济活动本质上是一种情感活动，受功利性的情感推动而产生，这种情感的动力与目标都与经济对象有关。经济活动必然涉及财富的交易以及积累，即财产权的转让与交易。事实上，经济活动中的财产权，不是财产具有的某种客观性质，而是体现了人的某种情感。如果说财产权具有某种客观的性质，那么，当财产权发生改变的时候，这个"物体"也要相应发生改变。然而，当人们进行财产权转让的时候，这个"物体"本身却不会发生任何改变。由此可见，人们对财物的所有权以及对财富的占有，本质上体现了人与人之间的情感关系。正如以外物为对象的情感必定体现具有功利性性质的可计算性特征一样，人类社会的财富必定存在大小多少的定量区分，由此必定产生经济不平等现象。经济关系背后所蕴藏的是人与人之间的情感关系，因此，当这种情感关系受到忽略的时候，经济不平等就直接决定了人与人之间情感上的不平等，并由此产生人与人之间的不平等。然而，每个人却天然被赋予了平等的权利，因此，追求平等是人内在的使命。自然科学视域下的情感所具有的功利性特征，决定了人与人之间难以实现真正的平等。要追求平等，我们必须还原经济行为的情感关系，并寻求对自然科学视域的超越，虚心接受那蕴涵在人性深处的自由情感。

---

① 哈奇森：《论激情和感情的本性与表现，以及对道德感官的阐明》，浙江大学出版社，2009，第127页。

二

在自然科学视域中的情感是没有自由的情感,要寻找自由情感,首先必须超越自然科学的视域。超越自然科学的视域,意味着情感必须以超越自然科学的自由本身为对象。对于处于物质与精神二元世界中的人而言,人的情感不能仅仅停留于自然科学的世界,不能仅仅只欲求或憎恶可见的、经验的、科学世界中的自然之物,它必须超越自然科学世界,走向以自由为特征的精神世界。精神性的理想生活是一种完全自由的生活,它必须作为人的特殊财富予以永久保存。精神性的自由情感孕育了人类灵魂的故乡,是人类自身价值的真正源头,就此而言,"神仅仅在精神之中,并不在彼岸,而是个人内心深处所固有的"①。保持这种自由性,就是保存人固有的神性。在自然中生活的人,功利性的情感构筑了圣洁的神庙,庙堂深处端坐着人之为人的自由与神圣。因此,生活在科学世界中的人,总是从两个方面表现人类情感的超功利特征,即超越主客二分的科学主义思维方式以及超越功利主义的审美气质。

首先,在内部结构上,超功利的情感必定超越主客二分之科学主义思维方式。所谓主客二分,就是把世界分为主体(subject)和客体(object),并以此作为观察世界的基点。主客二分,它"确信外部世界包括自然现象和心理现象存在的不言而喻性,以及人对外部世界的精确认识的不言而喻性"②。这是一种自然主义态度,这种态度以及由此演变的思维方式在"主体"与"客体"之间划出了一条鸿沟,决定了"你"与"我"之间的绝对界限。超功利的情感,在思维方式上首先必须超越主客二分,这种思维方式是超功利情感的内部结构的最典型表征。只有超越主客二分,才会超越"你"与"我"的区分,只有超越"你"与"我"的区分,我们才能沿着情感的道路回归灵魂的家园。蕴含于人性

---

① 黑格尔:《哲学史讲演录》第4卷,商务印书馆,1978,第5页。
② 戴茂堂:《超越自然主义》,武汉大学出版社,1998,第2页。

内部的自由性是人性的隐性结构，构成了人的精神与灵魂的生活。人之为人，不仅需要对它保持敬畏与崇敬，而且需要用我们全部的心思与意念去爱它、渴慕它，当我们的情感以超越主客二分的绝对自由为对象时，我们的情感就是以生命自身为对象，因为它就是生命自身。在它的面前，主客二分成了一个伪命题，因为欲求它，就是欲求生命本身和自由本身，在这里，宇宙万物作为生命而合一，你、我、他作为生命而同一，现实中的你我之间不再有对立与纷争，生活中的我自身也不再有身与心的矛盾与冲突。具有这种视野的人，虽活在生活世界中，但情感却总可以从这里寻找永恒的慰藉与动力。正是在此点上，"我们"作为人，可以真正做到与万物息息相通，因为这里是生命开始的本源。在这里，我们与万物一样，都共同起源于那原初的、本源的一切，这一切是绝对可靠的真，是完全可以信赖的善，也是值得人带着崇敬之心去仰望的大美。

其次，在外部特征上，超越功利的情感是具有审美气质的情感。审美是一种非常特殊的形象思维，具有最明晰的直接性，可以在当下以最直接的方式带我们进入永恒的精神世界。对审美的欲求，就是对"绝对自由"的热爱，也是对隐藏在人性深处的神圣精神的热爱，它看起来无形无象，却不仅是善的，而且也是真的，因为"超主客关系的审美意识貌似脱离实际，而从深层来看，它不仅能决定道德意识的水平，而且能促进科学、技术的发展，使科学、技术的发展有着明确的目标和动力"。[①] 在审美这种直接思维的带领下，当情感以精神自由为对象的时候，这种情感将直接超越主客对立而使自己成为自己的对象，从而演变为一种大美。生命本身就是爱，爱是生命的本质，然而，生命之爱的对象绝非自然事物，而是超越一切自然物的生命本身，它能展现存在本身，并具有绝对自由性。以生命为目标的情感是自由的，它在超越自然主义的过程中真正回到了永恒的家园，并淋漓尽致地展现生命深处最高和最大的美。在这里，美是爱的外衣，装点着爱的尊贵。在爱的天堂里，生命将超脱一切琐碎的兴趣，转而关注内在的永恒价值。这是一种神圣的

---

① 张世英：《哲学导论》，北京大学出版社，2008，第229页。

爱，它使每个人都成为快乐的天使，因为来自宇宙深处的大爱让每个个体的生命都极具穿透力，把我们自身的灵魂与他人的灵魂统一起来，把我们与万物的灵性统一起来。就此而言，如果说人类生存的最高任务就是要达到天地万物之相通相融，那么达到这个目标的最佳途径就是依靠具有审美气质的自由情感。要获得这种情感，就必须超越自然主义视域，必须超越科学主义以及由此而产生的功利主义，因为"自然的"科学事物彼此之间总是存在边界，存在边界就可以进行定量研究，而这会直接把人类一切活动推向功利主义的结局。因此，自然主义领域中的人类情感，总是摆脱不了超越性与功利性的矛盾，面对这种矛盾，要么如同近代英国情感主义哲学，为了功利（物质）而抛弃自由（精神），要么如同古代柏拉图哲学，为了超越（精神）而抛弃情感（物质），从而走向理性主义。然而，只有立足人本身，在科学世界和自然主义的尽头，我们才能很好地处理情感中的超越与功利的矛盾。在自然主义的末路，自由情感为我们展开了一个全新的视域，使我们在超越自己的同时真正成为自己。我们依靠自己内在的自由性而真正成为自己，这种内在自由性，是我们的灵魂找到的"返乡"的线索以及"回家"的方向，我们从这里能在无尽的感动中感知神的恩典。在这种审美情感的指引下，我们发现，作为人，"我们"既是有别于万物的一个特殊的被造物，也是与万物息息相通的被造物，因为在生命开始的本源，我们与万物一样，都共同起源于那原初性的、本源性的一切。

  同时，我们发现，唯有依靠这种自由情感，我们才能从情感上在人类社会真正消除经济不平等。这种"消除"，不是从客观上消除经济不平等，而是还原经济活动的情感本质，从而从情感上消除客观存在的经济不平等。当人与人之间面对经济不平等时，却在情感上保持一种平等的态度，这不是乌托邦式的自欺，而是体现了人之为人的内在尊严与价值。自然科学视域中的世界是物质的世界，物质的世界必然体现大小多寡和地位高低的差异，这是物质必然具有的特征。在自然科学的视域中，生活在物质的世界是人的宿命，财产权的转换，从本质而言是情感的转换，这种可转换的情感直接体现了人的物性。然而，人之为人，除了物质，除了与物质紧密相连的身体，还存在超越物质的精神，引导人走向这个精神世界的最好导师就是人的自由情感。唯有欲求与万物本源紧密相连的自由情感，人类情感才能在自由的世界中超越一切物质，超越一切与物质有关的财产权的转换，从而在主客不分中回归自我，回归永恒的精神家园。这种自我，不是科学视域下的主客二分式的自我，而是审美情感中的主客合一与万物一体。在这种情感的面前，即使现实中仍然存在经济不平等，我们也可以在情感上消除这种不平等，从而与众人保持平等，与万物保持平等，并在这种平等中培养对宇宙万物的敬畏之心和谦卑之情。如果说追求经济的发展，其终极目标是为了追求人的发展，那么，培养这种自由性的审美情感，或许是每个社会发展所欲求的终极目的。

论语言意识形态与语言秩序

——以美国孔子学院风波为例

郭熙煌[*]

摘　要：语言是文化传播的媒介，是了解一个民族文化的窗口，也是衡量一个国家软实力程度的重要指标。本文以美国孔子学院的风波为例，试图阐明语言和意识形态的内在关联，以及汉语推广与国际语言秩序之间的关系。

关键词：语言　意识形态　国际语言秩序

Language Ideology & Order: A Case Study of the Confucius Institute Incident in U. S.

Guo Xihuang

Abstract: Language is the media of culture communication, the window of ethnic culture, and the important index for the soft power of one country. Taking the Confucius institute incident as example, the paper intends to illustrate the inner connection between language and indology and the relationship between Chinese promotion and international language order.

Key words: language; ideology; international language order

---

* 郭熙煌，湖北大学高等人文研究院世界文化发展研究中心副主任，外国语学院副院长、教授。

据路透社报道，2014 年 9 月 25 日，美国芝加哥大学宣布停止与孔子学院合作之后，宾夕法尼亚州立大学于 10 月 1 日宣布，将于 2014 年年底终止与中国孔子学院已达 5 年的合作，不再续约，这是一个星期以来第二所与中国孔子学院停止合作的美国大学[①]。孔子学院（Confucius Institute）是中国国家对外汉语教学领导小组办公室（国家汉办）在世界各地设立的推广汉语和传播中国文化与国学的教育和文化交流机构。这几年，随着中国国力和文化软实力的提升，越来越多的孔子学院落户美国，在推动汉语学习和增进民间交流的同时，也引起了一些争议。部分美国学者认为孔子学院的政府背景和孔子的思想理念与美国主流价值观存在严重冲突，因此他们担心汉语文化推广是一种意识形态渗透，与美国核心价值体系不甚相符。美国孔子学院风波说明，语言与意识形态有着内在的关联。因此，在全球化时代的当下，如何构建和谐共生的国际语言秩序是我们必须仔细思考的问题。

1. 语言意识形态的内涵

语言在形式上是一组有序语符集合，但在功能上是表达、传递思维信息的载体，是思想交流的媒介。因此，它必然会对社会、政治、文化乃至科技产生影响，具有强烈的意识形态色彩。现代语言学之父索绪尔（Saussure）认为，语言是一种约定俗成的事情，既是一种社会制度又是一种表达观念的符号系统[②]。语言是传承一个民族的文化基因，其厚重的文化内涵和社会文化特征都蕴藏在其中，语言与文化有千丝万缕的联系。1400 多年前，查理曼大帝（Charlemagne）曾说：掌握一门外语如同拥有了另一个灵魂[③]。同样，美国人类语言学家 Sapir 说：语言的背后是

[①] http://news.ifeng.com/a/20141004/42138985_0.shtml.
[②] Saussure, F. *Course in General Linguistics*, Beijing Foreign Language Teaching & Research Press, 2001, pp. 11–12.
[③] Boroditsky, L. "Lost in Translation", *The Wall Street Journal*, July 24, 2010.

有东西的,而且语言不能离开文化而存在①。所有这些观点都意味着语言与文化的不可分离性,它们在相互影响中共同发展、共同完善。语言对文化的影响首先体现在语言是文化的载体。语言不仅蕴含着文化的内涵和特质,同时,它还是民族文化认同的基础。任何语言都具有双重特征,它既是交流的工具,又是文化的载体。文化因素渗透到语言之中,是语言形成和发展的基础,这种民族的文化基因在语言中得到充分体现。

意识形态(ideology)不是一个新兴概念,有着久远的存在。词源上它由希腊语 idea 和 logos 两个词素组成,意为"逻各斯学说"或"观念学说"。它或许可以追溯至古希腊哲学家柏拉图提出的"理念世界"(ideal world)和"洞穴比喻"(the allegory of the cave),这是柏拉图对意识形态问题的最初的猜测和思考②。18 世纪法国启蒙运动哲学家托拉西(Tracy)在创制出这一概念之前,人们已经生活在意识形态之中。今天意识形态通常是指思想、信念、观念、价值观等组成的系统,服务于某一社会集团,是一个社会集团所共享的信仰,其核心内容是价值观。

语言意识形态(language ideology 或 linguistic ideology)是人类学、社会语言学和跨文化研究领域的一个概念,用以表述语言使用者对其语言在现实世界中的信念、情感和态度③。作为文化、信念的载体,语言与映照客观世界的符号系统并非对应关系,它多半是意识形态的真实写照。Fairclough 指出,社会制度是由制度中与不同的社团相关联的各种意识形态话语结构(ideological discursive formation)构成的,一个语言社团(speech community)通常有一种意识形态话语结构起主导作用。每个意识形态话语结构相当于一个语言社团,而每个语言社团又有其独特的话语规范。这种话语规范隐含在意识形态之中,是意识形态的表征符号④。

因此,与意识形态一样,语言意识形态是关于语言的一系列信念、思想和价值观,是语言系统背后所隐含的身份认同。可以说,有语言的

---

① Sapir, E. *Language: An Introduction to the Study of Speech*. New York: Harcourt & Brace, 1921.
② 俞吾金:《意识形态论》,人民出版社,2009。
③ Kroskrity, P. *Language Ideologies*, Malden, Ma: Blackwell, 2004, pp. 496 – 517.
④ Fairclough, N. *Discourse and Social Change*, Cambridge: Polity Press, 1993.

地方就存在意识形态。当前，学界对语言意识形态有不同的解释，但大体如下。

（1）从性质上看，语言意识形态有三个层级。第一，语言意识形态可能是官方性质，也可能是民间性质。官方语言意识形态主要通过法律法规或某种机制来实现，如机关、学校、公共场所等地方的语言用语，而民间语言意识形态则可通过社会风俗习惯、价值取向等方式来呈现。第二，语言意识形态可能是有利于弱势语言的，也可能是危害弱势语言的，如话语、权利与身份认同的关系。第三，语言意识形态还可能是制度化的，如意识形态话语结构和权利权威结构。

（2）从内容上看，语言意识形态主要表现为语言的话语力量、语言与社会身份、语言与民族国家、语言社会达尔文主义[①]。语言的话语力量（power of discourse）是一种最基本，也是最重要的语言意识形态，通过词汇、句法等语言要素体现出来，如 Occupy Central/Anti-Occupy Central（占中/反占中）。因为语言只是篇章的形式，而意识形态是篇章的内容，因此语言形式通过意识形态得到解释。

其实语言与一个人的社会身份（social identity）密不可分，与意识形态关系非常紧密。如同服装是人的形体修饰，语言是个人素质的外在体现。一个人的话语风格并非固定不变，而是随着环境和对象的变化而变化。一个人的话语既有趋同倾向，又有趋异倾向。通过言语可以判断一个人的社会地位、教育程度、能力、智慧，甚至财富等。语言是一种工具，更是一种素质。在很多语言里，某些词汇、句法结构或者某些发音，常常与一个人的身份地位相关。比如，美国黑人英语（Ebonics）在句法上省略系动词 be，这种独特的不规范用法在美国社会中通常与黑人联系在一起。或通过某个词的发音（如 floor）是否带 r 音就能判断其身份地位[②]。这种将一个人的语言特点和风格用于身份识别的做法就是意识形

[①] Rumsey, A. Wording, Meaning, and Linguistic Ideology, *American Anthropologist*, 92（1990）: 346 - 361.
[②] Labov, W. *The Social Stratification of English in New York City*, Cambridge University Press, 2006.

态的表现。

语言与民族国家问题（ethnicity）历来是语言人类学界的重点，因为语言问题可能对一个国家，特别是多民族多语种国家产生重大影响，稍有不慎便会引发严重的社会冲突，对社会、国家、族群产生不利影响，如加拿大的法语区与英语区、比利时的荷语区与法语区、乌克兰的东部俄语区与中西部乌克兰语区。目前，全世界绝大多数国家是多民族、多语言国家。多民族国家在语言与民族问题的处理上比单一民族国家所遇到的挑战要大很多。一般而言，多数国家会采取行政立法手段确定某一种或几种语言在某一区域享有特殊地位，以维护民族认同。因此，官方语言的甄选与推广对该国民族关系所产生的影响特别重要。

与语言民族问题相反，语言达尔文主义（linguistic Darwinism）认为，人类社会中的"物竞天择，适者生存"是一种很自然的现象。一种语言的存活或消亡是语言本身的问题，与外界无关。一种语言如果生命力强自然会存在下去，否则就会消亡。这种社会达尔文主义观点十分荒诞，语言的消失有多种因素，如使用者人数、语言民族主义政策、拒绝吸纳外来语、语言扩张、缺乏代际传递，等等。

（3）从形式上看，语言意识形态大体可分为单语主义（unilingualism 或 monolingualism）和多语主义（multilingualism）。单语主义是指官方只推行一种语言的政策及现象，如美国、日本、法国、德国等国家通常被视为单语体系国家。多语主义是指社会群体或个人使用两种或两种以上语言的现象。多语主义源于对社会、文化、语言多元性包容的理念，是多元社会公平正义的可行之路。世界90%以上的人处于双语或多语社会中。

语言意识形态能对社会现实发挥巨大影响力。作为思想政治意识的参照系统，语言意识形态不但影响个人和社会的语言价值观，而且还左右个人语言的取舍和社会语言秩序的走向。语言秩序是社会现实，是现实中语言与语言之间的等级关系。在任何一个非单语的社区、地区、国家乃至国际社会都存在一定的语言秩序①。

2. 汉语推广与国际语言秩序

在经济全球化背景下，语言文化全球化或许将成为一个不可逆转的趋势。经济全球化突破了国家之间的经济藩篱，形成彼此依存、互为补充的交融局面，这一特征势必体现在语言文化全球化的进程中。当两种或多种语言同时存在于一个地区、国家或国际大家庭时，语言使用者会通过语言文化传播为自己的母语争夺主导权，推广自己的语言价值观、文化观。当今，语言文化软实力的作用越来越受重视。很多国家为了增强文化软实力，扩大自己语言的国际影响力，都在稳步实施各自的语言文化输出战略。中国语言文化走向世界的重点并非大规模输入文化产品，而是让中国的语言文化和价值观深入人心。语言推广只是载体，文化推广才是关键。

中国作为一个崛起的负责任的新兴大国需要尝试改变现行以英语为通用语（lingua franca）的国际语言秩序，让汉语上升为国际通用语之一。经济全球化为汉语提供了一个机会，使汉语有望走向国际化。中国政府充分利用这一契机，制定了汉语海外推广战略。目前由中国政府主导的孔子学院已成为体现中国软实力的窗口。

孔子学院是由国家汉办与国外机构合作在海外设立的非营利性教育机构，致力于适应世界各国人民对汉语学习的需要，增进世界各国人民对中国语言文化的了解，加强中国与世界各国教育、文化的交流与合作，发展中国与外国的友好关系，促进世界多元文化发展，构建和谐世界。

孔子学院成立10年来，得到了中国政府、教育机构以及企业的全力支持，在发展规模及影响力上大有赶超其他世界主要语言文化推广机构的势头。截至2014年9月，孔子学院已在全球建立465所孔子学院和

---

① 周明朗：《语言意识形态与语言秩序：全球化与美中两国的多语战略》，《暨南学报》2009年第1期。

713个孔子课堂，分布在108个国家或地区。孔子学院充分利用自身优势，开展丰富多彩的教学和文化活动，成为各国学习汉语语言文化、弘扬中华传统文化、了解当代中国的重要场所，也是中国文化走向世界的重要平台，受到当地社会各界的热烈欢迎。相比于世界其他主要语言文化传播机构，如法语联盟、歌德学院等，孔子学院创办起步最晚，但却在短短十年之间急速发展。其全球分支机构数目已跃居第一位，规模已超过拥有百年发展历史的法语联盟及但丁协会，成为中国对外文化传播的一张名片（见表1）。

表1 世界主要语言文化传播机构情况

机 构	创立年	分支机构数目
法语联盟	1883年	137个国家（地区）811个
但丁协会	1889年	60个国家（地区）550个
英国文化协会	1934年	110个国家（地区）229个
歌德学院	1951年	94个国家（地区）160个
塞万提斯学院	1991年	43个国家（地区）86个
孔子学院	2004年	123个国家（地区）1178个

一个合理的多语秩序能有效促进语言文化的和谐发展。与一个国家的语言秩序一样，国际社会也存在一个语言秩序问题，当前世界的语言秩序也有不同的等级和地位。在多语国家中，语言可分为通用语（如普通话）、区域语（如藏语）和地方语（如地区方言）。全球范围内，语言也可分为通用语（如英语）、区域语（如汉语）和国别语。今天的国际语言秩序以英语为通用语，其他大国语言为区域语，小国语言为国别语。从现行语言秩序看，虽然汉语是使用人数最多的语言，但是国际语言地位通常并非由使用人数的多寡来确定，而是由使用者的实力和影响力决定的。语言推广是实现汉语国际化的重要举措，在国际化征途中汉语还有很长的路要走。

语言意识形态和语言秩序决定语言市场上语言的价值。随着中国经济成为世界第二大经济体，全球化给中国提供了一个很好的机会，汉语有望在国际语言秩序中升级。国际语言秩序往往是大国综合国力竞争的平台，是政治、经济、军事领域博弈的场所。语言推广应处理好输出语言与其他国家语言之间的冲突与融合问题，使推广策略更趋合理。在语言对外推广和传播过程中，政治、经济、民族、国家关系等因素应纳入语言推广策略的研究范围。合理的语言推广策略是汉语国际化进程的有力保障。

总之，全球化对汉语推广是机遇与挑战并存，既可能改变国家和个人的语言意识形态，也可能改变世界的语言秩序。在全球化中，以美国为代表的英语国家力图维护并保持其现行国际语言秩序，而中国则试图通过语言推广提高汉语的国际地位。在文化全球化过程中，两种不同文明在接触中有可能产生误读引发摩擦与碰撞。这种冲突与对立既有两种文明间的物质性差异，也有双方的解读和认知差异。但文化冲突最终会走向文化认同，东学西渐会再一次对世界文化格局产生深远影响。

3. 文化传播的冲突归因

十年来，随着越来越多的孔子学院在世界各地建立，孔子学院在推动汉语学习和增进民间交流的同时，在对外文化传播的过程中也遭遇了挑战，引起了一些争议。中国经济的崛起使得文化输出较为急切，孔子学院首当其冲，成为"中国威胁论"新时代的实体代表。尤其是在孔子学院经过规模扩张阶段进入稳定发展的时期，在快速壮大的过程中积累的大量问题在现阶段爆发而引发争议甚至抵制，其中争议最大的就是汉办的政府背景和孔子学说与西方国家价值观之间的冲突。西方学者所担心的是，孔子学院的政府背景和孔子学说的君臣父子伦理与美国价值观之间存在严重冲突。

2013年2月，加拿大麦克马斯特大学（McMaster University）宣布于7月关闭本校的孔子学院。2014年5月，芝加哥大学百余名教授联合签署请愿书，呼吁芝加哥大学停止与孔子学院的合约。2014年7月，欧洲汉学学会第20届年会在葡萄牙召开，国家汉办总干事许琳要求撕去大会手册上有关蒋经国基金会的介绍，引发与会国际学者的不满。2014年10月，宾夕法尼亚州立大学（The Pennsylvania State University）宣布将于年底终止与中国孔子学院已达5年的合作。

孔子学院受到争议集中在2012年至2014年间，这正是孔子学院平稳快速发展的三年。对引发上述争议的原因进行理性分析，有助于厘清孔子学院发展中的问题。总的来说，争议与抵制主要集中在孔子学院分布最为集中的美国、加拿大及欧洲。这些国家或地区的本土教育机构质疑孔子学院通过语言推广输出意识形态与价值观、干预并试图操控本土大学教师招聘、干涉本土大学学术自由，等等。其中，最重要的还是意识形态问题。

孔子学院仅仅是一个以开展汉语教学为主要活动内容的中国语言文化推广机构、一个学汉语教汉语的地方。它比英国文化协会、法语联盟、德国歌德学院等其他国际语言文化传播机构更富有弹性、更独特，况且是教育机构合作，不是政府间合作。为什么其他机构没有受到过多的质疑和责难呢？这主要是因为有意识形态的因素，孔子学院有中国官方意识形态色彩和背景。对美国孔子学院的质疑来自美国保守主义杂志《国家》。该杂志2013年11月发表了芝加哥大学退休教授萨林斯（Sahlins）的长文，该文认为孔子学院审查课堂上的政治讨论，限制学生自由交流思想，因此建议美国大学取消孔子学院，美国大学教授协会在2014年6月的声明中再次提及这篇文章。

与萨林斯意见相反的是常春藤学府威廉与玛丽学院的汉森（Hanson）教授，他认为美国大学教授协会的声明可能来源于错误认知。美国大学教授协会认为汉办是国家机构，可能带来政治干涉，这是一种想当然。乔治·华盛顿大学的中国历史学家麦考德（McCord）在《外交家》杂志上发文反驳称"孔子学院威胁不了自由学术"。

由于政治上的疑虑，部分孔子学院在美国的一些大学里常常被边缘化，沦为夜校部或成教部那样的机构，只能开展业余汉语文化教育，不能成为高等教育的有机部分。孔子学院在美国的另一个争议是它的运作方式：一方面是不计成本的巨额经费投入，另一方面是对美国学生的免费。根据汉办的官方数据，每所孔子学院建设费用为50万美元，每个孔子课堂6万美元。虽然投资中美双方各占一半，但美方主要以硬件投入的形式投资，如办公和教学场地、家具和办公设备等。孔子学院对美国学生不仅免费，还提供奖学金，组织他们到中国学习培训、举办演出等。因此，中国政府承担着无限度的经济负担，不能不让人质疑这背后的动机。

此外，2010年，被誉为"史上最贵网站"的网络孔子学院进入公众视野，国家汉办中标金额高达数千万元的网站运营费用让人们咋舌，而中标公司法人代表的另一个身份又是国家汉办的主要负责人员，这不禁让人浮想联翩。

要化解孔子学院汉语推广遭遇的困境，消除隔阂和曲解，让世界知悉中国文化的内涵，必须提升公共外交理念，淡化政府背景，加大商业运作。孔子学院应适应当地的文化、法律，完善管理体系，科学评估发展环境，采取有效的合作模式，鼓励不同类型的商业机构、学术机构、民间社团等积极参与推广与交流。

总而言之，中国制定语言推广战略需要借鉴其他国家文化传播机构的推广经验，与国际接轨，按国际惯例行事，减少官方色彩，让汉语语言文化真正融入国际社会，实现国家语言战略，让汉语成为国际超级语言之一。

结　语

语言是文化传播的媒介，是了解一个民族文化的窗口，也是衡量一个国家软实力的重要指标，它传播的是民族文化传统和价值观念。如萨丕尔-沃尔夫假说（Sapir-Whorf hypothesis）所述，人类凭借语言符号将自然加以剪裁，任何人都做不到绝对客观自由地描写自然。人类通过语言所构造的心理范畴来观察和理解世界，语言的不同导致文化的不同。对语言惯常的、规则化的使用形成了该文化的思维定式，语言塑造了思维。既然语言塑造了思维，语言就必定是意识形态的体现。

我们相信,语言推广最终将由文化冲突走向文化融合与认同。正如习近平总书记 2014 年 9 月底在孔子学院建立十周年之际所说,孔子学院属于中国,也属于世界。中国政府和人民将一如既往地支持孔子学院发展。让我们一起努力,推动人类文明进步,推动人民心与心的交流,共同创造人类更加美好的明天。

强"魂"健"体":建设当代中国主流文化的关键

陈 俊 柳丹飞**

摘 要:当代中国的主流文化是中国特色社会主义文化,它是"魂"与"体"的有机统一。社会主义核心价值体系是其"魂",国民教育体系、公共文化服务体系、文化产业体系以及各种形式的文化产品和服务则是其"体"。处理好当代中国主流文化的"魂"与"体"的辩证关系,即强"魂"健"体",是建设当代中国主流文化的关键。

关键词:文化之"魂" 文化之"体" 主流文化

Strengthening the "Soul" and Improving the "Body": Key to Build up Contemporary Chinese Mainstream Culture

Chen Jun; Liu Danfei

Abstract: Contemporary Chinese mainstream culture is Socialist Culture

---

* 本文系国家社科基金重大项目"构建我国主流价值文化研究"(11&ZD021)成果之一。
** 陈俊(1976~),男,湖北孝感人,湖北大学高等人文研究院副院长、湖北大学哲学学院副教授、中央编译局战略部博士后,主要从事政治哲学、应用伦理学研究;柳丹飞(1992~),女,湖北荆州人,武汉大学哲学学院研究生,主要从事马克思主义哲学研究。

with Chinese Characteristics, which is an organic combination of "soul" and "body". The system of socialist core values is the "soul" of contemporary Chinese culture, while national educational system, public cultural service system, cultural industry system and all forms of cultural products and services are the "body". Properly dealing with the dialectic relationship between the "soul" and the "body" of Contemporary Chinese mainstream culture, that is, strengthening the "soul" and improving the "body" is the key to build up Chinese mainstream culture.

Key words: soul of culture, body of culture, mainstream culture

任何文化都是"魂"与"体"的统一,中国特色社会主义文化作为当代中国的先进文化,要确证其主流地位,必须处理好"魂"与"体"的关系。强"魂"健"体"就成了构建当代中国主流文化的关键。

一 文化应是"魂"和"体"的统一

什么是文化?人们历来有着不同的理解。从概念的外延来讲,在日常生活中,人们往往把"受过教育,掌握一定的知识"叫作"有文化"。这种理解上的"文化"是相对于"自然、本能"而言的,通常可以与"文明"一词相通。这应该是最狭义的文化概念了。从学术上来界定"文化",最通常的说法是"文化"是人类在改造生活于其中的世界(包括自然环境和人类社会自身)的过程中所创造的物质和精神成果的总和,包括器物文化、行为文化、制度文化、精神文化等从低到高的四个层次。这个意义上的"文化"成了一个几乎无所不包的广义概念。我们现实中所强调的"文化",则是特指"精神层面(或观念形态)的文化",通常表现为一定的价值观念、思维方式、意识形态以及生活态度,它们通过一定的理论知识、宗教信仰、文学艺术、道德法律、风俗习惯以及社会制度等表现出来。这种意义上的"文化"是介于狭义和广义之间的"中义"文化,实即"精神文化"。

从概念的内涵来理解"文化",则具有更大的模糊性。据统计,世界上给文化所下的定义有二百多种。但这些定义多是从不同学科和不同层次上来理解,都没有从根本上触及文化的本质。汉语中"文化"一词意为"人文化成"。"文"原指"纹理",引申为事物的"道理",即结构、秩序等;"化"则是"使……变成……"。所以汉语中的"文化"(人文化成)字面上的理解为:用事物的道理来改造对象,使"无序"变得"有序";进而引申为:用人的标准和尺度去改变对象的行为过程及其结果。在英语等外文中,"文化"(Culture)一词的原始含义是"耕作",后来引申为人工的、技艺的活动及其成果。英国著名的文化研究学者泰勒在《原始文化》一书中将"文化"界定为"包括全部的知识、信仰、艺术、道德、法律、风俗以及作为社会成员的人所掌握和接受的任何其他的才能和习惯的复合体"。[1] 德国的李凯尔特说得更明白:"文化"是一个区别于"自然"的概念,"自然产物是自然而然地由土地里生长出来的东西,文化产物是人们播种之后从土地里生长出来的"[2]。总之,尽管有许多不同说法,却可以看出其中共同的基本意思:文化就是按照"人"的方式和标准去改变环境和人自己的。或者说,文化就是"人化"和"化人"。"人化"是按人的方式改变、改造世界,使任何事物都带上人文的性质;"化人"则是用这些改造世界的成果来培养人、教育人、提高人,使人得到全面的发展。

从以上对"文化"本质的理解,我们可以看出,"文化"并不是一个静态的、已然存在的东西,"文化"更强调的是"化人",是一个动态的过程。人类在认识和改造世界的过程中形成一定的"文"(道理),然后用这些"文"(道理)去"化"人,而"化"人则需要将"文"通过一定的载体进行传播,被人们所认识并接受,进而得到人们的认同,这样,"文化"

---

[1] 〔英〕爱德华·泰勒:《原始文化:神话、哲学、宗教、语言、艺术和习俗发展之研究》,连树声译,广西师范大学出版社,2005。
[2] 〔德〕H. 李凯尔特:《文化科学和社会科学》,涂纪亮译,商务印书馆,1991。

的意义才能得以实现。"文化"说到底是"文"和"化"的统一。

我们也可以进一步这样来理解,任何"文化"都是"魂"(文)和"体"(化)的统一。要理解"文化"的意义和功能,我们不仅要识其无形的"魂",而且也要见其有形的"体"。任何形式的"有魂无体"和"魂不附体"都将无法实现"文化"育人、化人的功能,也无法实现文化的繁荣和发展。一种文化的"魂"就是其自身所蕴含的核心价值观,它处于文化体系最深层的内核位置,向外展现为一定的制度和规范体系,并经过长期反复的实践,最终落实为一定的风俗习惯。文化的"魂"决定着该文化的性质与方向,而文化的"体"则是指承载其核心价值的物质基础和传播手段的有机统一,它是文化实现其育人、化人功能的基本途径,并由此决定着该文化的影响力。文化的"魂"和"体"是相互依存、相辅相成的。离开了"魂","体"会变成失去内容的形式,没有思想性和生命力,变得空洞无物;而离开了"体","魂"会变成僵死的思想,无所依附,难以传播,文化的精神价值也会难以实现。

任何被大众所接受的文化都是有"魂"有"体"的文化,在这里,"魂"与"体"至少达到了一种基本意义上的统一,然而这并不意味着所有统一都是有效的。一种有效的统一应该达到这样一种状态,即文化的精神价值通过其物质载体有效传播开来,并为人们所接受甚至认同。这种统一我们可以将其称为一种有机的统一。在这里,"魂"与"体"有机统一于文化传播和文化认同的过程中,进而统一于文化建设的实践中,二者各自发挥其功能,并相得益彰。当代中国主流文化是中国特色社会主义文化,其文化之"魂"的核心概括就是"倡导富强、民主、文明、和谐,倡导自由、平等、公正、法治,倡导爱国、敬业、诚信、友善"。由以上价值观念所构成的社会主义核心价值观是在坚持马克思主义基本内核,继承中国优秀文化传统的基因以及吸收世界其他民族优秀文化成果的基础上提炼和建构起来的,是社会主义的先进文化。相比于中国社会存在的其他文化,在人们的接受、认同状况上,中国特色社会主义文化无疑有其独特的优越性。

但在社会主义主流文化建设实践中,往往存在两种偏向。一种是重视"魂"的提炼却忽视"体"的建设，造成"头重脚轻"。在这种情况下，"酒香出不了巷子"。再先进的文化如果不通过很好的形式进入人们的心中，都无法体现其先进性，最终难免会被历史所淘汰；另一种偏向则是注重文化的"体"，急于找到能够看得见、摸得着、抓得住的东西，却不知道它的"魂"是什么，造成"体大无脑"。在这种情况下，往往越"重视"文化建设，就越容易导致文化浮躁、形式主义和急功近利。浮躁本身是一种"魂不守舍"的文化——往往越想在文化上做出成绩，就越显得"没有文化"。这是因为，体和魂并不是固定不变的，二者之间更不是自然的一一对应的关系。在现实中，一"体"多"魂"、一"魂"多"体"的现象很常见。因此，正确理解和把握中国特色社会主义文化"魂"与"体"的基本内涵，厘清它们的精神价值与物质形态的辩证关系，并努力实现二者有机的统一，无疑是发展中国特色社会主义文化，推动社会主义文化大发展大繁荣的时代性课题。

二　强"魂"是构建中国主流价值文化的根本

前面已经指出，任何文化都是所蕴含的精神价值与承载其精神价值的物质基础和传播形态的有机统一。文化的精神价值是文化的"魂"，是文化思想性的根本体现；承载文化精神价值的物质基础和传播形态是文化的"体"，是文化实现教育功能、以"文"化"人"的基本途径。问题在于，我们究竟要以什么样的"魂"附什么样的"体"？

社会主义核心价值体系是当代中国特色社会主义文化之"魂"。它主要由四个方面的内容构成，即马克思主义指导思想、中国特色社会主义共同理想、以爱国主义为核心的民族精神和以改革创新为核心的时代精神、社会主义荣辱观，具体体现为"倡导富强、民主、文明、和谐，倡导自由、平等、公正、法治，倡导爱国、敬业、诚信、友善"这个核心价值观。作为当代中国特色社会主义文化的"魂"，社会主义核心价值体系是当代中国先进价值理念的集中体现，它对当代中国社会的历史命运和发展前途起着具有决定意义的灵魂作用。

第一，社会主义核心价值体系决定着当代中国文化的思想内涵，是当代中国文化的质的规定性，是当代中国文化立足于世界并区别于其他文化的内在根据。文化的性质在某种意义上讲，将决定它的历史命运和发展前途。一种文化主流地位的确立以及它的繁荣发展取决于它的性质是否与它所依附的国家性质一致。我国是以马克思主义为指导思想的、人民群众当家做主的社会主义国家。所以，以社会主义核心价值体系作为其内核的当代中国特色社会主义文化要想确立其主流地位，就必须是以马克思主义为指导的文化，而不是以其他主义为指导的文化；是社会主义形态的文化，而不是包括资本主义文化形态在内的其他文化；是服务于最广大人民大众的文化，而不是属于极少数人的文化；是有利于实现中华民族复兴的文化，而不是有碍于推进民族复兴伟业、实现伟大的中国梦的文化。所以，当代中国特色社会主义文化的先进性、合理性和优越性，归根结底取决于社会主义核心价值体系所规定的文化性质。

第二，社会主义核心价值体系决定着当代中国特色社会主义文化的方向。一个国家和民族的文化朝着什么样的方向发展，既关系文化自身的兴衰，也影响整个国家和民族的未来。在当代中国，社会主义核心价值体系不仅从指导思想、共同理想的高度给当代中国特色社会主义文化标明了发展方向，而且从传承民族精神与弘扬时代精神、提倡真善美与抵制假恶丑的价值理念上为当代中国特色社会主义文化标示了前进的路标。在社会主义核心价值体系的引领下，当代中国特色社会主义文化始终坚持为人民服务、为社会主义服务的根本方向，始终坚持面向现代化、面向世界、面向未来的发展方向，始终坚持民族的、科学的、大众的前进方向。朝着这样的方向发展，当代中国特色社会主义文化必将确立自身在引领社会发展中的主流地位，也必将得到希望实现伟大的中国梦的最广大人民群众的认同和接受。

第三，社会主义核心价值体系决定着当代中国特色社会主义文化的目的。一种文化坚持实现什么样的目的，是该文化的性质在价值追求和价值目标上的集中反映。作为社会主义核心价值体系内核的社会主义核心价值观，其倡导的"富强、民主、文明、和谐"是任何一个理性的社会和国家都为之奋斗的目标。"富强"是国家独立自主和人民普遍幸福的物质基础。只有在物质上实现独立,才会有精神上的独立与自由。因此,国家富强不仅体现了国家与社会的根本利益,更体现了人民的根本利益;"民主"是现代社会基本的政治制度,是保障人民当家做主,实现国家安定团结、社会有序的政治保障,而一个安定团结、社会有序的政治环境反过来又有助于实现国家的富强和人民的幸福;"文明"不仅是一个民族能立足于世界之林的必有条件,而且也是一个国家强盛的象征,在一个"文明"缺失的社会,人民的行为将有失规范,精神将日益匮乏,社会也将陷入混乱,人民的幸福也无从谈起。"富强""民主""文明"这三者将共同推进一个"和谐"社会的建立,而只有建立一个和谐的社会,才能容纳各种利益诉求,化解各种社会矛盾,从而为国家富强、民族振兴、人民幸福提供基本的社会保障。

第四,社会主义核心价值体系决定着当代中国特色社会主义文化的功能。一个社会的先进文化应当起到引领社会风尚、教化人民群众、促进经济繁荣以及推动社会进步的功能。当代中国特色社会主义文化作为当代中国的先进文化,应当具备并有效发挥引领风尚、教育人民、服务社会、推动发展的功能。当代中国特色社会主义文化要真正具备和发挥先进文化的功能,关键在于社会主义核心价值体系的先进性。社会主义核心价值体系所倡导的一切有利于实事求是、与时俱进的时代精神,国家富强、人民幸福的价值追求,公平正义、诚信仁爱的道德理想,全面展现了当代中国特色社会主义文化的先进性。因此,离开了社会主义核心价值体系这个"魂",当代中国特色社会主义文化就无法在全社会形成统一的指导思想、共同的理想信念、强大的精神力量、基本的道德规范。

文化之强源于"魂"强,而文化之魂欲强,贵在得人心。一种文化的命运,取决于它对人的发展的意义,即它是否能够反映社会发展要求和人民的利益?是否能为人的生存发展提供最大的资源,包括精神资源和制度资源?如果能,它就是先进的、有强大生命力的文化;反之,它就是落后的甚至反动的文化,必然衰落。中国特色社会主义文化之所以具有强大的吸引力和生命力，就在于它本质上是反映并服务于最广大群众的根本利益的文化。因为社会主义的本质和共同理想就在于"解放生产力，发展生产力，消灭剥削，消除两极分化，最终达到共同富裕"。可以说，实现全体人民在物质和精神上"共同富裕"是社会主义核心价值体系最核心的价值，也是中国特色社会主义文化所特有的精神实质和历史承诺。中国主流文化建设的全部任务要围绕实现这个最核心的价值来展开。

三 健"体"是构建中国主流文化的关键

中国特色社会主义文化之"体"有多种形态，主要包括国民教育体系、公共文化服务体系、文化产业体系以及各种形式的文化产品和服务等。这些"体"作为先进文化之承载基础，担负着宣传、弘扬社会主义核心价值体系这个"魂"的重大使命。因此，要使文化之"魂"得到广泛传播并日益深入人心，必须发展、完善文化之"体"。可以说，客观形势越要求看重文化之"魂"，就越要将建设强大的文化之"体"摆在重要的位置。然而，我们必须看到，社会主义先进文化之"体"还远远不够强健，这不仅表现在国内文化之"体"相对于文化之"魂"的落后上，也表现在国外文化之"体"对我国价值观念的渗透和侵蚀上；不仅体现在承载文化精神价值的物质基础建设的滞后上，也表现在文化的传播形态跟不上时代的要求上。这必然导致人民群众对社会主义核心价值体系的接受和认同面临巨大的挑战。因此，健"体"以强"魂"无疑成为当代中国特色社会主义文化建设的当务之急。

首先，从当代中国特色社会主义文化之"体"还不能完全承担起有效传播文化之"魂"的现实情况来看，强化当代中国特色社会主义文化之"体"的建设是时代提出的紧迫任务。虽然经过30多年的改革开放，我国经济建设取得了巨大的成就，政治制度建设获得了长足进步，人民的生活水平得到极大提高，但我们应该清醒地认识到，文化之"体"离文化之"魂"对它的现实要求还很远。当前，我国国民教育体系还不够健全，公共文化服务体系还不够完善，文化产业体系还不够成熟，各种形式的文化产品还不够充裕，文化传播手段和形式还比较落后。特别是在中西部广大农村，公共文化服务体系和文化产业体系尚处在起步阶段，各种文化产品和服务还远远不能满足客观需求。这必然会使当代中国特色社会主义文化之"魂"的广泛传扬并得到接受和认可受到极大制约。因此，我们必须高度重视文化之"体"的建设。

其次，从当前中国特色社会主义文化所面临的国际文化环境来说，加强当代中国特色社会主义文化之"体"的建设也是我们必须面对的一个严峻问题。虽然全球化的日益发展表明，国与国之间的相互尊重和合作以实现共同的繁荣发展已经在国际社会形成共识，但西方发达国家却始终没有放弃冷战思维，始终没有彻底放弃颠覆社会主义国家的企图。当前，西方发达国家进一步强化了对社会主义国家的文化渗透，试图借助其强大的经济实力，利用各种手段和途径向社会主义国家推销他们的价值观念，最终达到颠覆社会主义国家的目的。如今我国虽已牢牢占据物质产品输出大国的地位，但同时却又无奈地扮演着文化产品输入大国的角色。在各种思想文化交流、交锋、交融日趋频繁的国际背景下，与文化产品逆差同时而来的，必然是西方意识形态的渗透、价值观念的侵入。另外，全球化的发展也意味着国与国之间的竞争日益激烈，包括中国在内的发展中国家必须在构建更加公平公正的国际经济政治秩序上取得更大的发言权，这也需要我们增强文化软实力，传播中国的价值观，争取更大的国际话语权。面对这种情势，我们只有结合国情着力强健文化之"体"，使它能够以强劲的态势传扬中国的价值观念，才能构筑起坚不可摧的精神高地，为中国的和平崛起创造更好的文化环境。

再次，从当前社会主义市场经济条件下人们价值取向多元的发展趋势来看，强化当代中国文化之"体"以确立中国特色社会主义文化的主流地位也是需要解决的一个紧迫问题。随着我国改革的深入和市场经济的发展，人们价值取向的多样化日趋明显。多样化的存在意味着选择性增强了。多元价值并存并不一定导致多元价值冲突，但由于不同价值之间客观存在的差异性和不可通约性，"异域价值"与"本土价值"之间的矛盾和内在张力便不可避免。中国正处于社会转型过程中主流价值文化建构的关键时期，各种价值相互竞争、相互争夺、相互激荡，更加剧了原本多元交织的价值冲突。这一共时性的价值冲突必然使人们陷入主流价值的认同困境。价值的多元反映的是不同利益的分化。这就决定了社会主义核心价值体系的传播和弘扬必须在关注人们利益问题的同时，更加注重文化之"体"的吸引力和感染力。所以，人们价值取向的选择性越强，社会上可供人们选择的蕴含不同价值理念的文化之"体"就越多，我们就越要把自己的文化之"体"打造得更加出色，从而使社会主义核心价值体系这个当代中国特色社会主义文化之"魂"更多地被人们所接受和认同。

就当前中国特色社会主义文化之"体"的建设而言，以下几个方面是特别需要我们下功夫予以解决的。一是要改变落后、僵化的思想教育和文化传播理念和方法。思想教育不应成为一种知识性的灌输。平等的对话和沟通才能使受教育者完成对主流价值文化的体认，进而"入脑""入心"，真正内化为受教育者的信念和价值观。要把思想教育当作一种人文情感教育，通过情感的交流激发人们积极的情感体验，从而唤起人们自我教育的主动性，最终引起人的共鸣。主流价值文化的传播在一定意义上是一个"传心""交心"的工作，我们要做得不仅让人信服，而且更要人心服，这就需要我们大力改进和创新现有的传播方式。

二是要充分认识到，社会的公平正义是该社会所倡导的主流价值文化得以认同的心理基础。一种价值观念的认同在某种意义上讲就是一种利益诉求的认同。社会价值多元反映的是社会利益诉求的多元。当前，中国主流价值文化认同度不高的一个主要原因就是其在传播的过程中没有积极回应社会不同利益之间的分裂，许多的文艺作品和文化服务没有理直气壮地倡导公平正义的社会理想。渴望公正公平是人们一种本能的情感诉求，保证社会大多数成员的公平感是一个社会和谐的基本前提，同时也是确保其认同这个社会的制度和主流价值文化的根本所在。为此我们必须全力促进社会在政治、经济、文化和社会等各方面的公平正义。

三是要突出文化产业的社会价值。文化产业是把"双刃剑"。文化发展的市场化能繁荣文化市场，为人民群众提供更多的文化产品和文化服务，但是，在文化产品生产和消费的市场化的同时可能会出现为了追逐最大的经济利益而牺牲文化的社会效益的情况。因此，我们既要坚持文化产业的市场化发展道路，又要在尊重市场规律的基础之上，通过政府、公众等多方力量的共同参与来实现引导文化产品的创作者、传播者、市场经营主体的目的，使其自觉、自信地创作、传播出这样的文化产品：既能满足人民群众多样的精神文化需求，又能体现当代中国的时代和民族精神；既能以社会效益和经济效益的实现促进社会主义的精神文明和物质文明建设，又能鼓舞人民群众自觉地参与建构富有广泛影响力的主流文化。

康德谈两性关系*

徐 瑾**

摘 要：康德认为，与男人应有的"崇高"相比，女人应有的特征是"优美"；与男人擅长理性思辨相比，女人擅长感性直观及艺术。"性"是人类繁衍的客观的自然本能，但需要理性去节制情欲，使之转化为德性。婚姻、爱情归于一种基于相互尊重的平淡愉悦才能更加持久。两性关系的处理应当走向德性，只有道德修养的提升才是最终目的。

关键词：康德 两性关系 道德

On Relationship Between Man and Woman by Kant

Xu Jin

Abstract: The characteristic of man is sublime and woman is concinnity whose favourite is art. The sex is natural instinct but need to be controlled by logos. The marriage and love will be in harmony if man and woman can respect each other. The end of relationship between man and woman is morality.

---

* 本文系2012年湖北省教育厅青年项目"和谐社会需要什么样的性道德"（编号2012Q082）、2012年湖北大学人文社会科学基金项目"康德宗教哲学及其当代价值考量"（编号013 - 098326）的课题成果。

** 徐瑾，男，湖北蕲春人，湖北大学哲学学院副教授，湖北大学高等人文研究院研究员。

Key words: Kant, relationship between man and woman, morality

作为一代大哲的康德，不仅对于理性的认识能力有着深刻的批判，而且对于人性也有着深入的理解，对于男女两性关系有着非常精辟的论述。对其这方面的主要观点做一梳理，有助于我们更加全面地理解康德思想。

一 康德谈女人

康德是从男女有别的角度来谈女人的特征的，他认为男人具有较为明显的理性和对崇高的追求，而女人则具有感性的直观和追求优美的愿望。总体而言，男人的特征在康德这里表述为"崇高"，女人的特征则表述为"优美"："一个女性的全部其他优点都将由此而联合起来，为的是有高扬优美的特性，而优美乃是一个理所当然的参照点；反之，在男性的品性中，则崇高就突出显著地成为他那个类别的标志。"[1]

男人因为"崇高"的特征而更多地将注意力放在"大事"上，女人则因为"优美"的追求而更多地注重"外表"之类的琐事。康德对于女人爱美的天性理解得十分透彻，在他看来，"女性对于一切美丽、明媚的和装饰的洞悉，都具有一种天生的强烈感情。早在孩童时期，她们就喜欢打扮，而且一装束起来就会高兴。对于一切引起人厌恶的东西，她们是纯洁的而且是非常柔情的……她们很早就对自己有着一种端庄得体的作风，懂得赋予自己以一种美好的风度并且自矜……她们有许多同情的感受、好心肠和怜悯心，她们把美置于实用之前，并且很愿意把维持生活的节余储蓄起来，以便支付在争奇竞艳方面的消费"[2]。在这里我们看到，女人"喜欢打扮""把美置于实用之前""争奇竞艳""柔美敏

---

[1] 〔德〕康德：《论优美感和崇高感》，何兆武译，商务印书馆，2009，第29页。
[2] 〔德〕康德：《论优美感和崇高感》，何兆武译，商务印书馆，2009，第29页。

感"等特征康德都分析得入木三分，而男人往往相反，他们更加注重"实用""刚强""统治力"等方面。

正是因为女人往往注重外表的修饰，所以康德虽然将女人的特征表述为"优美"，但是认为女人相对于男人来说缺乏"深沉的理性"。男人擅长缜密的思维和严密的逻辑推理，而女人虽然天性敏感、心思细密，但并不擅长这种基于逻辑的推理，而擅长的是基于感性的直观，也更容易陷入情感的漩涡而失去理智（理智被遮蔽）。由此，康德建议："女人就不要去学习几何学；关于充足理由律或单子论，女性也只需要懂得那么多，只要足以尝尝我们冥思苦想的、没有趣味的男性所要钻透的那些闹剧之中的一点点咸味也就足够了。"① 当然这里康德并不是否认也有少数女人长于思辨，也并非歧视女人，而是就"女人"这种普遍化的抽象特征来说，大多数女人在日常生活中确实是缺乏理性的。

虽然女人并不擅长抽象思辨和逻辑推理，但是康德并不认为女人就会因此陷入不学无术的境地，恰恰相反，一个具有"优美"品质的女人一定要有与之相匹配的内在修养。在康德看来，这种修养最适合的就是"艺术"，这方面女人是有着天然优势的："至于对绘画表现的和音乐的感受——不是就其表现了艺术而是就其表现了感受而言——它们都精炼了或提高了女性的情趣，并且总是和道德的激情有着一定的联系。这些从来都不是冷静的和思辨的教导，而永远都是感受，并且还始终是尽可能地接近于她那女性的地位的。"②

二 康德谈性

两性关系中不可避免地要面临对"性"的认识，康德对于"性"有着自己客观的分析。他认为男女之间的爱情以及婚姻、家庭得以实现的可能契机是建立在"性"的自然本能基础之上的："整个这些，确实是

---

① 〔德〕康德:《论优美感和崇高感》，何兆武译，商务印书馆，2009，第31页。
② 〔德〕康德:《论优美感和崇高感》，何兆武译，商务印书馆，2009，第32页。

在性的本能的基础之上展开的。"① 虽然人们不愿意过多地谈论"性"的问题，一些人赞美性、沉溺性，一些人鄙视性、远离性，但是康德对于"性"却持非常客观理性的态度。在他看来，性并不是一个天生就"肮脏下流"或是"欢愉追求"的东西，性并没有天生的"善"与"恶"的界定，它只是一种自然赋予人类的生存本能。从人类繁衍的角度来说，"性"的存在使得人类能够不断繁衍生息下去，而不至于导致种族的灭绝。因而从这个角度来说，"性"不能因此而受到鄙视，"因为绝大多数的人类，就是靠着它而以一种非常简单和缺陷的方式在遵循着大自然的伟大的秩序的"。② 而且对社会上大多数人来说，"绝大多数婚姻都是由它促成的，而且还确实都是人类物种中最勤勉的那部分人"。③ 所以从自然生存的角度来说，离开了性，男女之间的爱情、婚姻、家庭都会成为一种不能实现的空中楼阁，人类存在的自然基础就会消亡。

"性"不应当受到鄙视，那么是不是就值得赞美呢？显然也不是。因为在康德看来，人类除了自然本能之外，更有自由的追求，"在有生命的地球居民中，人与其他一切自然存在的区别可表明为：利用事物的技术性素质（与意识相联系的机械性的素质），实用性素质（巧妙地利用别人达到他的目的），和在他本质之中的道德性素质（按照法则之下的自由原则来对待自己和别人）"。④ 如果说自然本能无法让人与其他一切自然存在物区别开来的话，那么就只有关涉科学的技术与实用素质以及关涉人际的道德素质才能使人类超越于自然万物。对于"性"也是这样，虽然康德认为"性"本能是一种自然的"伟大目的"，可以带来身体的"欢悦"，但同时因为"性"本能的"巨大的普遍性的缘故，它却很轻易地退化为放荡和轻佻"。⑤ 所以，康德提醒我们要警惕这种纵欲无度的危险倾向，从而对于"性"这种自然本能应该保持一种"情趣的单纯性"。

---

① 〔德〕康德：《论优美感和崇高感》，何兆武译，商务印书馆，2009，第38页。
② 〔德〕康德：《论优美感和崇高感》，何兆武译，商务印书馆，2009，第38页。
③ 〔德〕康德：《论优美感和崇高感》，何兆武译，商务印书馆，2009，第38页。
④ 〔德〕康德：《实用人类学》，邓晓芒译，上海人民出版社，2005，第261页。
⑤ 〔德〕康德：《论优美感和崇高感》，何兆武译，商务印书馆，2009，第42页。

康德主张以理性去约束情欲,以自由意志去约束自然本能冲动,"情欲不光是像激情那样,是一种酝酿着许多坏事的不幸的心绪,它甚至还毫无例外地是一种恶的心绪。即使那以道德领域的事物(按其质料来看)为主旨的最良善的欲求,如追求乐善好施,只要它是偏向于情欲的,它就(按其形式来看)不仅在实用上导致毁灭,而且在道德上也是可鄙的"。①康德在表述自己对于理想婚姻的观点时也这样认为,依靠性本能而结成的夫妻关系显然是不能保证婚姻幸福的,只要是偏向于情欲的,就会干扰理性,就会导致道德水平的下降,而道德追求才是人类自由的本质体现。所以对于任何家庭来说,"最为重要的则在于,男人作为男人应该成为一个更完美的丈夫,而妇女则应该成为一个更完美的妻子;也就是说,性的禀赋的冲动要符合自然的启示在起作用,使得男性更加高尚化并使得女性的品质更加优美化"。②

三 康德谈爱情、婚姻

在康德看来,爱情、婚姻不能基于一种性本能的追求,而应当基于促进双方道德的提高,即增进男人对于"崇高"品质的追求、女人对于"优美"品质的追求的一种相互完善。相对于质料性的"自然本能"来说,形式性的"自由追求"显然是更值得提倡的,对于男女双方的不同特征而言,应当在爱情、婚姻中形成一种相互补充、相互勉励、相互进步的关系,从而促使双方成为"道德人"。比如说,"男人根据经验会有更多的洞见,而且女性在其感受中也会有更大的自由和正确性,因而便产生一种心灵状态,它越是崇高,也就越发要把最大的努力目标置于所爱的对象的称心如意之中;而在另一方面,则它越是优美,也就越发力图以盛情来报答这种努力"。③爱情本身就具有一方为另一方无私奉献甚

---

① 〔德〕康德:《实用人类学》,邓晓芒译,上海人民出版社,2005,第185页。
② 〔德〕康德:《论优美感和崇高感》,何兆武译,商务印书馆,2009,第46页。
③ 〔德〕康德:《论优美感和崇高感》,何兆武译,商务印书馆,2009,第47页。

至牺牲自己的强烈情感,这种强烈的情感应当转化为促进双方道德的提升,越相互热爱,就越应当希望对方更加崇高或更加优美;婚姻也是这样,男女双方都有义务相互学习,促使双方改正缺陷、提升品性,使得双方变得更有道德,这样才能使得爱情或婚姻趋向于一种完满的状态。

康德不是"男权主义"者,也不是"女权主义"者,他主张一种基于平等人格上的相互尊重,"在这个目的秩序中,人(与他一起每一个有理性的存在者)就是自在的目的本身,亦即他永远不能被某个人(甚至不能被上帝)单纯用作手段同时自身又是目的,所以在我们人格中的人性对我们来说本身必定是神圣的"。① 所以,当在爱情、婚姻之中遇到难以调和的对立关系的时候,男女双方应当处于彼此平等的地位上,不能一方强迫另一方接受自己的主观意志,而应当相互理解、平等协商以达到解决问题并促进双方道德水平提升的目的,否则,"女性以这种暴力的调子妄自尊大,乃是极其可憎的;而男人则是极其低级下流而可鄙的"。②

由于对于大多数人来说,爱情和婚姻是基于情欲的,情欲不可能持久(否则因长久失去理智就会心理异化),所以康德也承认爱情、婚姻的开端总是包含着美好和甜蜜,充满着强烈的吸引力和占有欲,但是"随后就由于共同生活和家务操劳而逐渐变得日益迟钝"。③ 日益迟钝的原因是并不浪漫的现实生活会促使人们回归理性,情欲消退的同时就是爱情、婚姻走向平淡甚至破裂的过程。但是,康德认为肉体的相互占有绝不是爱情、婚姻的动人之处,相反,真正值得赞美的爱情或婚姻是在回想爱情的动人之处时能够保持一种愉悦的平静的欣赏或欢愉,这样才能保持家庭温情的持久。爱情的伟大"在于仍然能够保持这些东西的充分的残余,从而无所谓的态度和厌倦都不会勾销欢愉的全部价值,从而正是由于这个缘故,才唯有它是值得人们去做出这样的一种结合的"。④

可以说,在康德这里,爱情、婚姻不像常人想象的那样庸俗,庸俗

---

① 〔德〕康德:《实践理性批判》,邓晓芒译,人民出版社,2003,第180页。
② 〔德〕康德:《论优美感和崇高感》,何兆武译,商务印书馆,2009,第47页。
③ 〔德〕康德:《论优美感和崇高感》,何兆武译,商务印书馆,2009,第47页。
④ 〔德〕康德:《论优美感和崇高感》,何兆武译,商务印书馆,2009,第47页。

到仅仅是一种肉体欲望的满足和对对方的独占，而应当是一种基于精神的结合。当热烈的情欲逐渐消退的时候，精神与道德的力量就应当逐步显现出来。无论是对于爱情、婚姻还是家庭的态度，康德都认为："不管是处于哪种方式，人们绝不可以对生活的幸福和人类的美满有任何过高的要求；因为一个永远只不过期待着一切平凡的事物的人们所具有的优点乃是，事情的结果很少会违反他的希望，反之有时候意想不到的美满倒还可以使他喜出望外。"① 当爱情、婚姻因为现实的毫无浪漫的残酷甚至苦难而使得人们丧失热情时，理性精神会调整双方，追求一种面对社会压力的淡然的、知足常乐的生活态度。在理性地面对压力、保持恬静的愉悦的心境下，生活可能会回报给我们更多，这也正是康德一直主张的，"如果德性法则、圣洁和德行的形象在任何地方都应当对我们的灵魂施加影响的话，那么这种德性之所以能够施加这种影响，只是在它不掺加对自己的福利的意图而纯粹作为动机得到细心关照的范围内，因为它在苦难中才最庄严地表现出来"。②

四　两性关系以道德为旨归

康德对于两性关系的探讨，最终指向的是对道德的强调，而德性的获得必然要求理性对情欲的控制，"德性首先要求对自己本身的控制。……德性只要基于内在的自由，对人来说就也包含着一项肯定的命令，亦即把人的一切能力和偏好都纳入自己的（理性的）控制之下，因而是对自己的统治的命令，这种统治添加在禁令之上，即不让自己受情感和偏好的统治（不动情的义务），因为，若不是理性执掌驾驭的缰绳，情感和偏好就会对人扮演主人"。③ 对于男女关系中最重要的"性本能"即是如此，爱情、婚姻固然不能完全离开"性"，但作为理

---

① 〔德〕康德：《论优美感和崇高感》，何兆武译，商务印书馆，2009，第43页。
② 〔德〕康德：《实践理性批判》，邓晓芒译，人民出版社，2003，第212页。
③ 〔德〕康德：《单纯理性限度内的宗教》，李秋零译，中国人民大学出版社，2003，第420页。

性存在者的人更应当追求道德,而道德的达到必然要求理性对情欲的控制(这也正如柏拉图所说的对欲望的"节制"就是人们应有的美德一样)。

对于男人来说,由于男人在天赋中更加擅长理智思维,所以康德主张男人应当以理性的绝对命令(道德律)作为行动的指南。而对于女人来说,由于女人更多的是感性直观,更容易注重外表而忽视内心,所以康德认为女人必须克服与生俱来的几种缺点。在康德看来,女人的主要缺点是虚荣与无聊,虚荣意味着女人会在外表上花费大量的时间和精力,企图去博得别人的羡慕或欢心;无聊意味着女人不愿意探讨有深度的话题,而只热衷于一些(男人看来毫无疑义的)无聊话题。女人应当自觉地克服这些缺点,"尽可能地远远脱离这类令人厌恶的事",要以道德修养来提升自己。康德认为,女人首先应该保持"纯洁无瑕"的品行:"在美丽的性别身上就属于头等的德行,而且很难在她们身上被提升得更高了。"[①] 其次,对于女人来说,一定要有"羞耻心":"这种品质是尤其为美丽的性别所固有的,并且对于她们也是非常之相宜的。"[②] 最后,在社会生活及与人交往中,女人必须表现得"谦逊得体":"那是具有极大优越性的一种高贵的纯朴性和天真性。由此焕发对别人的一种安详的友好和尊重,同时还结合了对自己的某种高贵的信心和一种合理的自尊,那在一个崇高的心灵状态中总是可以被人发现的。……吸引人又敬重感动人;所以它就使得所有其余的光辉品质都能有把握地抵御各种责难和讽刺的恶意攻击。"[③] 只有女人以这三种主要德性加以熏习之后,才能克服女人自身的缺陷,才配得上"优美"二字。

在康德看来,两性关系还体现在对他人的爱和敬重上,这是一种义务:"它们可以分开(每一种独自)来考虑,也可以这样存在(对邻人的爱,尽管这位邻人可能很少值得敬重;同样,对每个人必要的敬重,

---

① 〔德〕康德:《论优美感和崇高感》,何兆武译,商务印书馆,2009,第36页。
② 〔德〕康德:《论优美感和崇高感》,何兆武译,商务印书馆,2009,第37页。
③ 〔德〕康德:《论优美感和崇高感》,何兆武译,商务印书馆,2009,第38页。

尽管他会被评判为几乎不配得到爱)。但是，它们在根本上按照法则来看是任何时候都彼此结合在一个义务之中的。"① 两性之间同样应当表现出这种品行，这里的"爱"就已经超越了狭隘的基于肉体欲望的"爱"，甚至超越了主要基于精神性的"爱情"，而变成一种对所有人的博爱、仁爱。这种爱是不寻求回报的，即使对方可能不值得敬重，可能配不上爱，但是作为每个人应有的德性，我们都应当"爱人如己"。

就整个人际关系来说，康德认为人之所以为人的本质特征乃是因为人的道德属性，"爱"是最重要的现实性的道德范畴，"爱的义务的划分。它们是：一、行善的义务；二、感激的义务；三、同情的义务"。② 无论是男人还是女人，无论处于爱情、婚姻之中还是处于普通交往之中，甚至是作为陌生人，每个人都应当行善而不是作恶，都应当对他人有同情之心而不是冷漠之心，对他人的任何好意或帮助都应当有感激之心而不是狡诈之心，如果这些能够做到并成为稳定的品质，那么家庭必定幸福美满，社会必定和谐稳定。

综上所述，康德对女人、性、爱情、婚姻的阐释最终指向的还是"道德"，这也正如康德一贯提倡的作为义务的"道德律"一样，做有德之人是每个人应尽的义务。

---

① 〔德〕康德：《单纯理性限度内的宗教》，李秋零译，中国人民大学出版社，2003，第459页。
② 〔德〕康德：《单纯理性限度内的宗教》，李秋零译，中国人民大学出版社，2003，第462页。

Hamka's Perspective on Economic Inequality and World Justice

A. L. Samian[*]

Abstract: Abdul Malik Karim Amrullah (1908 – 1981) or HAMKA is a renowned, autodidact social philosopher of the Malay World. Although much has been written about him, none so far has examined his perspective on economic equality and world justice in light of globalization. While it is imperative that we have to meet global challenges, we always need to revise our overall strategy in order to increase our private and public capacity for economic attainment and civil society, both at the local and international level. In other words, issues related to justice and economic achievements covers both the personal and social dimension. It includes freedom of speech and expression, discrimination against women, human trafficking, rights of minority, economic crisis, culture of fear, domestic violence, food shortage and distribution of wealth. The list, however, is not exhaustive. In this paper, an attempt is made to analyze some of these issues mainly from his *magnum opus Tafsir Al-Azhar* and his related books.

Key words: HAMKA; Economic Inequality; Justice

---

[*] A. L. Samian, Professor of Philosophy at the National University of Malaysia.

哈马克论经济不平等与世界正义

A. L. Samian

摘　要：哈马克（1908～1981年）是马来西亚著名的自学成才的社会哲学家。尽管有关他的研究很多，但到目前为止，尚无人从全球化视野下的经济平等与正义视角关注过他的学说。当我们不得不面对全球化挑战的时候，为了提高个人和社会的能力来获得经济效益，我们就总是需要一种整体战略。换句话说，正义和经济成就同个人和社会都有密切关系。它包括言论自由、反性别歧视、反对贩卖人口、少数人的权利、经济危机、文化恐惧、国内暴力、食品短缺以及财富分配等。不过，上述列举尚未穷尽所有内容。本文试图运用哈马克的观点及其相关著作来分析与上述问题有关的一些案例。

关键词：哈马克　经济平等　正义

1. Introduction

From the purely materialistic perspective, economic inequality means that only a few are rich at the expense of the many poor. It implies that natural resources are owned by a privileged few. It also describes a situation whereby unemployment rate is very high, access to capital, entrepreneurship, land and labor are restricted and there is no equal opportunity in terms of economic development. Minorities are sidelined and merit is not considered important in securing jobs and opportunities. It is not the case that from each according to its ability and to each according to its needs. At the macro level, economic inequalities promotes instability, dissent, revolutions, upheavals and reformations. At the micro level, economic inequality evokes individual stress, depression, anger, hate-ingredients for a cocktail for disaster. Economic inequality is reprehensible—irrespective of ideologies, political persuasions or geographical locations. It relegates human beings as unequal—for this phenomenon alone economic inequalities is bad and has to be avoided at all cost. At the very least, economic equality spells freedom from hunger because availability of food is a basic need for all and the foremost outcome of any economic development.

What is world justice? We have some sense about what the material world is. What is more abstract is to define justice. Justice in the Malay Language is *adil*. Traditionally it means that in the overall scheme of things, everything thing has its place and to be just implies to put a thing in its right place. To be unjust means to have things at the wrong place. A popular example would be that a hat is to be worn on top of the head, not on the foot. It is unjust to wear it at any other place. A vacancy is to be filled, an excess is to be trimmed. In terms of employment and capacity building, every staff has its place. In its unjust to have the president in office working as the janitor or to expect a child to behave like a grown up or for a car to be driven like a bike.

In a more sophisticated global sense, "world justice" has several meanings. It is unjust to take the right of others since everyone has equal rights as a human being. No one has more basic rights than another because everyone wants to live as others. No one wants anything less. At the very least, world justice means that everyone in this world wants freedom from fear—fear of having anything less than others, ie, food, rights, place, opportunity, time, future and of course, the past. The list is, however, not exhaustive. Suffice is to say that we have nothing to fear if we are living in a just world. In the language of humanity, to have freedom from fear is a good enough *reason d'etre* to strive for a just world.

2. The Issues

The received view pertaining to economic inequality and world justice normally focuses on distribution of wealth, the haves and the haves-not, the nouveau rich and the down trodden poor, terrorism, famine, war, aggression income per capita, poverty, human trafficking; matters that can sustain life, creature comfort, inflict bodily harm or injury, colonization, apartheid, human rights and rule of the law. To be economically sustainable means that there is no shortage of basic needs. A just society is a society that promotes equal opportunity, rule of the law and fundamental rights. Hamka views of economic inequality and world justice, by and large, is shaped by his view of what a man is, or basically, on the definition of man (Hamka 1987).

Throughout history, man has been defined in several ways. Aristotle states that main is a political animal; Plato construes man as a domesticated animal; Seneca has argued that man is "a rational animal". Hamka views man as a microcosm, that is an inward manifestation of the macrocosm. As macrocosm, man is not simply a being that "think", it is not the Cartesian case of "*Cogito ergo sum*". Rather, thinking is only one aspect of human existence (Hamka 1994). If we do accept without reservation the Cartesian doctrine, than economic equality and world justice means to have economic equality and justice security to the end that we can think freely. Yet, with or without security, we cannot stop ourselves from thinking, because in order for us to do that, we need to think.

As a microcosm, man consists of bodily parts which include "the vegetative self". Having economic equality and justice implies that man can develop his body unthreatened by anything. He has access to medication, food, exercise, and knowledge on how to develop his physical self. Translating this aspect to the societal level, physical security implies the availability of food more than anything else. It also means a just distribution of wealth. Anything which jeopardize the food supply amounts to a threat in security. A just distribution is essential because an unjust system anywhere is a threat to a just system everywhere since the entire world is organically related in so far as equality and justice is concerned. After all, mankind is *one big family* sharing planet earth (Hamka 1977).

Hamka neither over emphasizes nor reduces man's existence simply to matter. Even if a man could appease all his appetite, yet he still remain unsecured, as in the case of the super *nouveau riche*. We can be fed extremely well yet we are not emotionally happy. A prisoner may be more secured within the prison wall compared to his comrades on the street. The wife of an unfaithful restaurateur is well fed but emotionally unsecured. In view of this problem-situation, emotional security is no less important. All of man's phases of existence—as an individual, a family member, a member of the society, a citizen of his country, a denizen of the world—needs emotional security. In order to achieve *nirvana*, bliss, "*ananda*", or perfect happiness requires emotional security. Hamka has the opinion that emotional security lies in total submission to The Divine, the Most Secured, because all of the other forms of existence, be it artifacts, plants, animals, planets, theories, and dreams are spatial and temporal. If we love our family too much, we will suffer upon its loss. If our emotional security are directly proportional to our savings, we will be threatened when it depreciate in value because of the decrease in interest rate or rising inflation. A physically healthy man, in spite of his wonderful health, might still be unsecured if he is not emotionally secured. A just and economically equal world must take this aspect of emotion into consideration.

Even if a man is emotionally and physically secured, he might still think that he is not secured because of the ephemeral "emotional attachment" and the "temporal" physical needs. Put simply, it is impossible for a man to be fully secured if he "thinks" that he is not secured—we are influenced by what we think, namely, the effect (not so much the primacy) of mind over matter. According to Hamka (1998), it is impossible to place a man's mind behind bar. Man has a "thinking needs" —a man would think he is unsecured if his "thinking needs" is not fulfilled. A just and economically equal society should fully promote this innate ability to think independently.

What are the thinking needs of man? It is freedom to access information, freedom of speech, expression, problem appraisals, liberty to read and write. In short, to think whatever he wants to think about, on any subject that come to his mind, freedom to choose and solve problems. Life is a problem (*masalah*) solving activity and we need to think in order to solve problems. A good man, according to Hamka, is one that benefits his neighbor, that contributes to nation building, that helps to mitigate solutions for problems of his society (Hamka 2009). Any policies that restrict the flow of information, what more in cyber space or in the virtual world, is unjust since it is a threat to thinking and therefore needs to be carefully appraised.

Above all, human equality and justice requires "spiritual security". It implies the freedom to practise a man's chosen faith, because Hamka (1998) believes that there is no compulsion in religion. Faith is a matter of volition, similar to love, it can never be forced (Hamka 2008). We cannot genuinely love something that we are forced to love, existence of "force" admits the absence of consent. At the macro level, there must not be any element of "*paksaan*" in spiritual matters—while admitting the importance of observing "spiritual sensitivity". In a nutshell, in order for us to have "spiritual security", no man should be discriminated in a just world based on theological differences.

Thus far I have outlined Hamka's view of human justice and equality. It involves physical, cognitive, affective and spiritual aspects. The question is, if indeed, somehow, man could have justice and equality in all aspects, could we say that he is happy? Hamka will argue that 1) happiness, is relative—we could only be happy by way of comparison; and 2) like "success", it is more of a journey than a destination since there is no absolute happiness on this earth, whereby everything could be improved.

There is always the perplexing question of perfectly secure from inequality and injustice. Let's examine it from various angles, supposing that the problem of security exists objectively—it is more than a mental construct. Thus what is connected to it is security situation, implication of security, security network, kinds of security and security appraisal (akin to research priorities). The latter is most important because we cannot solve all problem of security at once.

Hamka would say that the most fundamental of all, especially in the current era of globalization, is security from hunger and fear (Hamka 1998). Why freedom from hunger? Food is man most basic need for survival. If there is enough food on the table, it is very unlikely that people would go to the street. Bereft of food, we cease to survive, what more to thrive. Food is as real as you could get of the material world for as the maxim goes, there is no love more sincere than the love to eat. Throughout the vicissitudes of civilization, there is always the haves and the haves-not, the material divide, the slums and the gated community. In principal, man should not die out of hunger because there is enough food for everybody. It is only because some have taken too much (*pembaziran*) that others are deprived. There must be intervention in order to have a just food distribution. In the current global economy, it seems that greed has been elevated to a sacrament whereby the wealth of 20 percent of the population equals to that of the 80 percent. There is enough food for everybody's need but not for everybody's greed.

In so far as human equality and justice is concerned, next to hunger is fear. This is "the fear factor". Hamka believes that mankind always has fear. Fear is innate in man in the sense that it is a potentiality. While it is not the case that "there's nothing to fear except fear itself", one can live a fearless life if one is only fearful of the Most Compassionate which is none—other than The Divine. It is perfect wisdom to fear The Creator rather than the created. Man survive because he learns to eat in as much as he learns to fear. If he is not fearful of anything, than he has excessive courage and that is a threat to his very own survival, i. e. , he is not fearful at all of his own safety.

If a man is full of fear, he would not produce, in short, he cannot create except objects of fear and destruction grounded on his belief that the world is unjust and economic inequality is everywhere, the best defence is offence. At the macro level, much resources will be siphoned to produce weapons of mass destruction. While it is commendable to anticipate the unexpected, phobia is a different matter altogether. Hamka's position is that in order to allay fear, we are to do good for a good act is a Godly act (Hamka 1998). The most destructive effect of fear is that it stymied man's creativity. To do nothing is to be nothing and it is in everybody's power to do nothing in our everyday life, what more in the era of globalization, where time and space shrink, and the only thing that we should not do is nothing. To instill fear is more than amputating the human body, it's to amputate his soul and spirit. Void of creativity, there is no much difference between man and other creation (Samian 2006). It is so destructive that no civilization worthy of its name in the history of mankind, can be constructed and developed mainly out of fear.

What is fear? Fear is not images, ideas or judgment. That fear is a kind of sensation, feeling, is self-evident because we always talk about afraid or feeling fearful and it is impossible for us to imagine something fearful that cannot be felt. Now the feeling of fear is totally different from ideas, image or judgment. Feeling hungry is the consciousness of being hungry and cannot be confused with ideas about food or images of fried rice or the judgment that our bodies are lacking calories. Idea, image and judgment refers to something outside of us; we always have idea about something, image of something, and judgment about something. "Fear" is an awareness which is neither cognitive nor part of the intellect. It is not physiological too, that is, it is not part of our physique.

It is a kind of feeling that is shared at the level of rats and chickens. It is one thing to "know" the amount of calories that we are lacking and it is another thing to fear of the implication of malnutrition. Since "fear" is an element of the affective aspect of our existence, and not so much of our cognitive and physical aspect, Hamka argues that fear is very real. If we know about the consequences of smoking yet we are not fearful of it, we would still smoke. Even though we know probability wise that it is safe to fly, that being in the plane is safer than in the car, we still would not fly if we are fearful of flying. Knowing is a necessary but not a sufficient condition of action. If we are fearful of something, we won't have the desire for it although we know about it since for a thing unknown there is no desire.

Freedom from fear entails freedom from the fear of doing good because even though you know something is good for you, you remain not doing it out of fear. So how does freedom from fear relates to an economically equal and just world? Having security means we feel free to do good. Knowing something is good is necessary but not sufficient condition to do good. It has to be enhanced by having no fear of doing good whatever "The Good" is—be it solely self—realization, the object of positive interest, vision of The Divine, power, love, pleasure, virtue or axiological pluralism. So if man *qua* man, abstain from doing good out of fear, how can a good society, which in this context an economically equal and just society, exists? Since the building block of a good nation is the presence of a critical mass of good citizens, it is very improbable that we can have a good state if the majority of the people in it are fearful of doing good. It follows that having food on the table is necessary but not sufficient condition. Doing good to people implies; "*Sakik dek awak sakik dek orang; sanang dek awak senang dek orang; nan elok dek awak katuju dek orang*" (Hamka 1977).

Is it good to have no fear at all? Total absence of fear is reprehensible as Aristotle has argued convincingly in his Nicomachean Ethics. The belief in the middle path in ethics and morals is shared by the Abrahamaic faith and

Buddhism as well. Hamka strongly advocates the middle path, or "*wasatiyyah*", i. e. moderation. It is praiseworthy not to have fear of doing good and it is blameworthy to have excessive courage to do good (Hamka 1982; 1987) The Malay proverb "*buat baik berpada-pada, buat jahat jangan sekali*" entails the need of doing many kinds of good, thus the "*berpada-pada*". It is wise to have a limit, a degree, in performing *the same kind* of good act since there is no end in kinds of goodness. There is no middle path in the intention of doing all kinds of good. An act of lesser good is still a good act; an act of lesser evil remains an evil act.

Human being is a complex creature. Not only does it has a physical self, it has the emotional non tangible component which gives values to the existence of being human. So we have the personal values and universal values, local wisdom as opposed to global wisdom, values as a person and national values subscribed by the leader of a nation. Knowledge wise we have personal knowledge, personal cognitive content, personal memory, as opposed to collective memory, conventionalists agreement on what counts as truths and global knowledge (as in the case of global history *vis a vis* regional history). Most fundamental of all of course is our spirits, the most important aspect of our existence that are embraced by all religions. All of these constitutes the core substance of being human and provide the parameters in defining human values, more so in making sense of human justice and equality.

Justice is, but by comparison. We can differ on judging what is right. In addition to Hamka's position and the traditional Malay definition of justice, I have argued at another occasion that it makes more sense in defining justice as having something at the right place and the right time rather than the traditional Malay definition of fairness (Samian 2012). For instance, the leader of the thieves could be fair in distributing their illegal gains yet it is a wrong act because the goods are not theirs at that time.

We like to have the goods that others are having. While we may not have equality in the sense of equal physiques, emotions, knowledge and spiritual attainment since no two human being are exactly equal, yet we should have equal opportunity in *trying* to have the goods since we are not equal in the first place. So equality means means equal chances, a level playing field for all.

3. Conclusion

In conclusion, Hamka prefers to look at security issue from a wholesome perspective grounded upon his belief of what a man is. In the wake of globalization, insecurity anywhere is a threat to security everywhere; injustice anywhere is a threat justice everywhere, inequality anywhere is a threat to equality everywhere. It is imperative for all of us to communicate, collaborate and cooperate in promoting justice and equality beyond our borders. For the sake of humanity *writ large*, it is far too important to leave justice and equality to mere chance. Striving for justice and equality is a necessary work in progress and so long as we are working on it, we are on the right track. The journey is more important than the destination. Paraphrasing Confucius, a thousand steps begin from one step and according to Hamka, the most important step of all, the way forward in order to have justice and equality in the long run, is to eradicate hunger and the fear of doing good.

References

Esposito, John L. "Hamka". In *Ensiklopidia Oxford Dunia Islam Modern*, Trans. by Ilyas Hassan, Bandung: Penerbit Mizan, 2001.
Hamka. *Keadilan sosial dalam Islam*, Kuala Lumpur: Pustaka Antara, 1977.
Hamka. *Kenang-Kenangan Hidup*, Kuala Lumpur: Pustaka Antara, 1982.
Hamka. *Tasauf Modern*, Jakarta: Pustaka Panjimas, 1987.
Hamka. *Falsafah Hidup*, Jakarta: Pustaka Panjimas, 1994.

Hamka. *Tafsir al-Azhar Juzu' 30*, Jakarta: Pustaka Panjimas, 1998.
Hamka. *Di bawah Lindungan Ka'abah*, Jakarta: Bulan Bintang, 2008.
Hamka. *Kedudukan Wanita Dalam Islam*, Selangor: Pustaka Dini, 2009.
Samian, A. L. "Satu Ulasan Tentang Definisi Manusia", *Jurnal Pengajian Umum*, 2006, (1).
Samian, A. L. *Memetakan Metamatematik*, Bangi: Penerbit UKM, 2012.

Education Without Indoctrination: The Ideal and Challenge of Ethical Training for Global Citizenship

Paul A. Swift[*]

Abstract: My paper addresses the objective weaknesses and strengths of five different approaches to ethics: divine command theory, utilitarianism, deontology, virtue-based ethics, and cosmopolitanism. I suggest that each ethical theory is vulnerable to different particular types of criticism and claim that recent approaches of cosmopolitan ethics by Anthony Kwame Appiah and others demand more from their proponents intellectually. This demand makes it unrealistic to expect everyone to become a proponent of cosmopolitanism. In spite of this ground for criticism, I suggest that cosmopolitanism is still the best equipped to engage issues of economic inequality from a global perspective. By drawing on elements of Rawls' theory of justice I claim that cosmopolitan ethics furnish us with the best tools for addressing the concept of world justice.

Key words: Kant, Divine Command Theory, Cosmopolitanism, Virtue-based ethics, Environmentalism, Rawls, Utilitarianism

---

[*] Paul A. Swift, PhD, Professor of Philosophy, Bryant University, USA.

无灌输的教育：全球公民理想与伦理挑战

Paul A. Swift

摘　要：本文客观地论述了五种伦理体系的优点与缺点：神命论、功利主义、道义论、美德伦理学以及世界大同主义。我认为，每一种伦理学理论都经不起批判，由安东尼·维姆·阿皮亚和其他伦理学家一起提出的全球伦理对其对手的批判要求更高，因为不可能指望每个人都成为世界大同主义的支持者。尽管有批判的基础，我还是建议把世界大同主义当作从全球视角出发解决经济不平等问题的最好方法。通过借用罗尔斯正义理论，我认为，全球大同主义伦理思想给我们提供了很好的方法，让我们可以较好地解决世界公正问题。

关键词：康德　神命论　世界大同主义　美德伦理学　环保主义　罗尔斯　功利主义

The resurgent interest in the ideal of Global Citizenship, or the cosmopolitan ideal, presents us with a broader and more challenging set of variables when considering what we mean by the term "justice". The cosmopolitan ideal is at least as old as the word from which it originates. In the chapter of the Lives of the Eminent Philosophers by Diogenes Laertius which is devoted to Diogenes the Cynic (VI 63), we find the first historical use of the term: when asked where he was from, Diogenes the Cynic claimed he was a man of no particular city, but a citizen of the world. Enlightenment thinkers like Kant, Wieland, and others championed cosmopolitanism as an important component for thinking about justice from an international perspective. I would like to address some specific challenges here to the ideal of cosmopolitanism which have implications for international politics, economic inequality, the question of justice, and what it actually means to educate people toward becoming global citizens.

One of the obvious criticisms of the cosmopolitan ideal is that its demand to consider obligations to people of distant regions is contrary to human nature. Anthony Kwame Appiah articulates this point in his consideration of the ethics of strangers. We evolved out of primitive small groups, with face to face negotiations, and for the most part formed packs which in some important ways are different than wolf packs. Whether wolves or humans, there are natural obligations to care for and help members of one's own pack (or clan, family, etc.) which do not extend to members who are outside of the pack, i.e., beyond one's immediate social circle.

Most of us recognize that we have some kind of ethical obligations to our family and friends that are different than the general public within our own communities. When does the consideration of strangers amount to a neglect of our duties to those within our own immediate pack? Consider, for example, what kind of parent or friend gives away her finite time and resources to those outside of her own network of family and friends; at what point does the consideration of the welfare of strangers make one negligently distant from those within one's own personal network of family and friends?

Yet even beyond this problem (that we probably do owe more to our friends and family than to strangers), there is the additional challenge to consider the significance of one's own nation state and other nation states. Getting people to recognize the importance of others in their own political states who are outside of their own circle of friends and family requires one to consider more abstract duties to others and the extent to which they are really binding. This in itself presents a difficulty for educating people to become global citizens, a point which I would like to address briefly from the perspective of the challenge of teaching ethics.

There is no shortage of corruption by individuals who dishonestly use public funds or use the local or national political structures to benefit themselves at the expense of others. This alone gives many persons caution to think that any cosmopolitan ethical ideal is workable. The challenge becomes far more daunting when considered from an international perspective: what are our obligations to people on the other side of the globe? What implications do these obligations have to our understanding of economic inequality from a global perspective? How far can a leader go before he or she is viewed as a "bad" leader in the concern for people outside of his or her own nation state?

Before addressing these challenges, let us consider the significance of education to address some of the difficulties associated with training people to think and act like global citizens. Although there are many different approaches to teaching ethics, virtually all surveys of ethical theory include utilitarianism, Kantian ethics/deontology, virtue-based ethics, and some kind of divine command theory. Cosmopolitanism also deserves inclusion into this list, the ideal of global citizenship.

Divine command theory (DCT) is probably the easiest to comprehend as an ethical theory, since it only requires obedience to a command by some God or gods. This is really not much different than legalism or authoritarianism as a political theory in its ethical foundation: what is good is whatever the political governing party claims is good, a view often attributed to Thomas Hobbes which resembles the "might makes right" theory advanced by Thrasymachus in Plato's *Republic*. The only difference here is one has an authority originating from a deity (DCT), the other has it originating from a political state. John Arthur and others have pointed out that both of these approaches are vulnerable to objections that they are arbitrary in their foundations and epistemologically suspect.

Among the competing ethical theories, utilitarianism (in whichever form, Bentham, Mill, Sedgwick, Singer) is also fairly easy to understand: calculating the greatest happiness for the greatest number (calculus without numbers!) is excellent for aiming at consideration of the common good. Understanding that perspective, as well as weaknesses associated with this approach such as the standard objections that utility based ethics may overlook the dignity of the individual are not too difficult to comprehend.

Invariably the objections toward utilitarianism lead some to consider the merits of Kant's ethics insofar as they take seriously the dignity of an individual. Although Kant had formulated some ideal of global citizenship, he is better known for his focus on the significance of aiming at the correct motives for ethical action. Astonishingly he rules out moral feeling for the basis of ethical action in his attempt to come up with an ethical theory through reason alone. Understanding the categorical imperative requires one to formulate a more abstract concept of morality and this is more challenging intellectually than DCT or utilitarianism. Kantianism is a bit more complex: to determine whether someone is ethical, it is not enough to simply examine the action of an individual. One most also know the motive. In this view, if someone provides assistance to those who are less fortunate, that in itself is insufficient to determine whether the action is good. This approach intellectually demands more than either DCT or utilitarianism to comprehend what is at stake in ethical evaluation. Actions can be observed fairly easily, but discerning what the motive is of an ethical agent is not so easy, requiring another level of interpretation.

The fourth approach to ethics, virtue-based ethics, is a little murky: this term is sometimes used to describe Aristotle's ethics, as well as Confucian ethics. In its Aristotelian incarnation, this approach focuses on both the intent of ethical agents as well as the consequences. In some ways this approach bridges the gap by incorporating both a consideration of motives (like Kant) but also focuses on consequences (like Utilitarianism). By training one's character to feel good about the right things, one can develop a well-formed character, one of the most difficult goods to take away from someone. Yet such an approach to ethics (doing the right thing in the right measure at the right time in the right ways) is reproached for being vague and imprecise. Indeed such an approach offers no specific rule to look to in order to definitively make conclusions like Kant does, or even like rule-based utilitarianism does. In spite of these criticisms, I think virtue-based ethics (at least how I have defined it here) is extremely valuable because motives do reveal something important about character, but (contrary to Kant), good motives and the categorical imperative are not the whole story about ethical engagement.

The point of briefly surveying these four approached to ethics is to advance a dialogue about ethical education which goes beyond a type of indoctrination. More importantly, the purpose of surveying these types of ethical theories is to suggest that some of them are more difficult than others to intellectually understand. One must know what is good to be able to aim at it. With this in mind, let's return to the cosmopolitan challenge, the ideal of global citizenship.

One of the chief difficulties of educating people toward the cosmopolitan ideal (beyond the earlier mentioned standard objections that it is contrary to human nature) is that it is intellectually demanding, even more than the four other approaches to ethics. It demands that people learn about things outside of their own community. Many individuals aren't even aware of what is going on in their own neighborhood; the obligation to be informed about the history, cultures, and traditions of communities outside of one's own is demanding. As an ethical theory, cosmopolitanism requires students of ethics to know more. It is therefore intellectually challenging in significant ways which the earlier mentioned other approaches to ethics are not.

If this view is correct, education toward global citizenship is intellectually more demanding than most standard approaches to civics and ethics since there is a much bigger set of variables to consider: one cannot default to learning a simple rule to apply (like DCT or authoritarian legalism). Nor can one simply invoke armchair philosophy of the Kantian abstract kingdoms of ends. In some ways the considerations of utilitarianism overlap with cosmopolitan considerations, but the cosmopolitan view presupposes a type of familiarity with many different cultures (an anthropological challenge in itself), as well as an understanding of Marxist critique and its relationship to economic inequality. Contemporary cosmopolitans must be post-conventional in Lawrence Kohlberg and Carol Gilligan's sense, but with a sensitivity and tolerance toward different peoples' histories and cultures.

There is a risk here of painting different approaches to ethics with broad brush strokes, since all of these approaches to ethics (DCT/Authoritarian, Utilitarian, deontology/Kantian, Virtue-Based, and cosmopolitanism as well), have different varieties and one could argue that there are other types of ethical systems not included in this list. Some cosmopolitans advocate for cosmopolitics and a world government, but some do not. Some view cosmopolitanism as best applied only to collecting or engaging art and culture, with varying and minimalist degrees of ethical directives.

Cosmopolitan ethics (at least Appiah's version) presents a type of challenge that goes beyond all the other approaches. Consequently it is unrealistic to expect everyone to become or identify themselves as a cosmopolitan. This is very different than the expectation from the proponent of DCT: the upshot of this is that we cannot expect everyone to identify as a cosmopolitan, at least not a type of actively engaged cosmopolitan, since active engagement may be a challenge which many persons simply cannot meet in terms of psychological and intellectual commitment. The concept of a universal sisterhood or brotherhood is friendly to the cosmopolitan ideal, but is so vague it means very little.

For the purpose of training people to be global citizens it is important to examine the significance of race and gender, important dimensions that have been ignored historically. How we think about sex and race in terms of the biological and anthropological sciences is important for contemporary cosmopolitanism. Those factors are absent or problematic in some versions of DCT, utilitarianism, Kantianism, and virtue-based ethics.

So the question of economic inequality from a global perspective and its relationship to justice is a tricky issue. The reason I have started with addressing education is because I believe that people are often indoctrinated into being locked into a way of thinking in which they believe they have the correct ethical perspective and others' views are simply mistaken. Cosmopolitanism tolerates difference and seeks out engagement with other viewpoints, rather than hostility. It is very understandable why some nation states have reified the "us vs. them" mentality, given the fact that there is a sort of consolidation of power and ease of organization by viewing the rest of the world as enemies. Indeed, this is a necessary condition of survival for most people in the history of the world.

In the US, jobs are fought over from county to county and state to state. The perception that jobs will leave the state directly influences popular elections: promising jobs is a good formula for attaining public office. When jobs disappear, people are understandably distressed. When jobs go overseas, it is quite natural for nationalism to kick in, reaffirming the "us vs. them" mentality. The theft of trade secrets and different interpretations of intellectual property rights have created divides between nations, stoking animosity between China and the US. Each nation acts on its own self-interest, perhaps out of a real necessity since that condition is necessary for survival, perhaps reflected in the most primordial form of organization in nature as a biological principle which is extended to the commonwealth.

One of the oldest political and philosophic challenges is formulating a theory of justice which can applied to this world. A theory which is unrealistic fails the pragmatist test of providing workable solutions. This is perhaps the most difficult objection against cosmopolitanism, but I believe a cosmopolitan ideal is still worth striving for in order to formulate a working concept of global justice.

Amartya Sen and others have pointed out that there has been a long discussion, but no univocal agreement in the West from the ancient Greek world up until the present about what the term "justice" actually means. Sen also engages this question from an Eastern perspective by considering the long history of the idea of justice present in the Indian context and the Chinese approach as well to a lesser extent. Although Sen criticizes John Rawls, Rawls' starting point of raising the question of fairness is still worth considering.

By considering what basic rights one has and how economic wealth will be distributed, Rawls' two principles are useful for thinking about how to make sense of the question of justice in terms of fairness. Rawls began presenting his work on this question before, during, and after the 1960s civil rights legislation in the United States. His theory has direct implications for dismantling apartheid.

Rawls' theory states that there are two principles and there is a serial order of these principles, which means the first cannot be compromised, even if the second should turn out to be more beneficial for society as a whole. The first principle suggests that no government can claim to be just without granting all of its citizens certain rights which ensure basic civil liberties (freedom of speech, freedom from arbitrary arrest, freedom to vote, assemble, etc.). The second principle states that economic inequality is permitted, provided that the most vulnerable are not made worse off.

Rawls defends economic inequality but also defends the poor, since some kind of compensatory benefits are granted to the poor. Rawls has been criticized in his theory because it might be usefully applied for specific nations or societies, but is difficult to apply to questions of international or global justice. Even if this is a valid objection, Rawls's theory can be used to think about economic inequality from a global perspective.

Rawls' theory can be applied to nation states by considering the disparity between wealthy and poor countries. If richer countries get richer by making the most poor countries worse off, this could be considered unjust. Rawls' theory suggests that there is nothing wrong with economic inequality as long as it doesn't make the most vulnerable worse off. This idea can be applied to relations between nation states.

At the minimum, pursuing this view would imply an ideology that seeks to minimize hostility to foreigners. To revisit the idea of justice as fairness is useful and friendly to the cosmopolitan ideal. The poor are the most vulnerable. If we can educate people toward the view that the poor should not be made worse off, we can craft a notion of international justice which recognizes that policies that benefit the world as a whole are worth pursuing.

This general theory could be applied to thinking about pollution of the planet and who the most vulnerable people are. The emerging field of environmental ethics is key to the future dialogue since we share the same planet which can be sustained or made much worse. Claims about environmental racism often boil down to environmental classism: the rich can afford to move and live in non-polluted areas. Crafting sustainable practices, especially so the poor are not made worse off, is a challenge to aim for in terms of seeking justice from a global perspective.

The precise obligations of wealthier nation states to impoverished countries is difficult to stipulate, but is not therefore empty. There are many arguments that suggest a large middle class in a nation benefits everyone in terms of quantifiable measurements of happiness. To what extent can that claim be expanded upon to think about the global aspirations to have many (relatively) affluent nations, rather than nation states which have increasing gaps in economic indicators?

What is true of the whole is not necessarily true of every part, so these are difficult questions. Some poorer nations have a few rich citizens so attempting to address the general problem of poverty by claiming richer nations have duties to poorer nations is problematic, since even if we admit there is an obligation of wealthy nations *not* to make impoverished nations worse off, what specific policies would this suggest? How do we know that an international policy will benefit those who are poor in the poor countries, rather than the anomalous few who are wealthy? These are important difficulties, especially when there are political obstacles, but there are plausible strategies to attempt to engage such problems which lie beyond my margins of inquiry here.

Conclusion

To formulate an ideal of global citizenship, I have surveyed different approaches to ethical theory, all of which are vulnerable to criticism, including cosmopolitanism itself. However, whichever ethical theory one pursues, the reality of environmental changes and their implications for current and future generations is vital to address. Traditional theories in the history of ethics which did not have the specific problem of environmental degradation usually prove to be very weak because none of them had to deal with the problem we have now. Cosmopolitanism may be the best equipped to deal with the challenge of the environmental hazards and their relationship to economic inequality since it requires that people think and be informed about their own communities, but also consider the implications of their actions and business practices from a global perspective. It is important for citizens of the world to recognize that the United Nations may be the most cosmopolitan institution there is: an important institution for the dialogue we must have with others because everyone matters.

学术争鸣

国际经济正义中的几个问题辨析

强以华*

摘　要：追求国际经济正义必须以清楚辨析相关的国际经济问题是否正义为基础。然而，在国际经济的问题上，长期以来一直存在颇多分歧，其中发达国家和发展中国家之间的贫富差距问题、国际分工问题和国际经济秩序问题是三个十分重要却分歧巨大的问题。我们认为，在这三个问题中，都存在明显的国际经济不正义的现象，但是，我们也没必要夸大它的不公正性。只有基于这样的理解，我们才能在如何消除国际经济不正义的问题上持更为务实的态度，才更有利于消除国际经济的不正义现象。

关键词：国际　经济秩序　正义　辨析

Some Issues in International Economic Justice

Qiang Yihua

Abstract: Pursuing international economic justice must be based on the clarification that some international economic issues are justice or not. However, there is long-lasting disagreement concerning these issues in which the main ones are the gap between developed countries and developing countries,

---

*　强以华，湖北大学高等人文研究院世界文化发展中心主任，哲学学院教授、博士生导师。

international division of labour and international economic order. We assume that there exists economic inequality in these three issues. Only by this kind of understanding, we can find a more practical attitude toward international economic unjustice and find an easier way to eliminate the phenomenon of economic inequality.

Key words: international; economic order; justice; analysis

"正义是社会制度的首要德性"[①]。国际正义包含了诸多方面，例如政治、经济、文化、教育等。但是我们认为，国际经济正义应该是国际正义的基础，它不仅影响着国际政治、文化、教育等方面的正义问题，而且还决定着一个国家、一个民族在争取、寻求和维持广泛的国际正义方面的实际话语权。因此，走向经济正义是走向广泛的国际正义的前提。但是，在走向国际经济正义的问题上，究竟何谓国际经济正义却是一个长期以来争执不休的问题。本文试图辨析国际经济正义中几个重要的争议问题，以有利于人们在国际经济正义问题上达成更多的共识，从而更好地帮助人们走向国际经济正义。

一　贫富差距问题

在当今的世界上，东西方的国家之间、特别的南北方的国家之间存在着严重的贫富差距，并且这种差距还有扩大化的趋势。问题在于：发展中国家和发达国家之间的贫富差距是否真的包含了国际经济的不正义从而使得它成为国际经济正义的研究对象呢？借用罗尔斯的观点来判断，我们可以认为：若是这些国家之间的贫富差距是这些国家自身的努力（包含勤劳、创造新的体制、发展科学技术等）程度不同所致，也就是说，若当今世界中发达国家的富仅仅是由它们自身的努力所致而发展中

---

① 〔美〕约翰·罗尔斯：《正义论》，何怀宏等译，中国社会科学出版社，1988，第1页。

国家的穷仅仅是由于它们的努力不够所致，那么，它们之间的贫富差距就不包含国际经济的不正义，它们也不构成国际经济正义的研究对象；若这些国家之间的贫富差距是由"与它们自身努力与否"无关的某种外在的偶然性所致，那么，它们之间的贫富差距就包含了国际经济的不正义，它们也就构成了国际经济正义的研究对象。为了弄清发展中国家和发达国家之间的贫富差距究竟是否包含了国际经济的不正义现象，从而是否能够成为国际经济正义的研究对象，我们应该分析导致它们之间贫富差距的具体原因，看看其中是否包含了与它们自身努力与否无关的外在的偶然性。

在当今的世界上，一个国家的贫富与否通常包含了三种主要原因，即：国内原因、自然原因、国外原因。其一，国内原因。国内原因指的是一个国家的政治制度、经济体制的先进程度，以及社会是否稳定、人民是否团结，它是经常处于和平状态还是经常处于战争状态，此外，这个国家的生产方式和科技水平等也应该是造成一个国家贫穷或者富裕的重要的国内原因。其二，自然原因。自然原因指的是一个国家的地理环境、气候条件、资源状况等。例如，有些国家有良好的地理环境和气候条件，它很适宜农业生产；另一些国家则土地贫瘠、常年干旱，甚至到处是广袤无垠的沙漠，显然无法从事农业生产。再如，有些国家的石油、天然气、有色金属等储量丰富，另一些国家则资源贫乏。在上述两种原因中，一般来说，国内原因是一个国家内部的事，它通常基于自身的不努力而非外在的偶然性，所以，贫穷的国内原因通常不能成为国际经济不正义的理由，它不应该是国际经济正义问题的研究对象。至于自然原因，尽管它作为与人的努力程度无关的偶然性应该成为国际经济不正义的理由，但是，由于当今并不存在能够超越国家层面并且有权进行国际资源分配的机构，所以，它不能构成"实际上"的国际经济不正义的理由。这样，若不同国家在贫富差距问题上确实存在国际经济不正义的话，那么，它一定与造成不同国家贫富差距的第三个原因即国外原因有关。其实，在经济已经一体化的当今世界中，任何一个国家的国内经济的发展或多或少成了国际经济整体的一个组成部分，因此，任何国家都不可能离开其他的国家、离开整个国际环境独立发展自己的经济。因此，当今世界中的任何一个国家的经济都必然会受到其他国家的影响，从而使得它的国内经济发展不"纯粹"是国内的经济发展，甚至使得它面对的自然环境也不是"纯粹"的自然的环境。来自国外经济的影响可能会导致如下情形：它有利于某些国家经济的发展而不利于另外一些国家经济的发展，从而可能进一步使某些国家更为富裕而另外一些国家更为贫穷。若真的存在这样的情形，那么，我们便可以说：在当今世界中，发展中国家和发达国家之间的贫富差距确实包含了国际经济不正义的事实，从而使得不同国家之间的贫富差距问题成为国际经济正义的研究对象。因此，我们应该进一步分析在当今世界国际经济整体中是否存在有些国家不正当受益或有些国家不正当受损的情形；并且，若有，它究竟表现在多大的程度上。这些分析有助于我们判断在不同国家贫富差距问题上是否存在国际经济不正义现象以及它的不正义程度，因此，它也有助于我们采取正确的方式去消除这些国际经济不正义的现象。

毫无疑问，发达国家的富裕与它的自身努力存在密不可分的联系。但是，另外，发达国家在成为发达国家从而成为富裕国家的过程中，也存在一些为了自己的经济发展不正当地对待发展中国家的情形。首先，它表现为发达国家把发展中国家当成廉价的原料产地和廉价的劳动力供应地，它还包含了发达国家和发展中国家之间的不公平贸易，它甚至包含了发达国家对于发展中国家的殖民掠夺。这些情形导致了发展中国家长期处于经济落后状态。就此而言，发展中国家的贫穷并不仅仅是自身不努力的结果，它也是自己在国际经济整体中遭遇的不公正对待所致。其次，它表现为发达国家通过各种方式（其中包含了一些不正当的方式甚至殖民掠夺）重塑了有利于发达国家的世界自然资源的布局。自然资源是经济发展的重要基础。在经济学上，资源总是短缺的东西，"短缺是指由于可供支配的资源有限而无法实现所有的追求目标"[①]。所以，短

---

① 〔美〕乔治·恩德勒等主编《经济伦理学大辞典》，李兆雄、陈泽环译，上海人民出版社，2001，第241页。

缺便会导致目标冲突。这里，有利于发达国家的自然资源布局不仅包含了历史意义上的不公正性，而且还作为现实的不合理性妨碍着发展中国家进一步发展经济。就此而言，发展中国家贫穷的自然原因并不仅仅是纯粹的自然原因，它也包含了人为的原因，并且它确实包含了这些国家在国际经济中遭遇的不公正对待。根据以上分析，在当今世界国际经济整体中确实存在发达国家不正当受益和发展中国家不正当受损的情形，也就是说，在贫富差距问题上，确实存在国际经济的不正义现象，它需要把发达国家和发展中国家之间的贫富差距问题作为国际经济正义的探讨对象。

然而，发达国家和发展中国家之间贫富差距问题的不正义现象并非全由国外原因造成。因此，它也不像有些人想象的那么严重。首先，发达国家的富裕和发展中国家的贫穷都包含了纯粹属于它们自身的原因，也就是说，包含了它们自身不同的努力程度。有些发展中国家固守着落后的经济体制，不愿意接受新的法制环境和管理制度，甚至不断地进行内部战争，这些都是它们贫穷的原因。因此，它们应该为自己的这些做法造成的贫穷承担责任。相反，发达国家的富裕则既是它们不断进行制度革命和科学技术革命的结果，也是它们辛勤劳动的结果。因此，它们也应该因自己的这些做法享受富裕。其次，虽然发达国家在成为富裕国家的过程中曾不公正地对待发展中国家并导致了它们的贫穷，但是，它们也在一定的程度上做了弥补。我们这里所说的弥补指的不是所谓的"援助""贷款"，而是发达国家在自己长期的发展过程中，为人类创立了先进的经济体制、管理方式和科学技术，并且，为了获得这些体制、方式和科学技术，发达国家不仅付出了艰辛的劳动，而且经历了大量的"试错"过程，也就是说，它们为此付出了大量的财力。当发展中国家直接利用这些体制、方式和科学技术时，它们不仅因此节约了大量的成本，而且也节约了大量的时间。

因此，在发达国家和发展中国家的贫富差距问题上，确实存在着国际经济的不正义现象，并且，它是表现在发达国家和发展中国家贫富差距问题上的基本现象，但是，它也不像有些人认为的那么严重。

二 国际分工问题

我们在说到当今世界上任何一个国家的国内经济的发展或多或少都成了国际经济整体的一个组成部分时，其实也就是说它们都是"国际经济分工"的一个组成部分，它们在国际经济分工中起着不同的作用。国际分工涉及方方面面，包含了诸多的内容。这里，我们只关注其中两个重要内容：其一，国际产业分工；其二，国际人力资源分工。在这两种分工中，发展中国家都处于非常不利的地位。

从产业分工来说，在当今世界的国际分工中，尽管发达国家和发展中国家都承担着诸如服务业、制造业等领域的工作，但是，相对地说，发达国家更多地承担着服务业（例如金融、贸易等）领域的工作，发展中国家则更多地承担着制造业（例如钢铁、汽车等）领域的工作以及原料供应和原料加工的工作；在制造业中，发达国家更多地承担着高端制造业的工作，发展中国家则更多地承担着低端制造业的工作。我们这里仅仅分析在制造业分工中发展中国家所处的不利地位。发展中国家所承担的低端制造业通常都是劳动密集型产业，在国际产业分工中，它们是一种受制于人的低利润、高污染产业。"二十世纪七八十年代，跨国公司为了降低成本并规避母国严格的劳动法规，开始通过在发展中国家设厂或寻找代工工厂的方式转移其劳动密集型产业，并最终形成了一个完善的金字塔形的产业结构链。在这个金字塔顶端的是掌握核心技术、品牌和市场终端的各大跨国公司……中间一层是通过订单为跨国公司生产产品或提供货源的代工工厂与制造厂商……处于最底层的则是工厂中的工人。"[①] 在国际分工的产业链中，由于发达国家处于顶端地位并且掌握着核心技术、品牌和市场终端，所以，它们控制着产业链下游的发展中国家的产业，从而控制着游戏规则和定价权力，迫使发展中国家不得不接受一些苛刻的合作条件，例如低利润和高污染。仅就污染来说，根据统计，20世纪60年代以来，

---

① 刘可风、龚天平、冯德雄主编《企业伦理学》，武汉理工大学出版社，2011，第244页。

美国已将39%以上的高污染的产业转移到了其他发展中国家,日本则将60%以上的高污染的产业转移到了东南亚和拉美国家。"我国也是发达国家产业转移的目标之一。根据我国第三次工业普查的报告,投资于污染密集产业的跨国公司有16998家,工业总产值4153亿元,分别占全国工业企业相应指标的0.23%和5.05%,占三资企业相应指标的30%左右。……外商正把我国视为他们的'污染避难所'。"①

从人力资源来说,正如我们刚才在引文中所看到的,在现代国际产业链的最底端是发展中国家低端制造业工厂中的工人。他们处于非常劣势的地位,不得不接受低工资、长工时的现实;不仅如此,与成年的男工比起来,还有大量女工和童工不得不接受更为苛刻的工作条件。根据2006年英国《星期日邮报》的报道,仅苹果iPad在中国深圳的代工厂就有超过20万的工人,他们的日工作时间通常长达15个小时,并且在原地一站就是几个小时;女工的工资比男工更低,她们的月收入(当时)仅为27英镑(折合人民币387元)。此外,尽管使用童工在西方国家已经明令禁止,但是,在发展中国家则不一样,例如,在印度每5人中就有2人生活在贫困线以下,孩子们为了养活自己和家人,被迫放弃学业出去工作。但由于种姓制度和缺乏教育,他们能找到的工作往往条件更差且报酬微薄。②毫无疑问,发展中国家在国际分工中处于的上述不利地位已经在一定程度上包含了国际经济的不正义现象,但是,若发展中国家自愿接受这样的国际分工,那么,其中包含的国际经济不正义就不那么明显。因此,为了更为准确地判断这些国际分工中是否存在国际经济的不正义现象,我们应该分析在这些分工中处于不利的一方接受这一分工是否是一种被迫的行为;并且,若是被迫的行为,被迫究竟是它自己造成的还是在这些分工中处于有利的一方造成的。对于这些分工中处于不利的一方来说,若这些分工是一种被迫的分工并且它们的被迫不是它们自己造成的话,那么,这些分工就是一种"不公正"的分工,其中

---

① 刘可风、龚天平、冯德雄主编《企业伦理学》,武汉理工大学出版社,2011,第251页。
② 刘可风、龚天平、冯德雄主编《企业伦理学》,武汉理工大学出版社,2011,第247页。

就存在国际经济的不正义现象。

表面看来,对于发展中国家来说,现行的国际分工似乎是它们自愿接受的分工。发达国家的资本输出曾被马克思主义经典作家看成资本主义侵略的一条重要路径,但是,我们发现,在当今世界中,发展中国家却把招商引资作为发展本国经济的重要渠道,甚至会在某个阶段将其看成发展本国经济的最为重要的手段。为了招商引资,发展中国家常常不惜开出一系列优惠条件,包括降低准入标准、税收优惠、放宽环保要求,等等。为什么这些发展中国家不惜开出一系列优惠条件来招商引资呢?因为它们知道,在它们现行的发展阶段,也就是说,在它们既没有资金也没有管理经验,更没有先进的科学技术的阶段,只有通过招商引资,让发达国家的外商来本国投资或者直接办厂,才能为其带来资金、管理经验和先进的科学技术,促进本国经济的发展。应该承认,基于当今世界发达国家和发展中国家所处的实际经济发展水平,发展中国家做出这样的选择应是最适当的选择,它们在无力承担国际经济产业链顶端的情形下,承担这一产业链的中端和低端才是发展它们经济的唯一路径,也是发展它们经济的最现实、最有效的途径。然而,细究起来,在发展中国家这种看似自愿的选择的背后却潜藏着一种强迫,也就是说,它们的自愿原则实际上是一种被动的自愿选择。由于它们制度、经济、科学技术发展水平落后,所以它们只能"被迫地"接受这样的选择。正是"被迫"才使它们不得不接受一系列苛刻的条件并使自己在国际分工中处于如此不利的地位。更为关键的问题是:造成它们"被迫"接受这样的国际分工的原因究竟是什么?也就是说,它们究竟是由于自身的原因造成了自己的落后还是由于其他的原因造成了自己的落后?在分析发达国家和发展中国家之间的贫富差距时,我们曾论证了发展中国家的贫穷既有自己的原因也有国外的原因,即它们在国际上遭遇了发达国家的不公正对待。落后与贫穷为伍。因此,造成发展中国家"被迫"接受现行的不利于自己的国际分工的原因也是双重的,也就是说,它既有发展中国家自身的原因,也包含了发达国家在国际经济整体中对于它们的不公正对待。

由于造成发展中国家"被迫"接受现行的不利于自己的国际分工的

原因是双重的，因此，我们认为，正如在发达国家和发展中国家贫富差距的问题上首先存在国际经济的不正义现象但也不能夸大这种不公正现象一样，在发达国家和发展中国家国际分工的问题上，我们也应该在首先承认存在国际经济的不正义现象的同时，不去夸大这种不正义的现象。

三　经济秩序问题

我们这里所说的经济秩序指的是国际经济秩序。早在 19 世纪末 20 世纪初，随着西方垄断资本主义经济体系的形成和发展，西方国家在世界经济的范围内确立了以国际分工为基础的国际生产体系、以交换为基础的国际贸易体系和以国际金融资本为基础的国际金融体系。这些体系其实就是西方资本主义世界的国际经济秩序。随着时代的发展，时至今日，这一国际经济秩序已经发生了很大的改变，但是，由于历史遗留的原因，它还保留了建立之初的一些基本精神。那么，我们应该如何评价这种国际经济秩序是否存在不公正的现象呢？我们可以从国际经济秩序的话语权是否平等、国际经济秩序的规则是否公平和国际经济秩序自身是否合理三个角度来评判国际经济秩序是否存在不公正的现象。

首先，我们认为现行的国际经济秩序存在不公正的现象。这种不公正的现象主要体现为国际经济秩序最早以西方资本主义世界的国际经济秩序的形式表现出来这一历史现象所造成的现代后果。我们曾经提到，国际经济秩序是随着西方垄断资本主义经济体系的形成和发展而首先出现的秩序，尽管它一开始就是国际经济秩序，但是，它最初主要是西方资本主义世界的国际经济秩序，也就是说，它最初主要是发达国家之间的国际经济秩序。因此，最初的国际经济秩序与当时的西方殖民体系存在内在联系，并且它的话语权一定属于西方发达国家，它的游戏规则一定是适应西方发达国家的国际分工、国际贸易和国际金融的游戏规则。然而，随着第二次世界大战的结束，大批殖民地、半殖民地国家相继在政治上获得了独立，并且，有些国家的经济也开始逐渐融入世界经济体系。当这些发展中国家进入世界经济体系的时候，由于它们直接面临的是已由西方社会主导并由西方世界制定的国际经济秩序，以及由于发达国家在经济上早已处于强势，所以，它们面对三种不公正：其一，在话语权上，它们根本没有或者没有足够的话语权；其二，在国际经济秩序的规则上，它们面对的是不适应发展中国家实际情况从而使它们处于劣势地位的国际经济游戏规则；其三，在国际经济秩序上，它们不得不接受不合理的国际产业分工、贸易分工和金融分工。这种不公正显而易见，所以，早在 20 世纪 60 年代，发展中国家就开始呼吁建立更为公平的国际经济新秩序。1964 年 10 月，第二次不结盟国家和政府首脑会议首先提出了建立国际经济新秩序的口号，接着，七十七国集团的部长级会议也强调建立新的国际经济秩序的重要性。1974 年 5 月联合国大会第六届特别会议通过了《关于建立新的国际经济秩序的宣言》和"行动纲领"。这些文件所体现的新秩序的主要内容是：各国对其自然资源和一切经济活动拥有充分主权，改革不利于发展中国家的国际金融制度和贸易条件，建立能够真正体现公平互利、尊重发展中国家的发展权并注重可持续发展的国际经济机制。当然，尽管经过发展中国家的努力，国际经济秩序已有了较大的改善，但是，国际经济秩序建立之初的有些有利于西方发达国家的基本精神还在或多或少地起着作用，它在一定程度上妨碍了国际经济秩序的公平性。若要完全建立国际经济的新秩序，发展中国家还需要进一步努力。

其次，我们依然认为不应夸大现行的国际经济秩序所包含的不公正现象。我们认为，至少有两个理由来支持我们的论断。其一，发达国家具备了更为先进的管理国际经济秩序的经验，因此更有能力制定完善的国际经济秩序的规则。由于发达国家先行进入国际分工和国际贸易的领域，所以，在长期的国际经济活动中，它们积累了更为丰富的管理经验，更加懂得如何制定更为有效、更为适用的维持国际经济秩序的规则。就此而言，它们主导建立国际经济秩序的话语权具有历史的根据。当然，我们这样说并不意味着否认在发达国家主导建立国际经济秩序的话语权时完全可能造成不利于发展中国家的情形，更不意味着认为发达国家应该始终主导建立国际经济秩序的话语权，我们只是强调，在一定的历史时期，从务实性和可行性的角度出发，只能由发达国家来主导建立国际经济秩序的话语权。但是，随着发展中国家经济实力的增强，特别是随着发展中国家在建立国际经济秩序的实践之中管理经验的不断积累，它们应该在建立国际经济秩序中拥有越来越多的话语权。其实，我们发现，无论是在世界银行，还是在国际货币基金组织以及世界贸易组织，发展中国家的话语权越来越大。其二，发达国家具备了承担高端服务业和高端制造业的条件。在国际经济秩序中，在产业分工中，我们曾说，发达国家与发展中国家处于双重关系中：发达国家侧重于服务业（特别是金融业）而发展中国家侧重于制造业；并且，发达国家侧重于高端制造业而发展中国家侧重于低端制造业。尽管发展中国家在这种国际分工中处于十分不利的地位，并且这种十分不利的地位也是它们在历史上受到某种不公正待遇的一个结果，但是，仅就这一结果是既成事实而言，发展中国家根本没有能力承担现代高端服务业（尤其是现代金融业）和高端制造业的工作，所以，在现行的国际分工中，这是一种各尽所能的分工，也就是说，这是一种务实并且唯一可行的分工。当然，随着发展中国家经济实力和管理能力的提升，以及随着它们的科学技术的发展，这种国际分工也应该发生相应的变化。

通过对于以上三个问题的公正与否的辨析，我们所得出的结论是：在当今国际经济领域，确实存在发达国家和发展中国家之间的不公正现象，它是我们判断国际经济公正与否的基础，但是，在此基础之上，我们也无须夸大它们之间的不公正性。我们认为，只有持这样的态度，我们才能在如何消除这种不公正性的问题上采取更为务实的态度，即：发展中国家若要彻底消除自己在国际经济领域中遭遇到的不公正性，最终还是应该依赖发展中国家提升自己的内在能力，包括提升经济发展的水平，完善自己的制度，发展自己的科技，等等。这就是说，不要等到有了公正的国际经济环境之后再去发展，更为重要的是，应在发展之中争取更为公正的国际经济环境。为此，发展中国家应在坚持不懈地反对各种不公正性的同时，把主要精力放在提升自己的内在能力方面。其实，中国目前所走的道路正是这样一条道路。

When Great Achievements Fail to Combine with Fairness: A Plea for Fairness by Economic Inequality and World Justice

Thomas Menamparampil*

Abstract: A society grows to greatness in proportion to the skill it develops to keep the components of its culture—the economic, the political, and the 'cultural'—in harmony with one another. In this paper I follow the main lines of argument that Arnold Toynbee developed in *A Study of History* in explaining the growth and destinies of societies and civilizations, leaving the readers to draw conclusions for themselves.

Key words: achievements; fairness; justice

伟业呼唤公义：经济不平等与世界正义对正义的呼唤

Thomas Menamparampil

摘 要：社会要变得强大，需要使发展技巧与文化内容保持协调一致。本文利用阿诺尔德·汤因比在《历史研究》中的观点来解释社会和

---

* Thomas Menamparampil, Professor of Philosophy, nominated for Nobel Peace Prize in 2011.

文明的成长与终极命运，希望读者可以基于该解释得出自己的结论。

关键词： 成就　公平　正义

1. Growing to Greatness

A society grows to greatness in proportion to the skill it develops to keep the components of its culture—the economic, the political, and the "cultural" — in harmony with one another. And if it does achieve the goal of growing to true greatness, it radiates its influence in all directions; a disintegrating one manifests opposite traits (Toynbee II, 140).

• **In this paper I follow the main lines of argument that Arnold Toynbee developed in *A Study of History* in explaining the growth and destinies of societies and civilizations, leaving the readers to draw conclusions for themselves.**

As societies emerge from their relative isolation and interact with other societies and civilizations, new psychic energies are generated; the **synergy** thus created makes amazing things happen. That is why it is good for us to reflect how societies and civilizations arise, what attitudes favour their growth, how they enter into relationship with others and promote the common good, and what can bring about their decline and even demise.

2. Earnest and Sincere Effort is the Only Way to Greatness

There is no shortcut to success: think, plan, work hard, be fair to people, be ready to pay the price for that which you wish to obtain. "If we ask what the right thing to do is, there are clear, fundamental answers. End poverty. Eliminate disease and squalor. Educate children. Teach women to read. In short clean up the mess." (Martin 25)

"A principle of a great civilization ought to be that it focuses intensely on how to *develop the capability latent in everybody. The more that is done, the more we all benefit from one another.*" (Martin 386)

One of Toynbee's central argument is that great civilizations rise on hard terrain, not on easy ground. Earnest and sincere effort is the only way to greatness. The Sumerian civilization for example came up on the jungle-swamps of the Tigris-Euphrates (Toynbee I, 95). The civilization of China rose on the marshy banks of the Yellow River (Hwang Ho) amidst jungles and high water (Toynbee I, 97); it came up on a river far more challenging than the navigable Yangtse (Toynbee I, 112 – 113). The Hellenic civilization took birth on the rocky and hard soil of Greece: while rich Boetia remained rustic, and its people cold and unimaginative, the austere land of Attica favoured the emergence of a creative and enterprising people. When Attica's pastures dried up and plough-field grew barren, the Athenians turned from stock-breeding and grain-growing to olive-cultivation; they exchanged the oil so produced for Scythian grain. The energies generated by these endeavours and creativity produced further energies: the Athenians explored the subsoil, developed silver-mines, and introduced currency. They built pottery, ships (Toynbee I, 113 – 114). The hard nature of their land only added strength to their sturdiness. "If Necessity is the mother of invention, the other parent is Obstinacy, the determination that you will go on living under adverse conditions." (Myres J. L.)

The measure of effort a society puts in for its very survival provides it with the stamina needed for further achievements. Toynbee asserts that it was the exertion that the early Romans put into transforming their barren soil that gave them the energy to build up their vast empire extending from Egypt to Britain (Toynbee I, 108). The neighbouring Capuans, on the contrary, who lived in luxury remained permanently weak, and were conquered repeatedly. In fact, Capuan luxury softened the character of Rome's arch-rivals, the Carthagenians, during a winter that Hannibal's soldiers spent in that city amidst plenty. The Carthagenian cause was lost at Capua. Greek epics describe how Odysseus who did not yield to the mighty Cyclops, fell to the charms of Circe and ended up in the pig-sty. The lotus-eaters could not resist the enticing invitation of the Sirens, nor the Israelites shed the memories of the "flesh pots of Egypt".

It was the hard soil of Tyre and Sidon that raised the Phoenicians to greatness. It is they who gave us the alphabet. They dominated the Mediterranean for a long time. Their venturesome spirit led them to found the city of Carthage in Africa and several colonies in Spain. In the same way, it was on the rocky hills of Judea that the Hebrews gained their religious insights which gave birth to two religious traditions (Jewish and Christian), and continue to inspire the world to this day (Toynbee I, 117 - 118). The badlands of eastern Germany produced the resolute Prussians who unified Germany and set a model for Europe in the areas of compulsory education and efficient social security system. The barren soil of Scotland brought up a well-educated people with a strong sense of economy and unlimited stamina; Toynbee could not notice the same grit and determination in the English. Amazingly the contribution of the Scots to the building the British empire was out of proportion to their numbers; they gave the Britain several outstanding Church leaders and Prime Ministers (Toynbee I, 120).

In our own times, the more successful nations can make a serious mistake if they decide to settle down to a comfortable way of life. For, as William James says, "...a permanently successful peace-economy cannot be a simple pleasure-economy. We must make new energies and hardihood continue" in the form of hard work and service, if we wish to survive (Barzun 673). Or else, sturdier peoples, working hard, will move ahead, leaving us right behind. This is already happening to early achievers.

3. Stimulus of a Challenge

"Soft countries invariably breed soft men", Cyrus, the Persian Emperor (Herodotus IX, ch. 122)

In earlier times the challenges were in the form pressures from other societies. Today challenges have changed. " In next two decades, this new international system will be coping with the issues of ageing populations in the developed world; increasing energy, food and water constraints; and worries about climate change and migration. " (Taroor 21) *Those who will give a creative response to these new problems will build their future.*

It is not only the challenge of the environment that stirs a society to achievement but also pressure or competition from other societies. The value of competition is widely accepted in the commercial world today. In the history of civilizations we notice that it a society under strong pressure that emerges to greatness; however, it does so only if it finds a way to offer an adequate response.

Toynbee adduces any number of examples to prove his point. He shows how the South of Egypt was prominent when political pressure was from the South and how North Egypt rose to prominence when the pressure was from the North (Toynbee I, 139); how the Byzantine challenge provoked the Turks to expand Westward into the European mainland (Toynbee I, 140); how the Orthodox civilization expanded Eastward reaching as far as the Pacific under pressure from those regions (Toynbee I, 141); how Charlemagne's empire grew most on the Eastern borders where it fought back the aggressive Saxons and Avars; how the Saxons in turn continued this Eastward strategy under threat from the ferocious Wends (Toynbee I, 144); how the Hapsburgs rose to power winning the support of the Hungarians and the Bohemians to halt the Ottoman pressure. It is interesting to note that the alliance broke up precisely in 1918, when the Ottoman power collapsed (Toynbee I, 145 – 146) .

In the same way, it was when Mercia was hard-pressed by the Celts that it grew. Later, when the pressure was greater on the Wessex side from the Scandinavians, king Alfred responded to the challenge and his kingdom became the nucleus of the future kingdom of England. Similar Scandinavian pressure made the house of Capet to take leadership in France and brought the French kingdom into existence. Thus it was Scandinavian pressure that gave birth to the powerful kingdoms of England and France (Toynbee I, 151). To escape penalization at home, English Puritans went over to America and laid the foundation of the United States (Toynbee I, 158).

The most interesting part of Toynbee's argument is that it was the Persian pressure that awakened the sleeping Greek states and ultimately led to the rise of Alexander; that it was the Carthaginian aggressiveness that stirred the Roman energies to throw back the invading forces and sent them conquering Gaul, Spain and North Africa, with the energies so generated; that the Westward expansion of Islam was a belated response to the thrust of Greece and Rome into Asia, and it was this Islamic pressure on the West that provoked the European society to gather strength not only to drive the alien forces out of the Iberian peninsula, but "carried the Spaniards and Portuguese overseas to all the continents of the world" (Toynbee I, 193). Their experience inspired France, Netherlands, England and others to build empires round the globe (Toynbee II, 238). Taking this argument further, we may see in the rise of many nations of Asia and Africa a belated response to the colonial pressure. Recent trends seem to show that the Third World economies are awakening in a big way.

We fervently pray that the negative experiences of the past may not be repeated all over again in either direction. This paper is an appeal to wisdom, sobriety and far-sightedness in a period of success. The future belongs to those who make the right options whether the change they choose "is moving in productive or destructive directions, and whether it is creating balanced growth across income classes, ethnic groups, and regions, or precarious imbalances" (Sharma 12).

4. A Society Responds to a Challenging Situation Guided by a Creative

Minority

"*Increasing inter-connectedness seems to lead to increasing interdependence, which in* turn demand new, ever wider, ultimately worldwide 'frameworks' for action, transcending old nations, blocs and civilizations." (Fernandez-Armesto 560) This is the challenge before creative thinkers in our times. A new future is possible.

The future belongs to those who make the right options whether the change they choose "is moving in productive or destructive directions, and whether it is creating balanced growth across income classes, ethnic groups, and regions, or precarious imbalances" (Sharma 12).

Toynbee believes that it is the manner in which a society responds to the challenge from the environment or from other societies that gives rise to a civilization. One can choose to cringe before a challenge and withdraw into an obscure corner merely to survive; one may opt to sink below other dominant societies and lose one's identity and allow one's genius to be stifled. Many have done that and have disappeared from history. Others may decide to take the challenge head on, plunge themselves into a determined struggle; it is this tenacity and determination that place them definitively on the way of progress.

This determination need not be in the area of military aggressiveness. Progress comes, says Bergson, when a society has "allowed itself to be convinced, or else allowed itself to be shaken; and the shake is always given by somebody" (Bergson H., *Les Deux Sources de la Morale et de Religion*, pp. 333, 373). Toynbee calls them creative personalities; they reshape others after their own thinking (Toynbee I, 251). Even if their ideas do not win acceptance immediately, those of a kin spirit take note of them, understand them, and begin to take after them gradually. New and creative ideas often come into the minds of several persons at the same time quite independently. That is the law of nature. Ordinary people have remained much the same all through history. They need creative personalities who think, reflect, transform themselves and introduce unforeseen changes into their society that lead them to new destinies (Toynbee I, 253 – 154). That is the mission we assign to intellectuals in the context of today's discussions.

There have been times when changes were introduced into a society by force and maintained through drill or mere mechanical imitation. Absolute rulers of every age have had recourse to force as the most reliable tool. But enforced changes have no future. But innovations, on the other hand, that are introduced through the inspiring figure of creative individuals or communities are true pointers to the future (Toynbee I, 255). They will remain on and win wide acceptance. Toynbee argues that it is an inwardly transformed person that takes up the challenge of assisting his/her fellow beings. The examples he adduces are of those who initiated religious and intellectual movements in human history. Plato believed that a nation is best led by a philosopher-king, a truly enlightened person (Toynbee I, 258). In the same way, Pythagoras and Neo-Platonists emphasized the importance of deep reflection and inner pilgrimages for self-transformation and social change. So, whether it be an individual, a team, a community, or a nation, that develops a new conviction through the power of inspiration (enlightenment, discovery of a new insight, a new set of ideas), it has something valuable to contribute to the rest of humanity. Such persons and communities alone will be able to offer a helping hand to the human family in its hour of its need.

5. Achievements Made by Means of Force Do not Last

All through history, there have been proponents of force as the sole means of shaping human destinies. Machiavelli was one of them. He said, " War should be the only study of a prince. He should consider peace only as a breathing-time, which gives him leisure to contrive, and furnishes an ability to execute, military plans. " (Friedman 37 – 38) But history shows that force is counterproductive; it is always confronted by force.

Referring to European history Fernando Braudel said, " The basic rule was always the same. When a State seemed to be too powerful…, its neighbours would jointly **tilt the scales** *in the opposite direction so as to make it more moderate and better behaved"*

(*Braudel 416*).

During the dynamic period of a civilization, the ideals and values of the creative minority win enthusiastic acceptance among the members of their society, and even among others. As long as the various elements of a culture or civilization are in harmony, it continues to grow (Toynbee I, 327) and win adherents. But at a later period of history some form of imbalance creeps into that society, inequality grows among its members, and the leadership and the upper classes become exploitative in the political and economic fields. Unfairness deepens. The creative minority atrophies into a closed clique of vested interests; it degenerates into a "dominant and exploiting minority" which seeks to maintain itself in power by the use of force. That is what happened to the leadership in Greek society. Its impressive democratic institutions ceased to function, and its energies were lost in internal struggles, and ultimately it had to submit to Macedonian imperialism.

Similarly the democratic traditions of the Roman senate gave way to the Augustan empire. The participative ruling styles prevalent in ancient India and China surrendered at a later stage to exploitative regimes and absolute rulers. And finally a stage comes when an exploitative society is forced to yield either to internal revolution or to external aggression. The greater the suppressing energies of the exploiting minority, the more violent the revolution (Toynbee I, 326 – 327). And ultimately the old system collapses, and a new creative minority takes over and drives things in a new direction. In Roman history the Plebeians withdrew their support from the Patricians. In France, Russia, China and Vietnam there were bloody revolutions. This is the destiny of any society that reaches a peak of achievement, but creates several forms of imbalances it within itself or in the neighbourhood. The old order is rejected and a new order comes into existence.

Something similar happens when a society becomes so complacent with its achievement that it begins to rest on its oars. Creativity dies; self-importance increases; idolatry of the self begins. Achievement in certain limited spheres of life, like economy, technology, military expansion is taken as total human achievement. And pride goes before a fall.

In this context, it may be good to point out that expansion of territory is not a sign of the advance of a civilization. During the colonial period European nations cannot be said to have reached the height of civilization just because they held much territory. They were in fact being inexorably driven by values that led them to the two suicidal World Wars and to their decline. Similarly, neither the military showmanship of Superpowers during the Cold War nor the present hegemonic pretensions of regional powers in Asia or in the rest of the Third World are signs of progress in civilization. For Toynbee, the rise of an empire or of military might is not the high point of a civilization, as it is often thought even today; it is rather the final effort of a society to rescue itself from collapse. Communities reach this position when the values that gave rise to their civilization have been enfeebled or lost. *Tao te Ching* says that "He who stands on tip-toe does not stand firm. He who takes the longest strides does not walk the fastest...He who boasts of what he will do succeeds in nothing. He who is proud of his work does nothing that endures". Aggressiveness and pretensions to greatness are not useful assets. It is good for the members of a society to ask themselves whether the values that their high performance possible are being forgotten, marginalized, or lost. It is to this exercise that this paper is inviting participants today.

Once a society gets divided into a dominant minority and exploited majority, force begins to play a greater role in its functioning. Compulsion comes into the picture and the ideals and goals that were greatly esteemed and enthusiastically pursued come to be imposed. The leaders cease to be admired or respected and ordinary people sink to the level of the oppressed. There may be a period of suppression, forced conformance, anarchy and uncertainty. Toynbee's main argument is that anything built on force in this way has no future. Violent solutions to problems only retards progress, does not promote it. Force does not pay in the long term, within the country or in the neighbourhood, despite immediate advantages.

The example he gives is the one of Sparta. She was a leading nation in the early period of Greek history. But once the Spartans had conquered the Messinians and subjected them to slavery, they had no option but try to maintain their dominant position by force. That compelled them to impose severe discipline upon themselves. Every Spartan had to keep himself ready for war at any time. This form of imposed discipline crushed the public spirit (Toynbee I, 214 – 215). Thus Sparta fell far behind Athens when the latter was becoming the marvel of the world during the 4th and 5th centuries BC (Toynbee I, 216). The Spartan citizen became no more than a war-robot. A Spartan training can contribute to immediate effectiveness, but in the longer term it damages the inner being of persons and communities (Toynbee I, 323). Machiavelli may not agree with this statement. He would say, when persuasion fails, use force (Toynbee I, 617). Many dictators and fascist leaders in modern times have admired the Spartan model and used it very successfully for some period of time, only to fail in the end. And their failure had disastrous consequences.

Excessive militarism is a perversion of the human spirit. Neighbouring states gather together in frantic self-defence against an apparent hegemonic threat. What results in the immediate context are tensions, and in the longer term, a fratricidal war. Toynbee's argument is that the art of war is always learned at the expense of the arts of peace (Toynbee I, 226). Everyone is the loser, both the winner and the loser. In the context of arms race between neighbouring nations in Asia, these reflections gain great importance. No one wins a war today except arms-producing corporations. They alone have the last laugh.

6. Use of Force, Violence and War Is Suicidal

George Friedman says, " *German, Japanese, French and British power declined not because of debt but because of* **wars that devastated** *those countries' economies....* " (*Friedman 17*)

Shashi Taroor gives us this warning, " *The terrible notion of a* ' *clash of civilizations*' *has entered our discourse, as the often benign forces of religion, culture and society have become causes of conflict, rather than succour, in many places.* " (*Taroor 17*)

Asia can collapse long before it rises, if a suicidal war takes place. So can any other part of the world. Wars or violence, internal or external, leave long term consequences behind. Culture and civilization stand threatened most of all. In the immediate context, technology related to war may seem to make progress, but it is humanity that takes the blow when one community inflicts cruelties on the other. The Hellenic society opted for a suicidal conflict when it made up its mind for the Peloponnesian war in 431 BC (Toynbee I, 305) . Thucydides calls it the "beginning of great evils for Hellas" . It does not matter whether the conflict is between states, classes, ethnic groups, religious groups, or communities within the same society or within the neighbourhood, the damage is in many directions.

The winners become irrationally cruel and the losers build up anger and begin dreaming of retaliation. At the moment of success, the Athenians were hard upon the losing Melians. The Romans became more and more harsh upon the conquered people in the later period of their history. Ultimately that cruelty itself turned against their best interests. Undue harshness returns to harass its perpetrators. The polarisation between classes, communities and interests in the Roman society led to such tensions and instances of violence that their democratic society had no choice but surrender an absolute ruler. The Roman empire was born over the dead bones of Roman democratic traditions

(Toynbee I, 344). The Republic was overwhelmed, and the ambition for money and power *devastated the "republican virtues"* that were the greatest pride of Roman citizenship (Friedman 31). Something similar would happen again in France after the cries of "equality, fraternity, and liberty" grew fainter; Napoleon emerged from the ranks with absolute power.

What begins with force returns to force again; violence of every kind is self-destructive in a society. That is the suicidal nature of army governance. The consequences of the Assyrian militarism caught up with their empire ultimately even though the Assyrians dominated southwest Asia for two and a half centuries. Their mighty power disappeared and even the name "Assyrian" was forgotten where it had held absolute sway. Xenophon was not even aware of such a name (Toynbee I, 390). No other factor was the direct cause of the breakdown of civilizations than violence: wars between neighbouring states, civil conflicts within the same state, social upheavals of all kinds (Toynbee II, 301). We are living through times when such tensions dominate the world scene at diverse levels. This paper is an invitation to reflect more deeply.

7. Victory Imposes Its Own Type of Punishment on the Winners

Hellenism withered from within. The free cities were torn asunder by **mutual hatred** *and by class wars. "They found no place for the greatest minds of the age" who had to take shelter with tyrants (Dawson 62).*

"Perhaps we are justly punished. We were insolent and unjust in our dealings with foreign nations in our day of power. Now in our adversity you trample us." Ahmed Vefik, referring to Ottoman humiliation before Western forces (Mishra 62).

Those who emerge victorious in a disastrous war are tempted to rejoice at their success. But victory imposes its own type of punishment on the winners. "Victory, like revolution, can devour its own children, particularly those who expect more from it than what it actually delivers. The idealists who realize too late that violence never achieve their goals are among history's most common losers in victory. " (Schivelbusch 98) Macedonians who went conquering nations right up to India turned against each other in a suicidal conflict (Toynbee I, 395) . That is again what happened to European nations which, after reducing the rest of the world to the status of the colonies, turned against each other during the two World Wars. It was a suicide-attempt on the part of mighty Europe. And today, many neighbouring nations in the newly emerging situation in the Third World are busy at the same game, learning little from the experiences of the Western World in the early 20th century.

Exaggerated forms of nationalism are fatal. In the nineteenth century, nationalism rose to have the status almost of religion in Europe, and wars became "total wars" involving the entire population. When democratic nations are in conflict every citizen is roused to anger. The consequences that such wars leave behind remain on for centuries. Continuous Roman wars reduced the highly populated areas of Italy to the state of Pomptine Marshes which were restored by Mussolini only after two millennia of disuse (Toynbee I, 301) . Malaria entered Greece only after the Pelopnnesian war and Latium after the Hannibalic war (Toynbee I, 301) . Exaggerated forms of political nationalism, that once led many Western nations into conflict, are taking many Third World nations in the same direction. And arms producers rejoice.

8. The Psychology of the Defeated

During the Great War " Shaw despaired of man's ability to overcome his **brutish instincts** *and his propensity to lie and mouth empty ideals" (Barzun 687) . In times of conflict, the hostile feelings that anyone may have against his fellowmen, employers, or state authorities find release in being turned against an anonymous foe (Barzun 700) .*

*World War I was represented as a war to " **save civilization** " . But later* historians have always wondered whether it was a civilized way of settling differences (Fenandez-Armesto 10).

The winners are tempted to think that once the enemy (another class, caste, ethnic group, economic or political interest or a Nation State) is humbled, their own future is safe. They lose all sense of realism and forget that they have just wounded a tiger; they do not know when it will bounce back to life. The same learning can be applied to inter-class, inter-ethnic, inter-religious, or inter-national conflicts. We know that to every action there is a reaction. Defeats often lead to resilience, like it happened to Rome after the *Clades Alliensis* (Toynbee I, 135). It was the humiliation of Carthage in the First Punic war that stirred Hamilcar Barca to conquer Spain which was bigger than the empire that Carthage had lost in Sicily. After the defeat of the Hannibal in the Second Punic war, Carthage paid off of the indemnity, recovered commercial prosperity, and got ready for another round of fight. Austria was stimulated by her defeat at Austerlitz in the Napoleonic war. Prussia decided to build up its strength after the humiliation it suffered at Napoleon's hand at Jena and Tilsit; she renovated her army, administration, educational system which led to the birth of German nationalism, leading to the later achievements of Bismarck (Toynbee, I, 136). In the Ottoman empire, the first spark of Greek nationalism kindled the first spark of its Turkish counterpart (Toynbee I, 161).

The humiliation of Athens by the Persians in 480 – 479 BC made her build up a fleet that led her to the victory of Salamis and to the glory of the Periclean times. Xerxes the successor of Darius took aggression to European Greece provoking a Hellenic counter-attack under Alexander (Toynbee I, 610). The Scandinavian onslaught helped the development of military skills in the affected parts of Europe (Toynbee I, 239).

There are always new responses to new challenges. The Mughals provoked the Sikh and Maratha resistance and the Osmanlis roused the Greek and the Serb eagerness for independence. When Charles XII of Sweden defeated the

Russians, Peter the Great said, "This man will teach us how to beat him." (Toynbee II, 239) The defeat of Germany in 1914 – 1918 and the French occupation of Ruhr Basin in 1923 – 1924 roused the Nazi claim to justice. People do not usually yield to disasters. After the disaster of 1918 the French repaired the Reims Cathedral; it was after the Athenian temple was destroyed that the Parthenon was built. The great fire in London was followed by the building of Wren's St. Paul's Cathedral (Toynbee I, 137). Every victory is a judgement, but the process starts again. Winners must be ready to face the contest. This is true not in the sphere of war alone, but today more especially in the area of economy, industry, marketplace, fashion, ideas, sports, competitions, political elections (Schivelbusch 2). But people seem to be slow to learn.

Usually the winners seek to humiliate the vanquished as much as possible in their own eyes with a view to destroying their self-confidence (Schivelbusch 6). They may glorify themselves any amount, but the defeat remains an injustice in the minds of the defeated which, they feel, must be rectified. A mood is created when all citizens want to fight for the nation (Schivelbush 11). Curiously, a national defeat is a moment when a nation looks back with pride at its glorious past and revive energies to rebuild a new future (Schivelbusch 31). And the struggle begins all over again. The contestants copy fighting skills from each other seeking to outwit the other. As the art of war develops, the greatest loss of all is the **weakening of culture** especially on the winning side. Nietzsche said in 1871 that "great victories pose great dangers and that the triumph of the German empire would lead to the demise of the German culture" (Schivelbusch 4).

9. Woe to the Winners!

"... *The more effective the terrorist attack is, the more frightened the population is, and the more compelled the government is to respond aggressively and visibly.*" *In other words*, **war against terror** produces **more terror** (Friedman 77).

The last shall be the first (*The Gospel of St. Mathew* 20: 16).

The victorious Romans used to cry, "Woe to the defeated", until they began to lose battles themselves. After every victory, there is a tomorrow: whether it is for a nation, community, class, caste, business interest, or political alliance. Fortune is a wheel that rotates. There is a central Christian teaching, "The last shall be the first." It is as simple as that. The great historian Renan used to say, "Today's victors are tomorrow's losers." Defeat comes from an earlier victory and prepares the ground for another one (Schivelbusch 126). The tables are turned, and victory comes in the opposite direction. The relationship between Germany and France from the time of Napoleon till World War II can provide abundant example of this, a drama that could be avoided in many parts of the World if there is sufficient good will.

The psychology of victory is more damaging than that of defeat: it brings to birth an aggressive generation. *Destructive heroism* becomes seductive on both sides. When the anger is high, all public statements are couched in aggressive terms. The "enemy" is always "barbaric, violent, predatory, uncultured, without spirit, disloyal, assimilative, imitative, servile, lacking in character" (Schivelbusch 159). Even well-meaning men take pride in making themselves the heirs and prisoners of a heroic past, but at the same time become victims of their own high rhetoric, unrealistic propaganda, and symbolic gestures. Today several situations in the Developing World remind us of this condition; people are made victims of political propaganda and commercial deception, the contestants adopting aggressive postures against each other within the country or beyond borders. Such anger may be expressed in contexts of polarizations between classes, castes, ethnic groups, political parties or alliances, or regional interests. Le Bon wrote, "Among the masses, ideas, emotions, passions, and systems of belief are transmitted with the same infectious capacity as microbes." (Schivelbusch 213)

10. In an Encounter of Communities and Cultures the Best Elements in Heritages should Be Exchanged not the Worst

"*Asia is one.* The Himalayas divide, only to accentuate, two mighty civilizations, the Chinese with its communism of Confucius, and the Indian with its individualism of the Vedas... Arab chivalry, Persian poetry, Chinese ethics and Indian thought, all speak of a single Asiatic peace...", wrote Kakuzo Okakura, a Japanese intellectual, to Tagore in 1903 (Mishra 230).

"Today, whether you are a resident of Delhi or Dili, Durban or Darwin, whether you are from Noida or New York, it is simply not realistic to think only in terms of your own country. **Global forces press** in from every conceivable direction." (Taroor 3)

When there is a conflict between nations, the weaker communities on both sides are the greatest sufferers. In earlier times, the conquered people were reduced to slavery. After the Hannibalic wars, whole hordes of slaves from the East were brought to work in the plantations of Southern Italy. They formed the working class from 2nd century BC to 6th century AD. (Toynbee I, 155). Unexplainably, a spiritual force can come into the picture to strengthen the weakest in their condition of helplessness. For example, during the interactions between the upper classes in Rome and their helpless slaves, the religious perceptions of the slaves won out in the end; their gods survived not the gods or the philosophies of the masters (Toynbee I, 156). The philosophies of the dominant classes were too abstract and too impersonal to appeal to the masses, and ultimately they yielded to the spiritual insights and divinities of the lower classes.

There were encounters of cultures not only in Rome, but also on the borders where the Roman top brass interacted with barbarians creating veritable "melting-pots" of cultures. There was mutual assimilation, both sides picking up bits and pieces of each other's culture, often the less worthy elements. It is not the noblest qualities that communicate fastest, but the art of war (Toynbee II, 142) or skills of exploitative trade. In the process of this mutual sharing, some representatives of the Roman elite sank to the level of the people they had subjugated (Toynbee II, 41). Similarly, in this globalized world an erosion of cultures and values is continuously taking place, every community picking up the less valuable elements from the other. There is no criterion for selection, there is no integrating principle. There is a danger that the worthless elements gradually will constitute the "common ground".

On the other hand, a meeting of cultures can be stimulating when the best is shared in each other's culture. In order that this may happen, there should be an appreciation of one community by the other. Pretensions to cultural or civilizational superiority on the side of those who are technologically or economically advanced is unrealistic. We need to give equal respect to the many streams of cultures and civilizations that contribute to the ultimate destiny of the human race. The great works of Greek thinkers and writers were introduced to the Western world by Arabic scholars (Toynbee I, 193). It was a great contribution of the East to the West. Modern society ought to be grateful to the wisdom and knowledge of ancient civilizations like those of Egypt, Greece, India and China which have gone into shaping the modern world today. Civilizations progress through mutual borrowing. The Arabic numerals, for example, are of Indian origin; the printed word of Chinese. Similar Asian contribution in the past has been great (Mishra 299). More is possible, and it will be all the greater when our debt to the West is also equally recognized.

11. Technical Progress Alone Is not Civilization

Unfortunately in our times, ".... mass education, cheap consumer goods, the popular press and mass entertainment are combined with deeply felt **rootlessness**, confusion and *anomie*" (Mishra 302) .

"*Dharma*" *is rooted in culture than in politics* (Das 60) .

Unfortunately, today we judge a society's stature by its technological advance. Toynbee considers it exalting the *Homo Faber* above *Homo Sapiens*, placing the technician above the philosopher. He contends that a civilization has often declined while technique moved ahead, and vice versa. For example, *Homo Pictor* has declined while *Homo Faber* has flourished; art has suffered while industry has bloomed (Toynbee I, 230) . He says, it was precisely when the Athenian economy expanded with plantation-farming for export that they introduced slavery into the colonies of Agrigentum and Sicily. This was not a step forward for the Athenian civilization (Toynbee I, 232) .

Something similar would happen again during the post-Hannibalic period in Roman history when oriental slaves were brought on a large scale to work in the estates owned by the Roman elite. While it brought increased productivity and profits, it drove the pauperized peasants into the cities creating a parasitic urban proletariat. It was the beginning of the collapse of the Roman system which was to reach its climax in the 4th century (Toynbee I, 233) . The mass production-centres in our times give a similar impression. Unless there is intelligent evaluation of the newly emerging situation in the new **urban agglomerations** in the Developing World, especially in Asia, major difficulties can arise in the days to come. The saving factor remains that "family customs have been among the slowest of all Asian Institutions to change" (Jacques 158) .

We do not deny that technological skills and economic assets are of enormous importance; however, what is even more important are the less visible assets like the values that a society lives by, relationships that hold it together, ideals it places before its members, spiritual dreams it assiduously pursues. These make *Homo* truly *Sapiens.* In the East, the wise man is held in high esteem. We need to affirm this, because in today's globalized society the invisible values that gave birth to different cultures and civilizations are getting marginalized and forgotten. The manager or the technocrat of our days stands for impersonal technology, not for the community or its interests (Schivelbush 256); his task is to rationalize processes, which means increased production and greater competitiveness. It is true, rationalization helps to reduce prices and ensure easier availability of the goods produced; and the improvement in the quality of consumer goods adds to their competitiveness (Schivelbusch 279).

However, we cannot afford to forget the human person and his/her individuality, communities and their values, human society and civilizational heritages. There is an abundance of moral rhetoric in today's political statements, but there is no seriousness. "None of the mission statements I have come across says anything worth saying, unless you are a fan of badly written platitudes." (Hobsbawm 2)

12. Economic Success Is not Everything; It Must be Guided

Intelligent human beings can act in a contradictory manner. For example, as John Steinbeck says, "The things we admire in men, kindness and generosity, openness, honesty, understanding and feeling, are the concomitants of failure in our system. And those traits we detest, sharpness, greed, acquisitiveness, meanness, egotism and self-interest, are the traits of success. And while men admire the quality of the first they love the produce of the second." (Das 182)

A new educated elite has emerged with special advantages, "superior classes", presumptuous and morally unsatisfactory elite enjoying economic and cultural privileges. This is the new class division: university certificate holders and others. They amass money, their fortunes come from business and political power, they flaunt wealth—football players, media stars, lottery winners (Hobsbawm 200).

Schools of Economy today forget that even an economic world order could not be built on economic foundations alone (Toynbee I, 337). Universal values of fairness cannot be sacrificed to the self-interest of a few who control affairs. While it is true that the market is productive and raises living standards, it tends to concentrate wealth in the hands of a few, pass on environmental costs to society and to abuse workers and consumers. "Markets must be tamed and tempered." (Stiglitz xiii) Big corporations and bankers should not be allowed to have recourse to fraudulent and unethical ways (Stiglitz xxiii) nor take advantage of the weaker sections of people. Democracy cannot be limited to a ritual of periodic elections, it must listen to people's voices. Poor governance in many countries is due to too cosy relationship among business houses, civil servants, and politicians. Large business houses have excessive power (Das 158).

The Government should play a regulating role, when, for example, producers seek to make profit by making their products more addictive or are indifferent to the damage they inflict on the environment (Stigltiz xviii), or consumer interests are ignored. The ethical consciousness in society has to be kept alive and the Market too must be given a "moral character". The movers of the economy seem to have lost their "moral compass" (Stiglitz xvii). The consequence is the constant restlessness we notice in society. Anger is intensifying. The Spanish Youth, marginalized by their economy, called themselves "los indignados" (the angry) (Stiglitz x). When genuine grievance gets mixed up with anger engineered by people with political interests, matters become more complicated. In many places we are in such situations. Our options become limited.

Certainly street revolutions are not always the right answer to social problems. However, we are still to find other effective alternatives. People do not have sufficient confidence in the ideas or in the sincerity of the leadership. Today, it is not only the anger of the working class that is growing, but that of the "middle class" as well. There is too much of the sense of frustrated expectation among them. Moises Naim says that the middle class is the faster growing segment in the world, "and it will be the main cause of coming conflicts. They have anger from unfulfilled expectation. The middle class is shifting from rich countries to the poor countries" (Das 179). This is what makes it difficult to say whether street demonstrations are signs of regeneration and self-confidence or of anarchy (Das 19), or plain political irresponsibility. If the prompters of protest inspire violence in addition, the scenario changes dramatically. There are enough instances of violent citizens making themselves stronger than the state, joining politics and becoming lawmakers. Criminality in politics is in the ascendant (Das 200 – 203).

In any case, if a political structure only reinforces the unfair system rather than correct it, hard days are ahead. The anxiety is that the rewards of the new economy are not always going to the most deserving. "Much of this vast rise in private wealth has gone to a small segment of the ultra-rich...." (Hobsbawm 50) Ram Charan says, "Some who are in the know tell me that the key decisions in the global financial system are made by a cozy group of fifty or fewer people from these firms. They move frequently from one company to another." (Charan 42) Even considering this statement an exaggeration, there seems to be some truth in it. The 1% that are earning most are not great thinkers or innovators (Stiglitz 27), they are self-rewarding executives. They are people, it is alleged, who know how to manage the Government machinery for their own interests. They know how to skirt the law, shape it in their favour, take advantage of the poor (Stiglitz 37); who know how to win monopolies, get control over natural resources (Stiglitz 49), sell to the Government above market prices (Stiglitz 40), get taxes and wages lowered (Stiglitz 63), silence unions (Stiglitz 64), fire workers (Stiglitz 67), marginalize minority groups (Stiglitz 68); push austerity programmes to the areas of medical care, health, education in aid of the poor (Stiglitz 230 – 231). For them even unemployment serves a useful purpose, since it will create a climate that favours the lowering of wages (Stiglitz 263).

"Inequality and unemployment grow as highly mobile corporations continually move around the world in search of cheap labour and high profits, evading taxation and therefore draining much-needed investment in welfare systems for ageing populations. " (Mishra 296) Monopolists in general are not good innovators (Stiglitz 46) . The mighty task they seem to perform may be described as macro-mismanagement. And ultimately the bubble bursts (Stiglitz 82) . Looking more closely at the Third World, we notice that "Much of the 'emerging' world now stands to repeat, on an ominously large scale, the West's tortured and often tragic experience of modern 'development' . In India and China, the pursuit of economic growth at all costs has created a gaudy elite, but it has also widened already alarming social and economic disparities" (Mishra 307) . Uneven distribution prompts people to join populist movements, or follow ethnocratic politicians, or fundamentalist radicals, nationalistic fanatics (Mishra 308) . This is the context in which inter-national rivalries get accentuated (Mishra 309) . The tragedy is that the privileged Third World minority aspire for nothing higher than the conveniences and gadgets of their Western consumer counterparts (Mishra 308) .

13. Human Values and Fairness Must Be Given a Place in the Economy

A Call for Social Responsibility

"*Companies are competing against countries—not just other companies.*" (*Charan 7*)

Following Hegel " *One might describe history as a dialogue between societies, in which those with grave internal contradictions fail and are succeeded by others that manage to overcome those contradictions*" (*Fukuyama 61*) .

Growing inequality in the economy can spell doom for the economy itself, because it impairs efficiency by weakening the motivation of the workers and undermines growth by distorting market mechanisms or introducing asymmetries and unfairness in competition (Stiglitz 6) . If you create wealth, society is enriched. If you take it from others through dishonesty or raising prices or adulterating goods, it is impoverished (Stiglitz 32). Unequal societies create continuous political instability; here Stiglitz quotes the example of Latin America (Stiglitz 83 – 84). On the contrary, in more egalitarian societies people work hard and seek to preserve social cohesion (Stiglitz 77). It is in such societies that high levels of social responsibility are achieved and rules for environment protection respected (Stiglitz 100). There, people see the need to invest in infrastructure, education, health and research (Stiglitz 93). Mutual trust is generated. Business leadership with high sense of *dharma* will be trusted (Das 160). It is such a society that creates a climate for good economy. Mutual trust is an invaluable social capital (Stiglitz 121).

So it is evident that human values must be given a place in economy for the very success of economy. The Market becomes inefficient if it ignores the human dimension (Stiglitz xi-xii). Freedom for enterprise and venture must combine with responsibility for the common good (Toynbee I, 339). Some of cities in the Developing World are growing up as monsters, serving a vigorous economy but not the interests of communities nor the natural environment. Unskilled workers are reduced to conditions less than human. Meanwhile consumerism keeps sapping physical stamina, moral energies getting exhausted, sources of ethical inspiration going dry. Consequences can be summarized in the words of Sebastian Haffner writing about his own country in 1923: It is as though "an entire generation had a spiritual organ removed: an organ that gives human beings constancy, balance, even gravity". No space is left for "conscience, reason, wisdom of experience, fidelity to principles, morality and piety" (Schivelbusch 270).

The slave-owning states of America and the slave-using plantations of the later Roman period were prosperous. But that prosperity was built on exploitation. The only difference is that today's "slaves" are better paid, better fed and better entertained. But we should not forget that the Roman slaves also were provided with "bread and circus" (food and entertainment). The painful reality was that their destinies were not in their own hands. People in our times little realize how much of their self-determination (freedom) and self-articulation (creativity) is stifled under an oppressive economy. Our society is fast becoming more and more impersonal with scope for human growth narrowing every day. This type of economic success cannot become the measure of civilization. The true measure of civilization according to Toynbee is the ability for self-determination and the art of self-articulation (Toynbee I, 225). The economy of our days needs values to give it a direction and a destiny. "When there was neither kingdom, nor king; there was neither governance, nor governor, the people protected themselves by dharma." (Mahabharata, XII. 59. 14)

Dawson says, as life passed out of Hellenic civilization, there was the gradual disappearance of those vital traits in which the spirit of their earlier culture was embodied... and individual native qualities came to be choked within the context of a formless, cosmopolitan society, with no roots in the past and no contact with a particular region. This was the degradation of the Greek type (Dawson 63). Is some form of degradation of our cultures and civilizations taking place at a massive scale today?

14. Any Effort towards Regimentation Invites Resistance

"*Rome became more and more a predatory state that lived by war and plunder, and exhausted her own strength with that of her victims.*" (*Dawson 67*)

The global crisis is that the publics of the major countries do not trust the political or financial elites...Hence the political elite find it hard to manage affairs. "*Without public trust, it is impossible.*" (*Friedman xxi-xxii*)

The era of the World Wars introduced many elements of regimentation into social life. The memories of military discipline, straight lines, similar dress for men and women, imposition of ideas from above lingered on even afterwards. Rationalization of the economy and production turned out to be another form of regimentation: rigid schedules, mass assemblies, record performance. Mass-produced goods came in abundance in compensation, but that alone could not satisfy human longing for spontaneity. There was a reaction, more especially in Western society: rejection of restraints, chaotic movement of tourists, weird fashions, deafening jazz and rock, irresponsible movies (Schivelbusch 268). The conclusion of the War brought further rejection of restraints: e. g. the rigidities of the military code, the high ideals of nationalism, ideological zeal, and hypocritical moral codes. The external expressions of such reactions were imitated in Asia and other continents with little understanding of the reasons for the trends in the world's leading nations.

Then came the Cold War, each side over-confident about its ideologies and theoretical stands. It created a climate of fierce challenging of opponents, denunciation of each other's points of view, and production of abundant propaganda material (anti-communist on the one side and anti-capitalist on the other) with evident exaggerations on both sides. There was diverse reading of history in support of each one's ideology and military strategy. Everyone was too sure of his/her theoretical stand; everyone wanted to play the "prophet". Denunciation of what you differ from became close to a moral precept.

Once again there was a reaction to excessive ideological zeal. Recent postmodernist trends have been to reject all ideologies, meta-narratives, any pretension to a comprehensive explanation of reality (religious or philosophical), as having no validity. More and more people begin to adopt the attitude that each person is "thrown into the world" to make meaning and shape codes of conduct in the best way he/she can.

Existentialism arises out of harsh experiences like those that society experienced during the World Wars: a recognition of "man's incapacity to direct civilization along any precise course" and "the gap between the actions of men and their stubbornly professed ideals" (Barzun 755). For many, this was evidence enough that humanity has no destiny. But self-reduction to helplessness is not an intelligent solution to problems. But in this sense of impotence, people began to make some meaning of life, accommodating to the rationalization of the economy, rejoicing in high levels of production and yielding to ardent habits of consumerism. If this path of rationalization is pursued to its furthest possible limits, human beings will be reduced to the status of mere producers and consumers, victims of mind-manipulation by commercial advertisements and political propaganda. Society gradually becomes impersonal and even inhuman.

The War-era also brought defence policies of nations too much under the influence of industrial giants who produced weapons. And the long term disadvantage of it was that arms-producing companies and nations developed a vested interest in keeping international tensions, insurgencies, and local conflicts, going. Arms control became impossible; arms-race became not the "sports of kings" like in medieval times, but the source of income for arms-producers. Today, people engaged in ethnic wars, ideological dissenters, secessionists... all fall victims to the manipulations of arms-traders, though they little realize this truth. Poor Third world countries are the greatest victims. But they consider themselves heroes when they keep struggling against their neighbours. Toynbee says that the stature of a civilization is to be judged by the progress towards self-determination (Toynbee I, 324), not an abundance of consumer goods. It should stand for freedom for thought, intellectual activities, self-organization and self-expression, with utmost scope for creativity, always with a strong sense of social and cosmic responsibility. This is what is precisely lost in a value-less economy.

15. Social Idealism Leads to a Spiritual Search

"*The central conviction which has dominated my mind ever since I began to write is the conviction that the society or culture which has lost its spiritual roots is a dying culture, however prosperous it may appear externally.*" (Dawson xxxi)

Spiritual blindness gives rise to a " a kind of hubris which leads to the frustration of social idealism and society's turning away from those principles it professes to be following" (Mulloy at Dawson xxxix).

Under pressure of circumstances people are compelled to develop new skills. That is how different societies develop different skills and different attitude to life. Forbidden to engage themselves in other forms of economic activities in the West, Jews developed the skill for trade and finance; so did the Parsees in India and the Armenians and Georgians under the Ottomans (Toynbee I, 164). People's outlook also is conditioned by their historic experiences. Greeks developed an aesthetic outlook, Indians a religious vision of reality, the West a fascination for machinery and parliamentary system and military mobilization (Toynbee I, 284). This is how cultural/civilizational differentiation takes place between communities. Taking such diversity for granted, today we are in search of a universally appealing worldview or perspective, a leading concept or vision, and generally acceptable moral norms which people have called "global ethics", which would give even to our material culture a transcending quality.

Toynbee argues that progress of a civilization is to be measured by its capacity to move steadily to higher levels of human activity, e. g. from the enhancement of practical efficiency to achievements in aesthetic and intellectual fields, thus moving from lower sphere of action to a higher one. He calls it "etherialization". At the earliest stages of the existence of a society, it seeks to defend itself against the harshness of nature or pressure from a neighbouring adversary. If it is successful in this endeavour, it begins to address the challenges it faces in a higher sphere of action, moving on to various forms of self-articulation and self-determination (Toynbee I, 236) . Thus a growing civilization moves its concern from its achievements in the outer sphere to those in the inner, thus enriching the collective personality of the civilization (Toynbee I, 246) . This inward journey is nothing unfamiliar to the Asian peoples. Rabindra Nath Tagore, while rejoicing over Japan's victory over Russia in 1905, said, " Asia today is set to realizing herself consciously, and thence with vigour. She has understood, know thyself—that is the road to freedom. In imitating others is destruction. " (Mishra 225) Mahatma Gandhi's understanding of civilization was something similar; he said that " true civilization is about self-knowledge and spiritual strength" (Mishra 228) .

This movement from the outer to the inner becomes necessary when a society is compelled to make certain basic options, especially in the moral sphere (Toynbee I, 244) , e. g. when the latest technical advance a society makes becomes a tool for enslaving its weaker members or is used for the destruction of a sister-society or a sister-civilization. The construction of the pyramids, for example, stood for a great measure of technical advance; but they were built on oppression (Toynbee I, 245) . Napoleonic wars carried the liberating ideas of the French Revolution and the advanced technology of the French nation, but these blessings went only to aggravate the horrors of war (Toynbee I, 330) .

Toynbee laments that today's mass education does not include what he calls "etherialization" of interest and motivation (Toynbee I, 339) . Writing in our own days, Gurucharan Das expresses a similar concern, emphasizing the need of education in citizenship and "public dharma" (Das 148) . He insists on inculcating moral habits rather than shouting moral slogans (Das 140) . The present system of education, Toynbee feels, is defective; it leads to the "vulgarization" of tastes in our society, as it happened in the case of the urban masses in Rome who were happy enough to be supplied "bread and circus" . Ardent consumers in our times little realize how much they are being "used" by profit-makers, being treated to the trivializing entertainment provided by commercial entrepreneurs and taken advantage of by the propaganda of interested parties like political ideologues or media barons. This is the modern form of slavery to which we already referred. The pity is all the greater when the victims are not aware how they are being 'used' (Toynbee I, 340).

16. The Future Belongs to the Weakest

"For nearly all of world history the richest and most developed societies have been in Asia." (*Ponting 9*)

"For most people in Europe and America the history of the twentieth century is still largely defined by the two world wars and the long nuclear stand-off with Soviet communism. But it is now clearer that the central event of the last century for the majority of world's population was the **intellectual and political awakening of Asia** *and its emergence from the ruins of both Asian and European empires."* (*Mishra 8*)

Hobsbawm calls the present period of history an "era…that has lost its bearings and which in the early years of the new millennium looks forward with more troubled perplexity than I recall in a long lifetime, guideless and mapless, to an unrecognizable future" (Hobsbawm ix). However, as Toynbee sees it, there is redemption for all. In the hardest times, destiny unfailingly intervenes in behalf of the weakest. The future belongs to the exploited masses who allow themselves to be led by the enticement of 'etherilization'. They have aspirations, they have energies. Philosophical theories and ideologies developed by the elite ate abstract, cold, distant, impersonal and elusive. But spiritual insights entertained by the oppressed masses are dynamic. But they have to make a decisive choice between a violent approach or a peaceful one: 1) ongoing exploitation can create to a sense of helplessness, stir up collective anger and end up with a revolution; that is what happened in France, Russia, China and other places. 2) But it can also lead to the stirrings of the inner person for a new search for deeper meaning and fulfilment. The energy so generated can provide new spiritual insights lighting up a new path to unforeseen destinies. Nietzsche said, "One must possess a chaos within to give birth to a star."

It is at the breakup of an old order, that a new one comes into existence. Toynbee sees Abraham emerging at the disintegration of the Sumerian civilization, Moses during the decadence of the "New Empire" in Egypt (Toynbee I, 442), each time from among the most oppressed people. Judaism takes birth among the Jews who were most hard-pressed and helpless during their Babylonian exile, "by the waters of Babylon". In fact, Toynbee believes that the Babylonian exploitation called into existence two religious movements: Zoroastrianism and Judaism. Christianity rose from among the exploited Roman labour-class. Buddha and Mohammed too appeared when an old order was passing away. A new world can be born only through a "tremendous spiritual travail" (Toynbee I, 443). Possibly, we are beginning to experience the pains. While the globalized economy seems to offer better living conditions to more human beings than ever before, wherever people are condemned to live in a society without really belonging to it (in it, not of it), it is exploitation; the choice that remains is between a violent and a gentle way of facing the ordeal.

Marx proposed a violent solution. It has been tried out in different ways and different places, with different results. A milder approach too has been attempted. Buddha had no violent answers, but he changed the world (Toynbee I, 457). The message of Jesus too was one of peace. His inspiration caught the imagination of the oriental slaves in Roman Italy who needed to cling to a spiritual ideology for strength and inner motivation. It was their example that inspired their Roman masters who were living in a spiritual vacuum. And the spiritual spark caught on. Hindu reformers like Chaitanya, Tukkaram, Mirabai, Ramakrishna, Aurobindo, Vivekananda, Sankardev, Mahatma Gandhi and others did not suggest violent solutions to the problems of the weaker communities. But they sustained their hopes. In the Western world, groups like the English Quakers, the German Anabaptists in Moravia, the Dutch Mennonites sought to offer a gentle approach to the problems of the down-trodden people whom Toynbee calls the "internal proletariat" (Toynbee I, 456). Quakers prospered and they ceased to belong to the proletariat, showing the validity of maxims like "meek shall inherit the land", and "honesty is the best policy". Buddhism brought solace to the proletariat in China. The Taoist and Confucian formulae too were peaceful, but world-transformative.

Keeping true to Toynbee's vocabulary, the "internal proletariat" of the globalized world today are seeking a new Inspiration, a Fresh Enlightenment, a relevant spiritual insight, a Peaceful Revolution. Only, it has to be made intelligible by the creative minority that proposes it. That is the mission of intellectuals today. The proposal should be based on the emerging realities (Toynbee I, 489) and should make an appeal to the subconscious psyche of the communities concerned (Toynbee II, 316). Norms proposed for inter-relationship among people and communities should reflect the infra-personal layers of the subconscious psyche (Toynbee II, 317). They should mirror the internal harmony that the creative leaders has consciously cultivated (Toynbee II, 317 – 318). For, we know too well "We are betrayed by what is false within" (Meredith, G, *Love's Grave*).

17. The Mission of Intellectuals: to Become the "Creative Minority" that Helps Society to Make the Right Choices for the Common Good

An interlocking of interests is taking place. "The growing ties between nations over the last decade have made every one of them less inclined to allow their trade partners to go under." (Sharma 252)

The British military historian Basil Liddell Hart said, "I used to think that the causes of war were predominantly economic. Then I came to think that they were more psychological. I am now coming to think that they are decisively 'personal' arising from the defects and ambitions of those who have the power to influence the currents of nations." (Khanna xxiii) *A transformation of the individuals is called for.*

In this respect, the globalized world offers a vast variety of ideas and choices. But society itself seems to be in the grip of diverse uncertainties. Not every concept generated in one part of the world or by a civilization finds ready acceptance in another. While Western technology found ready welcome, neither the concepts of social relationships nor the attitude to religion prevailing in the West have found equal acceptability. While the traditions of Western democracy have attracted several Asian countries, certain regimes believe in unlimited powers. While Western theories about free enterprise are winning favour day by day, not all feel equally convinced.

Moreover, certain new trends seem to be emerging: "Wealth is moving from North to South, and so are jobs. Companies in the south, big and small, have a fierce entrepreneurial drive. Many are revelling in double-digit revenue growth, bringing jobs and prosperity to their home countries." (Charan 5) Further, "Postwar Asian experience demonstrated that later modernizers were actually advantaged relative to more established industrial powers, just as earlier liberal trade theories had predicted" (Fukuyama 101) . Reflecting carefully over these statements, we need to remember that economic breakthroughs are not everything. Many perceptions and hopes are mere bubbles, and are based on passing trends.

When any Region of the World rejoices overmuch on its economic or military achievements, the following words may have a sobering effect, "What is most striking… is the speed of the Roman Empire's collapse. In just five decades, the population of Rome itself fell by three-quarters. Archaeological evidence from the fifth century—interior housing, more primitive pottery, fewer coins, small cattle—shows that the benign influence of Rome diminished rapidly in the rest of Western Europe. What one historian has called 'the end of civilization' came within the span of a single generation" (Ferguson 292). Ferguson was addressing this message to the leading nations of the world with falling populations. None needs to be too sure.

There may be differences of perceptions among nations about free enterprise or regulated economy, but there will not be much difference about the need for a global ethic, and an equitable world order, a spiritual vision of the human and cosmic reality. We have no choice but to respond to reality. "This active response is an awakening to a sense of unity which broadens and deepens as the vision expands from the unity of mankind, through the unity of the cosmos...." (Toynbee I, 492) This takes place spontaneously when there is a true encounter of cultures and civilizations. "The great civilizations of the past have often been focused on their own cultures. In the future, they will increasingly *study the greatness of other civilizations.*" (*Martin 388*) *For example,* Toynbee holds that "*The spiritual event that had liberated Gandhi's 'soul force'* was an encounter, in the sanctuary of the soul, between the spirit of Hinduism and the spirit of the Christian Gospel embodied in the life of the Society of Friends" (Toynbee II, 251). This is an amazing statement. No matter how alien the spark, a stimulus is welcome when and where it is needed (Toynbee I, 488). Today we long for such stirring stimuli through genuine encounters between the geniuses of different societies/civilizations.

Also in this case, it will not be the philosophy of the elite that will bring salvation, but the spiritual dynamism of the masses. Though Horace said *Odi Profanum Vulgus* (I hate the vulgar crowd), Carl Jung is of the opinion, "Great innovations never come from above; they invariably come from below... (from) the much-derided silent folk of the land—those who are less infected with academic prejudices than great celebrities are wont to be" (Modern Man in Search of a Soul pp 243 – 244, as quoted at Toynbee I, 549)

. Elevated discussions are too elitistic, high-brow, fit for few. It touches the intellect, not the heart. Its main weakness is a lack of vitality. It fails to attract the masses and motivate its propagators. The defeat of ideological theories is a foregone conclusion, unless they link themselves in some manner with the vision of the newly rising generation (Toynbee I, 548). The Possibility is that a stage comes when the philosophy of the dominant classes meets the popular spirituality of the proletariat (Toynbee I, 547). When the heart and the head meet, human life becomes more complete. Scientifically formulated theology too may prove like a philosophically formulated theology an ephemeral success, it does not satisfy the soul. Diverse forms of achievements are possible. Our greatest achievement would be a deeper insight into human nature.

In spite of the immense importance of science, "The most important questions that Man must answer are questions on which Science has nothing to say". He/she must look deeper into himself/herself. Toynbee feels that the agonies of the World Wars helped the Western man to attempt searching his subconscious depths. At that level the human being discovers his/her deeper identity with all his/her weaknesses, but also where he may find himself "wiser, more honest, and less prone to error than the conscious self" (Toynbee II, 119). Bergson H. thinks, "The natural man is buried under the acquired characteristic, but he is still there, practically unchanged." (Toynbee II, 123) It is at the deeper level that a person stands face to face with his true self and the Ultimate Reality. The global agonies today may be an invitation that we look deeper into ourselves to discover certain hidden strengths that got "buried" under acquired tastes and artificial priorities.

Fully in keeping with his thesis, Toynbee argues that it is precisely because spiritual concerns are under strain in modern society that we can be confident that they have a future. Just as physical challenges stimulated physical achievements, so too spiritual challenges may lead modern society to spiritual achievements. "Physically hard environments are apt to be nurseries of mundane achievements, and, on this analogy, it is to be expected that spiritually hard environments will have a stimulating effect on religious endeavour." (Toynbee II, 135) Material prosperity and spiritual poverty will serve as a double-stimulus (Toynbee II, 136). Hosbasbawm says that today's anti-intellectual and crudely materialistic society too "has a greater need of people who have ideas, and of environments in which they can flourish" (Hobsbawm 202). When the intelligence of such great minds meet the spiritual insights of the masses, wonders take place (Hobsbawm 203).

But a creative minority must show the way. That remains the mission of the intellectuals who are transformed by such reflections as we hope we do today. They must return to the masses and help them to move in a new direction. Human destinies are interlinked. We are not at the parting of ways, but at the converging point of human destinies. A transformed society might open up "some hitherto unknown avenue for an unprecedented spiritual advance" in order to prevent fratricidal wars among aggressively nationalistic states (Toynbee II, 322), classes, castes, ideologies, ethnic groups, economic and political interests. "Confucius's pious zeal for the revival of the traditional code of conduct and ritual, and Lao Tse's quietist belief in leaving a free field for the spontaneous operations of the subconscious forces of Wu Wei, had both been inspired by a yearning to touch springs of feeling that might release a saving power of spiritual harmony...." (Toynbee II, 323)

References

Braudel, Fernand, *A History of Civilizations*, Penguin Books, London, 1993.
Charan, Ram, *Global Tilt*, Random House Books, London, 2013.
Danielou, Alain, *India: A Civilization of Differences*, Inner Traditions, Rochester, Vermont, 2005.
Das, Gurucharan, *India Grows at Night*, Allen Lane (Penguin), London, 2012.

Dawson, Christopher, *Dynamics of World History*, ISI Books, Wilmington (Delaware), 2002.

Eric, Hobsbawm, *Fractured Times*, Little, Brown New Delhi (Noida), 2013.

Fernandez-Armesto, *Civilizations*, Pan Books, London, 2001.

Ferguson, Niall, *Civilization*, Allen Lane (Penguin), London, 2011.

Friedman, George, *The Next Decade*, Anchor Books (Randon House), New York, 2012.

Fukuyama, Francis, *The End of History and the Last Man*, Penguin Books, London, 1992.

Jacques, Martin, *When China Rules the World*, Penguin Books, London 2012.

Khanna, Parag, *The Second World*, Allen Lane (Penguin), London, 2008.

Martin, James, *The Meaning of the 21st Century*, Eden Project Books, London, 2006.

Mishra, Pankaj, *From the Ruins of the Empire*, Allen Lane (Penguin), London, 2012.

Ponting, Clive, *World History*, Pimlico Publishers, London, 2000.

Roberts, J. M., *The New Penguin History of the World*, Penguin Books, London, 2004.

Schivelbusch, Wolfgang, *The Culture of Defeat*, Granta books, London, 2004.

Sharma, Ruchir, *Breakout Nations*, Allen Lane (Penguin), London, 2012.

Stiglitz, Joseph, *The Price of Inequality*, Allen Lane (Penguin), London, 2012.

Taroor, Shashi, *Pax Indica*, Allen Lane (Penguin), New Delhi, 2012.

Toynbee, Arnold, *A Study of History*, D. C. Somervell's Abridgement, Vol I & II, Dell Publishing Co., New York, 1969.

Inequality and Justice in a Global World: The Distant Poor

Lydia Amir[*]

Abstract: Poverty is a worldwide phenomenon. I propose that cosmopolitanism is one of the ways for us to eliminate poverty. However, there seem to be difficulties, then, in attempting to ground a worldview that will motivate us to ease global poverty, as well as tensions between capitalist views and the critique of limitless wealth-maximizing and power-seeking that may be necessary for such an endeavor. This essay explores these difficulties.

Key words: poverty; cosmopolitanism; difficulties.

全球不平等与正义：遥远的门扉

Lydia Amir

摘 要：贫困是一个世界性的现象。我认为，世界大同主义是消除贫困的一种有效方法。然而，用世界大同主义来消除贫困，存在很多困难。本文对这些困难进行了详细讨论。

关键词：贫困 世界大同主义 困难

---

[*] Lydia Amir, The School of Media Studies, College of Management Academic Studies, Rishon Lezion, Israel.

The famous French Catholic priest, Henri Grouès, known as Abbé Pierre, said that the first step toward fighting poverty is to face a poor man. Perhaps the 1st century B. C. poem, *On the Nature of Things*, written by the Roman Epicurean philosopher Lucretius, can help explain why this is hard for most of us: poverty seems to be a slipping toward death (III. 59 – 67) . Thus, the greedy accumulation of wealth makes its possessor feel further from death, which, in our thirst for immortal existence (III. 10003 ff.) , we all unconsciously and somewhat consciously fear. Lucretius links the fear of death with a large number of activities destructive either of self or of others, all of which allegedly give expression to a thirst for some sort of continued existence. "The longing for being, the oldest and greatest of all forms of *eros*," which Plutarch describes, is associated with the relation to the things we love and find delightful. For our fear, is above all, a fear of losing, according to Axiochus in the Pseudo-Platonic dialogue of the same name, "this light and the other good things" (365 B-C) .

Fear, then, is a response to value (Nussbaum 1994: 201) , and our fear of loosing translates into a fear of poverty. This leads to a frantic attempt to differentiate ourselves from the poor, in order to sustain the illusion that we are immune to poverty. We entertain ideas that hold the poor responsible for their condition, which, as Candace Clark has shown in her *Misery and Company*, make us feel less sympathy for them, as we reserve that feeling for undeserved misfortune (Clark 1997: 84) . Consequently, we often avoid the domestic poor and ignore global socioeconomic human rights, such as those formulated in Article 25 of the *Universal Declaration of Human Rights* (1992): the right "to a standard of living adequate for the health and well-being of oneself and one's family, including food, clothing, housing, and medical care". As extremely poor people—often physically and mentally stunted owing to malnutrition in infancy, illiterate owing to a lack of schooling, and much preoccupied with their family's survival—can cause little harm or benefit to the politicians who rule them, they too often ignore them. And, as a narrow view of self-interest has been characteristic of American foreign relations policy at least from the end of the Second World War through the Cold War (see Mandle 2006: 28 – 37), we feel entitled to tend to our own gardens, so to speak, and avoid the distant poor.

But in our global world poverty is also created by citizens of affluent Western countries (see Mandle 2006: 114 – 116). Thus, one great challenge to any morally sensitive person today is the extent and severity of global poverty. Since Peter Singer put global poverty on the moral agenda in 1972, Thomas W. Pogge has been leading a sustained campaign against the complacency of the world toward poverty. He has argued convincingly, I believe, that most rich people are not merely failing to help those who are in desperate need, but are responsible for grave injustices. "That the academic justice industry has, by and large, ignored this phenomenon is a stunning failure," he remarkably notes (Pogge 2002: 75); for this indicates that those who live in protected affluence have managed to reconcile themselves, morally, to severe poverty and oppression.

Fifty years ago, the eradication of severe poverty worldwide would have required a major shift in the global income distribution, imposing substantial opportunity costs on the advanced industrialized societies, he argues. Today, the required shift would be small and the opportunity cost for the developed countries barely noticeable. Moreover, earlier generations of European civilization were not committed to moral universalism. Today, by contrast, the equal moral status of all human beings is widely accepted in the developed West. While these two historical changes make our acquiescence in severe poverty abroad harder to justify than it would have been in the past, we are still quite tolerant of the persistence of extensive and severe poverty abroad when it would not cost us much to reduce it dramatically.

John G. Abbarno has convincingly argued for the deficiency of both

Utilitarian and Deontological accounts of justice for the global poor, for the need to supplement the Kantian account with empathy, and for the mutual strengthening of information and feeling needed for actually acting according to one's empathy (Abbarno 2009; 1988).

Whilst repeated broadcasting of pictures and stories has been indeed proven effective in moving politicians to action ("the CNN effect"), I am skeptical about the capacity of the media to consistently create the sort of proximity needed for acting on empathy fed by knowledge. Let me explain. Empathy is a new concept, often used to designate an imaginative reconstruction of another persons' experience, without any particular evaluation of that experience. But psychologists and psychoanalysts sometimes use the term "empathy" to mean some combination of imaginative reconstruction with the judgment that the person is in distress and that this distress is bad. So used, it come close to being pity, although it still might not be identical with it (if, for example, we conclude that one may have pity without imaginative reconstruction).

Although the terminology in these issues is notably confusing, as we often use uncritically terms of empathy, sympathy, compassion, pity, and mercy, I understand from Abbarno's analysis that he considers empathy close to pity. However, we know, and Abbarno acknowledges this as well, that the intensity of pity varies according to proximity. I suggest that two additional components are necessary in order to overcome the partiality of empathy or pity. First, the spectator of poverty should hold either some form of cosmopolitanism or a philanthropic vision of indiscriminate love of humanity. This second option may be what Abbarno has in mind when he writes that "what makes the identification possible is the metaphysical relation which binds humanity" (Abbarno 2009: 93), without explaining what it is. Second, the worldview of the spectator of poverty should be informed by a critique of limitless wealth-maximizing and power-seeking in order to actively work for alleviating poverty.

Whilst urgently needed in contemporary society, this form of critique is rarely approached head on by moral philosophers in capitalist countries. And, whilst both Eastern and Western accounts of love of humanity exist, they have been deemed dangerous, utopian, and unnecessary for the imaginative move described by proponents of "empathy" (however referred to) that drives one to help the distant poor. But I believe that, in contradistinction to the sporadic sympathy for poverty occasioned by catastrophes, the imaginative move that enables one to help needs a worldview to sustain concern and duty to the global poor. Cosmopolitanism, which can sustain such a vision, tends to be viewed as opposed to nationalism or statism; and, as recent events in the news keep showing us, may be contrary to most persons' psychology. There seem to be difficulties, then, in attempting to ground a worldview that will motivate us to ease global poverty, as well as tensions between capitalist views and the critique of limitless wealth-maximizing and power-seeking that may be necessary for such an endeavor. This essay explores these difficulties, beginning by a clarification of the terminology involved.

1. Emotions

In discussions of world poverty, the often uncritically used terms of empathy, sympathy, compassion, pity and mercy, occasion much confusion. Various philosophers have tried to shed light on the erroneous view that these terms are interchangeable. To take a few examples, Irving Singer differentiates between sympathy, compassion and empathy (1994: 111 – 112), Aaron Ben-Ze'ev distinguishes between mercy, pity and compassion (2000: 131) and Martha Nussbaum between compassion, empathy and mercy, whilst acknowledging that her own account and endorsment of compassion is to be viewed as synonymous with pity (2001: 364 – 368).

Lauren Wispé's account of the difference between empathy and sympathy is significant (1986): sympathy "refers to the process whereby the pain of the sufferer is brought home to the observer, leading to an unselfish concern for the other person. Empathy refers to the process whereby one person tries to understand correctly the subjectivity of another person, without prejudice" (Wispé 1986: 320). It may be hard to muster sympathy for a murderer, but one could empathize with that person in order to try to understand him, while still disapproving of his or her actions, Wispé explains. This may be the reason empathy is the notion most psychoanalysts and psychologists prefer.

I will elaborate on pity, compassion, and empathy later on. Let me mention here that "sympathy" is frequently used in British eighteenth-century texts to denote an emotion equivalent to pity. In contemporary usage, pity may be more intense and suggests a greater degree of suffering, both on the part of the afflicted person and on the part of the person having the emotion. People who are wary of acknowledging strong emotion are more likely to admit to "sympathy" than to "pity". But sympathy as standardly used today, in contradistinction to Adam Smith's use (1976), for example, is very different from "empathy": a malevolent person who imagines the situation of another and takes pleasure in her distress may be empathetic, but will surely not be judged sympathetic. Sympathy, like pity, includes a judgment that the other person's distress is bad.

The Greek words *eleos* and *oiktos*, the Roman *pietatem* (nominative *pietas*) or *misericordia*, itself a translation of the Hebrew "hesed", are at the origin of the French *pitié*, the Italian *pietà*, the English *pity*, the German *Mitleid* or *Mitgefruhl*. Compassion has its Latin medieval history (*caritas*), and is sometimes used interchangeably with pity, such as in the sixth chapter of Thomas Hobbes' *Leviathan* (1996).

A. Pity

Plato, Seneca, Epictetus and Locke, Spinoza, Kant and Nietzsche, among others, criticized pity. Following Aristotle, a second tradition, featuring Rousseau as a notable advocate, adopted pity as an ideal. Aristotle argued that pity is a painful emotion directed at another person's misfortune or suffering (*Rhetoric* 1385b13 ff.). Three cognitive elements define the emotions, of which each is necessary and they are jointly sufficient. The first cognitive requirement is that the suffering is serious rather than trivial. The second is the belief that the person does not deserve the suffering. The third is the belief that the possibilities of the person who experiences the emotion are similar to those of the sufferer. This last requirement is exchanged by modern proponents of pity, such as Martha Nussbaum (2001: 300n6), by the view that implicit in the emotion itself is a conception of human flourishing and the major predicaments of human life, which reflects the onlooker's ethical vision (310).

I consider pity problematic on three accounts: first, it weakens, and thus reduces one's capacity to act. Second, it is paternalistic, as it involves our own view of human flourishing even in cases where it does not necessarily fit into the norms of another society (for example, lack of freedom is seen by Western onlookers as a terrible restriction). But, third, and most importantly, it involves judgments that may impair the help needed for the global poor. Judgments of this kind involve the view that poverty is deserved (it's their, or their politicians', fault).

I believe that in order to help the distant poor, a more compassionate and less judgmental view is needed, which overlooks the condition of deserve or undeserved misfortune. Various forms of indiscriminate love of humanity—usually referred to as philanthropy or compassion—have been advocated by Western as well as Eastern thinkers.

B. Eastern and Western Views of the Love of Humanity

The account of Western ideals of an indiscriminate love of humanity should begin with the Stoics, whose idea of *kosmou politès* (each of us is a citizen of the entire universe), was complemented by their innovative notion of philanthropy or love of humanity. However, the Stoics rejected pity for the same reason that they rejected any kind of suffering: it was not conducive to peace of mind.

Their lack of pity or compassion has often been criticized. Moreover, Martha Nussbaum associated the Stoics' ideal of eradicating the emotions with their failure to make social and political reforms: "To respect a slave as a human being is, as Stoic texts make clear, perfectly compatible with perpetuating and endorsing the political institution of slavery," she writes, "By contrast, compassion [synonymous with pity, for Nussbaum] which makes the slave's pain real for oneself and acknowledges its significance, would naturally lead in the direction of material and institutional change." (Nussbaum 1994: 503)

The Stoics did not acknowledge the significance of pain as an absolute value, as they emphasized that virtue is the sole value. Still, it is them who introduced the ideal love of humanity in the West: from its very beginnings in the 3rd century B. C. Stoic thought was anti-sectarian and anti-nationalist, turned firmly against the narrow loyalties that make politics focus on competition between groups rather than on rational deliberation about the good of the all. This revolutionary thought, found also in the Cynics, is better appreciated when compared with Judaic thought.

Although one of the most important laws in Judaism is to love "one's neighbor" —that is, *any other human being*, as oneself, the Jewish view needed the mystical expression of the *Kabbalah* in order to overcome the separation between the Jews and the Gentiles. The *Zohar*, the central text of the Jewish mystical tradition (known as the Kabbalah) made that law the foundation of everything (Epstein 1959). Especially within the *Musar* (self-perfection) school, founded by Rabbi Yisrael Salanter (1810 - 1883), the premise was that if we grow in our relationship to God, we should also grow in our ability to relate in a positive way to our follow human beings (Kaplan 1985: 161 - 165).

Through its emphasis on the love of enemies, Christianity stands out in its call for a love of humanity and rectifies thereby the more narrow traditional Jewish view. This revolutionary Christian vision was early on qualified by St. Augustine's influential commentary, however, on the grounds that it was impossible to implement. Without denying the holiness in loving humans indiscriminately, regardless of propinquity or family ties, as Christ has done, St. Augustine argued that we exist in a moral universe that must extend outward from our intimate and daily relations with one another. No one could have contact with all other people, or even a significant number of them, and therefore our love for persons in the actual groups to which we belong requires our special attention. Through love for the human race is inherently commendable, it would have to be secondary or modulated in its effect: "All... men are to be loved equally; but since you cannot be of assistance to everyone, those especially are to be cared for who are most closely bound to you by place, time, or opportunity, as if by chance. " (Augustine 1958: 126)

Christians—for instance, Martin Luther (1955) —sometimes argue that by his nature man is unable to love: we can only be vehicles of God's love; others, such as Thomas Aquinas, insist that God bestowed the capacity for love on human nature as an act of grace (Aquinas 1945; 1960). Irvin Singer might be right is remarking that "in either event Christianity, which calls itself the religion of love, must face the anomaly of believing that its own practitioners, however devout, cannot love anything except in a secondary manner" (Singer 1994: 117). In practice, moreover, the Christian love of humanity has been refuted by its long history of war against avowed or suspected heretics, and by other values it endorses that undermine love as the sole or central value even in relation to other Christians.

It is in the Eastern traditions that we find more reliable views of indiscriminate love of humanity. In a radical departure from the past in China, Confucius formulates an entirely new ideal, the superior man, one who is wise, humane, and courageous, who is motivated by righteousness instead of profit, and who "studies the way [Tao] and loves man". He never explains how it is possible for one to become a superior man, but seems to imply that "by nature men are alike but through practice they have become far apart".

Mencius, one of his major followers supplied the explanation of how we can know that man can be good. From the fact that all children know how to love their parents and that a human being seeing a child about to fall in a well will instinctively try to save him, Mencius concludes that human nature is originally good, possessing the "Four Beginnings" —humanity (*jen*), righteousness (*i*), propriety (*li*) and wisdom (*chih*) —and the innate knowledge of the good and the innate ability to do good.

A common problem that confronted all the thinkers of the classical age was how to bring order out of chaos. By Mo Tzu's diagnosis, the chaotic was brought about by selfishness and partiality, thus, "partiality should be replaced by universality". Universal (or undifferentiated) love (*chien ai*) is the keystone of Mo Tzu's teaching. Dissatisfied with Confucianism for its gradation in benevolence or "partial love (*pieh ai*)", Mo Tzu exhorts everyone to regard the welfare of others as he regards his own. He urges people to love other people's parents as they love their own, whereas the Confucians, especially Mencius, insist that although one should show love for all, one should show special affection to his own parents. Otherwise there will be no difference between other people's parents and one's own, and family relationship would collapse. Convinced that the practice of universal love would bring peace to the world and happiness to the human being, Mo Tzu took pain to demonstrate that the principle of universal love is grounded simultaneously in its practicability on earth and its divine sanction for Heaven.

Universal love for Mo Tzu is at once the way of man and the way of God. He advocates Love without distinctions, or universal love as superior to graded love. In contrast to most Chinese philosophers, Mo Tzu spoke of Heaven with feeling and conviction; his conception of it is similar to the Western conception of God. The will of Heaven is to be obeyed by the human being and should be the standard of human thought and action. Heaven loves all men, and it is the will of Heaven that men should love one another (Mo Tzu 1963; see Pei 1934).

In the Taoist Chuang Tzu's view, even Mo Tzu's conception of universal love is still narrow and partial. The proper "object" of love is the totality of all things (processes), designed as the Tao. One should not only be in love with life but with death, ugliness, injustice, war, crime and all the other evils (Chuang Tzu 1968).

Most people can feel sympathy for another human being. Buddhism deems it insufficient, for it can be shallow, both morally and emotionally, it scarcely specifies the nature of our bond and it does not indicate that we will do anything to help the other person. We feel that the world is alike for us, but otherwise our sympathetic response may be wholly vague and indeterminate. The kind of love that compassion fosters makes our identification with another human being more consecutive in our behavior than sympathy. The imagination then presents the other not only as a human being who resembles us (if it is a human being) but also as one whose suffering we are prepared to alleviate or take upon ourselves even if we could avoid it.

Among the world religions, Buddhism best understands this employment of the imagination. It seeks to awaken compassion or loving kindness (*Karuna*) and Love (*Metta* in Pali; *Maitri* in Sanskrit) for all equally (*Upekha* in Pali; *Upeksa* in Sanscrit). The Buddha may be revered as a divinity, but he originates as Gautama who progressively earns the reward of Nirvana but then refuses to accept it. His perfection consists in attaining infinite compassion. That is why he refuses to enter into paradise unless all the rest of suffering life is also admitted: "As a mother watches over her child, willing to risk her own life to protect her only child, so with boundless heart should one cherish all living beings, suffusing the whole world with unobstructed loving kindness." (Monroe 1995: 143)

This gesture of universal love constitutes the supreme holiness of the Buddha, but it is also available to other men and women. They themselves, without Christ and without grace, learn how to work out their salvation through the diligence of a comparable love (Cooper 1996) . It is true, though, that this kind of love, as other moral requirements, is only instrumental to salvation; once you are enlighten, you have no need of them.

The Iranien school is one of the most important of the other Eastern religious views. There is no human community, no unity of civilization that is inspired any more of Zarathustra's Mazdeism; and never there has been one that was inspired by the Sufis' mysticism. Yet both proposed concepts of the human being and of love that are homologue to the Christian concepts, that is, to love one's neighbour in the sense of *any human being* (de Rougemont 1996: 228 – 232) . In his impressive survey of world philosophies, David Cooper emphasizes that " many Sufis—at least until they fell foul of Islamic Orthodoxy—liked to stress the affinity between their doctrines and those of Christian anchorites, or even Buddhists " (Cooper 1996: 186; see Monroe 1995: 226 – 228) .

In the West, following mostly the ideal of Christianity, various Modern philosophers, such as Henri Bergson, Arthur Schopenhauer, George Santayana, and Bertrand Russel, defended versions of indiscrimiate love of humanity.

Bergson distinguishes between "closed morality" and "open morality" in the hope that human beings will someday attain a universal society in which the latter supplants the former. As he defines the relevant terms, closed morality arises from instinctual bonds that impose a sense of obligation upon each individual, while open morality consists in sympathetic identification with the creative vitality in all people.

In the open society, which Bergson recognizes to be utopian, we love all members of our species with a love that is God himself. We do the right thing not because the voice of conscience tells us to, but rather through a spiritual impulse to bring the world closer to an absolute goodness. According to Bergson, that is what motivates the saints and the heroes who thereby transcend the limits of their own origins in a particular family, tribe, or country. Nature has provided us with instincts that enforce our allegiance to closed societies such as these. But the saints and heroes experience a love of humanity that Bergson deems superior. It represents a force in nature more ultimate than mechanisms of group survival or solidarity. Through this type of love, as Bergson describes it, the closed society is wholly displaced by the open society that truly shows forth our ultimate being (Bergson 1977).

Bergson thought that the love of humanity is fundamentally different from the love of one's family or even of one's country. David Hume had made a partly similar assertion. He called attention to the fact that the feelings we have for people who are remote from us are much weaker than our sympathy for intimates. He nevertheless thought that humanitarian love is strong in many persons and that it bestows upon strangers or unknown individuals a sympathetic concern that resembles what we experience toward those who are closely related to us. Since sympathy itself is limited in its scope, Hume concluded that we render our sentiments more general through an act of rationality. Our judgments tell us that all humans are alike and so we treat them in a similar fashion, even though the sympathy we actually feel is addressed only toward people we encounter (Hume 1888). At this point Bergson disagrees. To explain how the love of humanity differs from other social loves, he invokes a separate mode of feeling, an intuitional faculty that goes far beyond the intellect.

Arthur Schopenhauer's universal compassion is another ideal worth probing. The kind of love Schopenhauer proposes derives its import from the fact that someone cares enough about others to treat them as joint manifestations of life while also recognizing that they are different realities. Every love of persons does something similar, but only in sympathy and compassion does one focus on the fellowship of living together in a largely hostile world and suffering in the way that animate creatures do. One does not have to agree with

Schopenhauer when he claimed that suffering results from merely being alive, wanting what we need but do not have and never feeling completely satisfied with what we get (Schopenhauer 1969; 1965). Still he might be right in thinking that sympathy and compassion or *Mankelieb* can be directed toward whatever suffering does occur, and that these responses unite us most effectively with all the rest of life.

According to Schopenhauer, no loving response could be more religious or more truly metaphysical than this. He considered his philosophy to be a systematic account of what Western and Eastern mystics intuited, and developed his conception of ethics in contradistinction to the Kantian view which excludes all kinds of fellow-feeling. Although he scarcely tells us how we may attain the sympathy and compassion he so greatly admires, we can infer from his description of the conditions for the salvific negation of the will to the conditions for attaining to compassion: it is through personal tragedy or through conceptual understanding of his philosophy that ethical change can occur.

Adhering to Schopenhauer's philosophy involves accepting that individuation is illusory, however; and, adhering to Bergson's view needs us to accept the mystical implications of Bergsonian intuitionism. Judaism and Christianity are religions, as is Mazdeism, and Mo Tzu's view is based on an argument about Heaven. Sufism is a mystical view and Buddhism requires (few, yet hard to stomach) metaphycial assumptions. This is why I have attempted to establish an ethics of compassion through the thesis of *homo risibilis* or the ridiculous human being, which grounds a philosophy of vulnerability and faillability without metaphysical nor religious assumptions (Amir 2014: 219 – 286).

George Santayana will make clear the difference between a love of humanity based on reason and one based on spirituality. Deemed a "Catholic atheist", this true follower of Schopenhauer attempted in his philosophy to unite materialism and Platonism. The result was, among other things, a very interesting theory of love. A chapter in *Dialogues in Limbo*, entitled "The

Philanthropist", is especially relevant to our concern. In this dialogue Socrates and the Stranger converse about the two ways in which mankind can be loved. One is love coherent with what Santayana calls the life of reason and the other is love which issues from pure spirituality.

Socrates defends a conception of humanistic "philanthropy", against which the Stranger advances the vision of "charity". Philanthropy is a love of mankind which Socrates describes as really being "the love of an idea, and not of actual men and women" (Santayana 1925: 155). Philanthropy directs itself toward what is truly good for human beings; it is geared to the realities of their nature and aims for a "perfect humanity" that ideally would provide fulfillment, regardless of what some individual may happen to desire. The Stranger claims that "any adoration of mankind is mere sentimentality, killed by contact with actual men and women. Towards actual people a doting love signifies silliness in the lover and injury to the beloved, until that love is chastened into charity" (ibid.). Santayana employs the word "charity" in approximation of the mediaeval concept (*caritas*) and not as the word is more commonly used nowadays. He considers charity godlike even if it exists only in human beings. The Stranger calls it "a sober and profound compassion … succoring distress everywhere and helping all to endure their humanity and to renounce it" (ibid.).

In this notion of charity we may recognize the disposition that Santayana generally assigns to pure spirit. Transcending the search for perfection and aspiring towards emancipation from the world, the spiritual life is an exclusive commitment to charity. The Stranger remarks that charity "is less than philanthropy in that it expects the defeat of man's natural desires and accepts that defeat; and it is more than philanthropy in that, in the face of defeat, it brings consolation" (139). Socrates sums this discussion with the suggestion that "philanthropy is a sentiment proper to man in view of his desired perfection, and charity a sentiment proper to a god, or to a man inspired by a god, in view of the necessary imperfection of all living creatures" (156 – 157).

Santayana leaves the dialogue with this minimal synthesis between the two ideals, the Greek and the Indian. The former seeks a harmony of interests, whereas the latter is a single-minded pursuit that would seem to cast aside everything but itself. The humanistic and pluralistic reach of Santayana's philosophy of love appears more prominently in his posthumous essay entitled "Friendship". His remarks there serve as a corrective to the charge that Santayana's later philosophy seeks to orient all human relations toward the achievement of spiritual purity. For he insists on the differences between friendship and charity. The latter "not being intrinsic either to love or to friendship requires the intervention of imaginative reason, by which we detach ourselves from our accidental persons and circumstances and feel the equal reality of all other persons in all other plights" (Santayana 1968: 88). Santayana extols the infinite beauty in charity, but he points out that love or friendship or philanthropy can also be beautiful.

Finally, George Santayana's friend, the great British philosopher Bertrand Russell, testifies in the first lines of his autobiography that three passions have governed his life: "The longing for love, the search for knowledge, and unbearable pity for the suffering of mankind." (Russell 1967: 9) He sounds like Schopenhauer when he writes, "united with his fellow-men by the strongest of all ties, the tie of a common doom, the free man finds that a new vision is with him always, shedding over every daily task the light of love." (Russell 1918: 56) He relates himself to Buddhism when he says, "Buddha is said to have asserted that he could not be happy so long as even one human being was suffering. This is carrying things to an extreme and, if taken literally, would be excessive, but it illustrates that universalizing of feeling of which I am speaking." (Russell 1956: 182) And, Russell relates himself to Spinoza when he describes the latter thus: "Spinoza, who was perhaps the best example of the way of feeling of which I am speaking, remained completely calm at all times, and in the last day of his life preserved the same friendly interest in others as he had shown in days of health." (183 – 184)

Closely parallel to the development of impersonal thought is the development of impersonal feeling, Russell argues, which is at least equally important and which ought equally to result from a philosophical outlook. This is so because our desires, like our senses, are primarily self-centered, and their egocentric character interferes with our ethics. In the one case, as in the other, what is to be aimed at is not a complete absence of the animal equipment that is necessary for life but the addition to it of something wider, more general, and less bound up with personal circumstances. We should not admire a parent who had no more affection for his own children than for those of others, but we should admire a man who from love of his own children is led to a general benevolence. We should not admire a man, if such a man there were, who was so indifferent to food as to become undernourished, but we should admire the man who from knowledge of his own need of food is led to a general sympathy with the hungry (see Kuntz 1986: 107f).

Russell argues that what philosophy should do in matters of feelings is very closely analogous to what it should do in matters of thought. It should not subtract from the personal life but should add to it. Just as the philosopher's intellectual survey is wider than that of an uneducated man, so also the scope of his desires and interests should be wider. A man who has acquired a philosophical way of feeling, and not only of thinking, will note what things seem to him good and bad in his own experience, and will wish to secure the former and avoid the latter for others as well as for himself.

Wisdom has an affective aspect, since "comprehensiveness alone... is not enough to constitute wisdom. There must be, also, a certain awareness of the ends of human life... perhaps one could stretch the comprehensiveness that constitutes wisdom to include not only intellect but also feeling. It is by no means uncommon to find men whose knowledge is wide but whose feelings are narrow. " Such men lack what Russel is calling wisdom (Russell 1956: 174) . For example, the best way to overcome the fear of death, according to Russell, is to make one's interests gradually wider and more impersonal, until "bit by bit the walls of the ego recede, and your life becomes increasingly merged in the universal life" (52) . "The good life," he writes, "is one inspired by love and guided by knowledge. " (Russell 1957: 56)

I am not sure whether Russell advocates an ideal of indiscriminate love, although at times, he sounds as if he is. But as Russell is an admirer of Spinoza's ethics, as Kenneth Blackwell convincingly argues (1985), his is a dynamic vision that emphasizes the *process* of extending comprehensiveness, both intellectual and emotional. Such emphasis characterizes Spinoza's ethics.

Many thinkers criticized the ideal of indiscriminate love. Sigmund Freud's and Karl Popper's critiques are worth mentioning, I believe, for the popularity of the former and the political implications emphasized by the latter.

Freud recognizes that civilization itself develops by means of a love that is essential for its existence. This is the love that binds the members of a group who have common interests. It consists of sublimations that have turned into religious or humanitarian love—the love of God as well as attempts to love one's neighbor and even one's enemy. Freud considered such love to be aim-inhibited since he believes that all love, however remote from apparent sexuality, reduces to the drive for libidinal satisfaction. Though he is convinced that religious and humanitarian types of love are generally unrealistic, and therefore morally suspect, Freud explains their occurrence in terms of civilization's justifiable need to use them as instruments for the control of human aggressiveness (Freud 1949a; 1949b; 1961) . He criticizes the possibility and even the desirability of the Judeo-Christian's precepts about a universal love of mankind. In his opinion, they are unreasonable, irrational and they even violate the original nature of man (Freud 1961: 56 – 59) .

Karl Popper views the love of humanity as neither possible nor desirable, yet for different reasons. It is impossible to love mankind as a whole, for we cannot feel the same emotions toward everybody, he argues. Emotionally, we all divide men into those who are near to us, and those who are far from us. "The division of mankind into friend and foe is a most obvious emotional division; and this division is even recognized in the Christian commandment, 'Love thy enemies!'" (Popper 1962: 235) We cannot really love "in the abstract"; we can love only those whom we know. Thus the appeal even to our best emotions, love and compassion, can only tend to divide mankind into different categories. And this will be more true if the appeal is made to lesser emotions and passions.

Consequently, there is a political danger in the rule of love, for he who teaches that not reason but love should rule opens the way for those who rule by hate. Socrates, he believes, saw something of this when he suggested that mistrust or hatred of argument is related to mistrust or hatred of man. Those who do not see that connection at once, who believe in a direct rule of emotional love should consider that love as such certainly does not promote impartiality. And, it cannot do away with conflict either. There would be heaven on earth if we could all love one another, undoubtedly; but the attempt to make heaven on earth invariably produces hell. "Thus we might say," writes Popper, "help your enemies; assist those in distress, even if they hate you; but love only your friends." (237)

Popper is quite prepared, however, to admit that the Christian idea of love is not meant in a purely emotional way:

"I admit that the emotions of love and compassion may sometimes lead to a similar effort [of our imagination]. But I hold that it is humanly impossible for us to love, or to suffer with, a great number of people; nor does it appear to me very desirable that it should, since it would ultimately destroy either our ability to help or the intensity of these very emotions. ...A direct emotional attitude towards the abstract whole of mankind seems to me hardly possible. *We can love mankind only in certain concrete individuals.* But by the use of thought and imagination, we may become ready to help all who need our help. " (Popper: 240; italics added)

As Popper's views concord with contemporary views on the role of empathy in our moral vision, I suggest we probe this relatively new notion.

C. Empathy

Empathy is used to designate an imaginative reconstruction of another persons' experience, without any particular evaluation of that experience. So used, it is quite different from pity and compassion, and is insufficient for both. It may not even be necessary for them. For example, Mother Theresa acted on her compassion regardless of how Indians, possibly influenced by Hindu views of suffering as deserved, felt about their suffering. But psychologists and psychoanalysts sometimes use the term "empathy" to mean some combination of imaginative reconstruction with the judgment that the person is in distress and that this distress is bad. So used, it come close to being pity, although it still might not be identical with it (if, for example, we conclude that one may have compassion without imaginative reconstruction) .

Empathy is a mental ability highly relevant to pity, although it is itself both fallible and morally neutral. Yet, empathy does count for something, as we suspect a person without empathy of an incapacity to recognize humanity. Empathy is obstructed by rejecting unacceptable parts of the self, such as vulnerability, and projecting them unto others. As I have shown elsewhere, reclaiming one's less appealing aspects through the compassionate criticism that intra-personal and self-directed humor is, is conducive to greater empathy.

As empathy understood in this way is insufficient and not even necessary, that which is required to attend consistently to the distant poor is either an indiscriminate, non-judgmental, love of humanity that comprises *an egalitarian worldview*, such as the Christian *caritas* (we are all sinners, thus all suffering) , or the Buddhist *karuna* (we are all ignorant, thus all suffering) , or Schopenhauer's compassion (we all necessarily suffer because of the illusion of individuation), or my own *homo risibilis*-based compassion (we are all equally ridiculous in refusing to acknowledge our necessary failure, vulnerability, and fallibility); or, alternatively, if these loves are considered too mystical (Bergson, Schopenhauer, Chuang Tzu), spiritual (Santayana), religious (Christianity, Mo Tzu) or metaphysical (Buddhism), to attend consistently to the distant poor requires adhering to a form of cosmopolitanism.

2. Cosmopolitanism

Cosmopolitanism means being a "citizen of the world" (from the Greek *kosmos*, "world" and *polis*, "city"). It is usually contrasted with nationalism or statism. Its relevance to the topic at hand is that both nationalists (whose allegiance is to the nation), or statists (whose allegiance is to the state) can justify their preference for attending to domestic social ills. Thus, some form of cosmopolitanism seems to be needed in order to help the distant poor.

Being a cosmopolitan does not necessarily imply the existence of a global state, however. Steven Vertovec and Robin Cohen (2002) have identified six major ways of understanding cosmopolitanism: as a socio-cultural condition, a worldview, a political project to build transnational institutions, a political project based on the recognition of multiple identities, a mode of orientation to the world and a set of specific capabilities allowing adapting to other people and cultures. What unites those visions is a "fundamental devotion to the interests of humanity as a whole" (Robbins 1998: 1); a devoted cosmopolitan, Martha Nussbaum defines it as the ability to "recognize humanity wherever it occurs, and give its fundamental ingredients, reason and moral capacity, our first allegiance and respect." (Nussbaum 2002: 7)

Three major tenets are commonly identified as forming the core of cosmopolitanism (Held 2003: 169; Pogge 1992: 48 - 49): first, individualism—

the individual is the ultimate unit of concern and analysis; second, universalism—every person, irrespective of class, gender, race or religion is equally worthy of respect and recognition by others; finally, generality—the whole humanity (and not just those sharing certain objective characteristics) is entitled to fair and impartial treatment.

Cosmopolitanism has been described as a "middle-path between ethnocentric nationalism and particularist multiculturalism" (Vertovec and Cohen, 2002: 1). On the one hand, it is different from multiculturalism in that it is not limited by the frontiers of individual nation-states. It advocates the recognition of cultural diversity and openness across the globe as a whole, whereas multiculturalism simply accepts difference within nation-states and promotes collective rather than individual identities. On the other hand, cosmopolitanism should be distinguished from nationalism. The most relevant to the present discussion points of disagreement between them concern cultural aspects.

Nationalism denies the general and celebrates the importance of the specific. Nationalists tend to provide ample justifications for why each nationalist movement is unique. For nationalists individuals are culturally and socially embedded beings, the needs of the nation take precedence over individual interests. Cosmopolitanism maintains, amongst other points, that identities are fluid and not geographically or culturally bounded. Most authors who have contributed to the debate have identified themselves as being either on the nationalist or on the cosmopolitan side, although some recent voices have argued that cosmopolitanism is not necessarily exclusive of nationalism.

Because our world is set up on the model of individual, sovereign states, many people believe that each country should take care of its own. However, this sort of parochialism fails because the boundaries of states are not natural facts but socially constructed conventions. The way we parse ourselves (via geography, language, or culture) is rather arbitrary. There is a much stronger sense (based on human biology) that our existence as Homo sapiens is the only real robust boundary that counts among our species.

But recent political events, such as the disintegration of some states into national or religious communities seem to go against the possibility of human identification with the whole of the human race. In the Hellenistic empire as well, there were definite signs that, in contradistinction to the Greek *polis*, too big an empire comprising conflicting cultures was impossible to envisage as a political entity worth identifying with. Although this empire occasioned the birth of the complementary Stoic visions of cosmopolitanism and philanthropy or rational love of humanity, Stoicism remained an ideal.

Even as an ideal, however, a cosmopolitan vision seems insufficient to move citizens to ease global poverty. We can infer this from the following obvious fact: nationalists do not necessarily attend to domestic poverty. A critique of limitless wealth-maximizing and power-seeking seems necessary as well.

3. A Criticism of Wealth and Power

Commenting on the social critique of the Hellenistic and Roman schools of philosophy, Stoicism and Epicureanism, in her groundbreaking *The Therapy of Desire* (1994), Martha Nussbaum writes:

"Nothing seems more urgent in contemporary society than the reasoned critique of limitless wealth-maximizing and power-seeking. And yet these goals are rarely approached head on by moral philosophers, especially those in capitalist countries. " (Nussbaum 1994: 501)

She explains that economic Utilitarians officially endorse wealth-maximizing as a rational end. Other Utilitarians modify the picture in various ways, but rarely as much as the Hellenistic argument requires. Even the contemporary Kantian theory of John Rawls includes wealth and income as among the "primary goods" of which more is always better (see Rawls 1971). She emphasizes that only theories with a clear affiliation to the ancient Greek world—such as the neo-Aristotelian theory of Amartya Sen (see Sen 1982, 1985; Crocker 1992) — clearly state that financial goods are only means to human functioning. Thus, the vigorous and detailed critique of our values that the Stoics and Epicureans attempted will need to be heard today again (502).

It may be important in pursuing this critique to distinguish the psychology of moneymaking from that of power-seeking. Recall that both Adam Smith and Samuel Johnson have argued, in different ways, that the person who is occupied in making money is a relatively innocuous character whose virtues will include frugality and self-discipline, and will not be likely to be given to acts of fanatical hatred or brutality. A person like that may also do good for society as a whole (502n17).

These comments can be generalized and formulated in terms of philosophers' historical role within their societies. From Socrates on, philosophers' views of virtue were enacted on a criticism of society's values, such as pleasure, wealth, and power or honor. Consider Baruch Spinoza who is exemplary here:

"Most things which present themselves in life and which, to judge from their actions, men think to be the highest good, may be reduced to these three: wealth, honor, and sensual pleasure. The mind is so distracted by these three that it cannot give the slightest thought to any other good." (Spinoza 1985: 7)

Thus, Spinoza begins his *Treatise on the Emendation of the Intellect* with the remarkable sentence, "after experience has taught me that all things which regularly occur in everyday life are empty and futile...I resolved at last to try to find out whether there was anything that would be the true good...." (8) Spinoza introduces the driving thought of his philosophy by describing the fundamental conflict between the values of philosophy and those of society.

Unless a criticism of these latter values, especially those which unnecessarily emphasize hierarchical differences, as well as a critique of limitless wealth-maximizing and power-seeking are undertaken, we will attend to the distant poor only sporadically. This means that once again, philosophy is called in contemporary societies to perform its timeless job.

4. Conclusion

Both cosmopolitanism and indiscriminate loves of humanity are visions that are hard to implement because they seem to go against the grain of human psychology. The latter ideal has been also criticized as harmful. Problematic as both these ideals are, either cosmopolitanism or an indiscriminate love of humanity seems to be necessary, yet insufficient, for actually combating world poverty. A critique of limitless wealth-maximizing and power-seeking is necessary in order to enable a shift of values and an ensuing change in actual social possibilities. This is so because in states in which everything is bought by money and power, it is understandable that regular parents (in contradistinction to celibate, yet often poor, monks, either Christian or Buddhist or Schopenhauerian deniers of the will to live), would find it hard to deprive their children of a penny in order to help the distant poor. Yet, this critique is rarely undertaken head on by philosophers in capitalist countries. These are some of the factors, I suggest, that contribute to the bad faith with which we generally address the issue of the global poor.

References

Abbarno, G. John. "Ethical Approaches to Poverty." In J. Yan and D. Schrader (eds.), *Creating a Global Dialogue on Value Inquiry*. Lewiston: Mellen Press, 2009, 85–96.

---. "Empathy as an Objective Value." In S. H. Lee (ed.), *Inquiries into Values*. Lewiston: Mellen Press, 1988, 161–171.

Amir, Lydia B. "The Role of Impersonal Love in Everyday Life." In H. Herrestad, A. Holt and H. Sware (eds.), *Philosophy in Society*. Oslo: Unipub, 2002, 217–242.

---. "The Affective Aspect of Wisdom: Some Conceptions of Love of Humanity and their Use in Philosophical Practice." *Practical Philosophy*, 7/1 (2004): 14–25.

---. "Que Podemos Aprender de la Filosofia Helenista?" ("What Can We Learn from Hellenistic Philosophy?"). *Sophia: Revista de Filosofia*, 5 (2009): 81–89. Much longer English version in www.revistasophia.com, 1–32.

---. "The Value of Spinoza's Ethics in a Changing World." *Journal of Axiology and Ethics*, 1 (2010): 301–320.

---. "Spinoza's Ethics in Global Management." *The Journal of Global Studies*, 4/1 (2012): 123–138.

---. *Humor and the Good Life in Modern Philosophy: Shaftesbury, Hamann, Kierkegaard*. Albany, NY: SUNY Press, 2014.

---. "Philosophic Humor for Women (and Men)." In P. Raabe and L. de Paula (eds.), *Women in Philosophical Counseling: The Anima of Thought into Action*. Lanham, MD: Lexington Books, Rowman & Littlefield (forthcoming).

Aquinas, Thomas. *Summa Theologica: Basic Writings of St. Thomas Aquinas*. New York, NY: Random House, 1945.

---. *On Charity (De Caritate)*, trans. Lottie H. Kendzierski. Milwaukee, WI: Marquette University Press, 1960.

Aristotle. *The Rhetoric of Aristotle*, edited by John Edwin Sandys, commentary by Edward Meredith Cope. Hildesheim: G. Olms, 1970.

Arnim, von, J. *Stoicorum Veterum Fragmenta*. 4 vols. Leipzig: Teubner, 1905–1924.

Augustine, St. *On Christian Doctrine*, trans. D. W. Robertson Jr. Indianapolis, IN: Bobbs-Merill, 1958.

Beck, Ulrich. *Cosmopolitan Vision*. Cambridge: Polity Press, 2006.

Ben-Ze'ev, Aaron. *The Subtlety of Emotions*. Cambridge, MA: MIT Press, 2000.

Bergson, Henri. *The Two Sources of Morality and Religion*. Notre Dame, IN: University of Notre Dame Press, 1977.

Blackwell, Kenneth. *The Spinozistic Ethics of Bertrand Russell*. London and Boston: George Allen and Unwin, 1985.

Boylan, Michael. *Morality and Global Justice: Justifications and Applications*. Boulder, CO: Westview Press, 2011.

Buber, Martin. *I and Thou*, edited and translated by Ronald Gregor Smith, 2nd ed. New York, NY: Charles Scribner's Sons, 1958.

---. *Between Man and Man*. New York, NY: Macmillan, 1967.

Callan, Eamonn. "The Moral Status of Pity." *Canadian Journal of Philosophy*, 18 (1988), 1–12.

Cartwright, David. "Kant, Schopenhauer, and Nietzsche on the Morality of Pity." *Journal of *the History of Ideas*, 45 (1984): 83 - 98.

Chuang Tzu. *The Complete Work of Chuang Tzu*, trans. Burton Watson. New York, NY: Columbia University Press, 1968.

Clark, Candace. *Misery and Company: Sympathy in Everyday Life*. Chicago, IL: University of Chicago Press, 1997.

Cooper, David E. *World Philosophies: An Historical Introduction*. Oxford: Blackwell, 1996.

Crocker, David E. "Functioning and Capability: The Foundations of Nussbaum's and Sen's Development Ethic." *Political Theory* 20 (1992): 584 - 612.

Epstein, Isidore. *Judaism*. Harmondsworth: Penguin, 1959.

Freud, Sigmund. *Three Essays on the Theory of Sexuality*, trans. James Strachey. London: The Alcuin Press, 1949a.

————. *Group Psychology and the Analysis of the Ego*, trans. James Strachey. London: The Hogarth Press, 1949b.

————. *Civilization and its Discontents*, trans. James Strachey. New York, NY: W. W. Norton, 1961.

Held, David. "From Executive to Cosmopolitan Multilateralism." In D. Held and D. Archiburgi (eds.), *Taming Globalization: Frontiers of Governance*. Cambridge: Polity Press, 2003, 160 - 184.

Hobbes, Thomas. *Leviathan, or The Matter, Forme, & Power of a Common-wealth Ecclesiasticall and Civill*, ed. Richard Tuck. Cambridge: Cambridge University Press, 1996.

Hume, David. *A Treatise of Human Nature*. Oxford: Clarendon Press, 1888.

Kant, Immanuel. *Critique of Practical Reason*, trans. Lewis White Beck. Indianapolis, IN: Bobbs-Merril, 1956.

————. *The Metaphysics of Morals*, trans. Mary Gregor. Cambridge: Cambridge University Press, 1996.

Kaplan, Aryeh. *Jewish Meditation: A Practical Guide*. New York, NY: Shoken Books, 1985.

Kierkegaard, Søren. *Works of Love*, trans. Howard V. and Edna H. Hong. London: Collins, 1962.

Kuntz, Paul G. *Bertrand Russell*. Boston, MA: Twayne, 1986.

Kupperman, Joel J. "The Emotions of Altruism, East and West." In J. Marks and R. T. Ames (eds.), *Emotions in Asian Thought: A Dialogue in Comparative Philosophy*. Albany, NY: SUNY Press, 1995, 123 - 138.

Lewis, C. S. *The Four Loves*. London: Collins Fount Paperbacks, 1985.

Long, Anthony A. *Hellenistic Philosophy: Stoics, Epicureans, Sceptics*. Berkeley and Los Angeles, CA: University of California Press, 1974.

Lucretius. *On the Nature of Things*. Translated by Alicia Stalings. London: Penguin Classics Books, 2007.

Luther, Martin. *American Edition of Luther's Works*. Philadelphia, PA: Muhlenberg Press, 1955.

Mandle, Jon. *Global Justice*. Cambridge, UK: Polity Press, 2006.

Monroe, C. R. *World Religions: An Introduction*. New York, NY: Prometheus Books, 1995.
Mo Tzu. *Basic Writings*, trans. Burton Watson. New York, NY: Columbia University Press, 1963.
Nussbaum, Martha C. *The Therapy of Desire*. Princeton, NJ: Princeton University Press, 1994.
———. *Upheavals of Thought: A Theory of the Emotions*. Cambridge: Cambridge University Press, 2001.
———. "Patriotism and Cosmopolitanism." In J. Cohen (ed.), *For Love of Country: The New Democracy Forum on the Limits of Patriotism*. Boston, MA: Beacon Press, 2nd ed., 2002, 3-17.
Nygren, Anders. *Agape and Eros*, trans. Philip S. Watson. Chicago, IL: University of Chicago Press, 1982.
Outka, Gene. *Agape: An Ethical Analysis*. New Haven, Conn: Yale University Press, 1972.
Pei, Y. P. *Motse: The Neglected Rival of Confucius*. London: Arthur Probsthain, 1934.
Plato. "Phaedo." In *The Portable Plato*. New York, NY: The Viking Press, 1948.
Plutarch. *Moralia*. Translated by Frank Cole Babitt. 15 volumes. Loeb Classical Library. Cambridge, MA: Harvard University Press.
Pogge, Thomas, W. "Cosmopolitanism and Sovereignty." *Ethics*, 103/1 (1992), 48-75.
———. *World Poverty and Human Rights*. Cambridge, UK: Polity Press, 2002.
———. "The First United Nations Millennium Development Goal: A Cause for Celebration?" *Journal of Human Development* 5/3 (2004): 377-397.
Popper, Karl R. *The Open Society and Its Enemies*, Vol. 2: *The High Tide of Prophecy: Hegel, Marx, and the Aftermath*. London: Routledge, 1962.
Portmann, John. *When Bad Things Happen to Other People*. New York and London: Routledge, 2000.
Pseudo-Plato. *Axiochus*. Translated by Jackson P. Hershbell. Michigan, MI: Scholars Press, 1981.
Rawls, John. *A Theory of Justice*. Cambridge, MA: Harvard University Press, 1971.
———. *The Laws of People*. Cambridge, MA: Harvard University Press, 1999.
Robbins, Bruce. "Introduction Part I: Actually Existing Cosmopolitanism." In P. Cheah and B. Robbins (eds.), *Thinking and Feeling beyond the Nation*. Minneapolis and London: University of Minnesota Press, 1998, 1-19.
Rougemont de, Denis. *Les Mythes de l'Amour*. Paris, Albin Michel: 1996.
Rousseau, Jean-Jacques. *Emile*, translated by A. Bloom. New York, NY: Basic Books, 1979.
Russell, Bertrand. "A Free Man's Worship." In *Mysticism and Logic*. London: Allen and Unwin, 1918), 47-57.
———. *The Conquest of Happiness*. London: Allen & Unwin, 1930.
———. *Portraits from Memory*. London and New York: Routledge, 1956.
———. "What I Believe." In *Why I Am Not a Christian and Other Essays on Religion and Related Subjects*, ed. Paul Edwards. New York, NY: Simon and Schuster, 1957, 50-56.
———. *Autobiography*. London: Unwin Paperbacks, 1967.

Santayana, George. *Dialogues in Limbo*. New York, NY: Scribner's, 1925.

————. *Dominations and Powers: Reflections on Liberty, Society, and Government*. New York, NY: Charles Scribner's Sons, 1954.

————. "Friendship." In *The Birth of Reason and Other Essays*, ed. Daniel Cory. New York, NY: Columbia University Press, 1968.

Schopenhauer, Arthur. *On the Basis of Morality*. Indianapollis: Bobbs-Merrill, 1965.

————. *The World as Will and Representation*, trans. E. F. J. Payne. New York, NY: Dover Publications, 1969.

Sen, Amartya. "Equality of What?" In A. Sen (ed.), *Choice, Welfare, and Measurement*. Oxford: Oxford University Press, 1982, 353 – 369.

————. *Commodities and Capabilities*. Amsterdam: North-Holland, 1985.

Singer, Irving. *The Nature of Love*, 3 vols., vol. 1: *Plato to Luther*; vol. 2: *Courtly and Romantic*, vol. 3: *The Modern World*. Chicago, IL: The University of Chicago Press, 1984 – 1987.

————. *The Pursuit of Love*. Baltimore and London: John Hopkins University Press, 1994.

Singer, Peter. "Famine, Affluence and Morality." *Philosophy and Public Affairs* 1 (1972): 229 – 243.

Smith, Adam. *The Theory of Moral Sentiments*. Oxford: Clarendon Press, 1976.

Spinoza, Baruch. *The Collected Works of Spinoza*, vol. 1, edited and translated by E. Curley. Princeton, NJ: Princeton University Press, 1985.

Turner, Bryan S. "Cosmopolitan Virtue, Globalization and Patriotism." *Theory, Culture and Society*, 19/1 – 2 (2002): 45 – 63.

UDHR (*Universal Declaration of Human Rights*). In *Twenty-Four Human Rights Documents*. New York: Columbia University Center for the Study of Human Rights, 1992.

Vertovec, Steven and Robin Cohen. "Introduction: Conceiving Cosmopolitanism." In S. Vertovec and R. Cohen (eds.), *Conceiving Cosmopolitanism: Theory, Context and Practice*. Oxford: Open University Press, 2002, 1 – 22.

Voronkova, Anastasia. "Are Nationalism and Cosmopolitanism Compatible?" http://www.e-ir.info/2010/11/25/are-nationalism-and-cosmopolitanism-compatible/, Nov 25 2010.

Weil, Simone. *L'Enracinement*. Paris: Gallimard, 1949.

Wispé, Lauren. "The Distinction Between Sympathy and Empathy: To Call Forth a Concept, A Word Is Needed." *Journal of Personality and Social Psychology*, 50/2 (1986): 314 – 321.

Re-thinking Global Justice and Moral Responsibility

G. J. M. Abbarno[*]

Abstract: The paper will address the economic disparity between the poor and the wealthy from a global perspective. I shall not focus on homelessness in this paper but on the larger global plight of some populations and examine the conditions that account for the economic inequality and what, if any, moral duty one has to rectify the injustice among people.

Key words: economic disparity; global perspective; population

反思全球正义与道德责任

G. J. M. Abbarno

摘 要：本文从全球视角论述了穷人和富人之间的经济差距问题。文章不只关注美国本土的穷人，而且以全球的穷人为对象来讨论导致经济不平等的原因，并探索在消除不正义的问题上我们所负有的道德责任。

关键词：经济差距 全球视角 人口

---

[*] G. J. M. Abbarno, Professor of Philosophy at D'Yourille Callege, USA.

The scholarship on poverty is replete with evidence of the economic inequality among people both locally and globally. The condition of homelessness in the United States, for example, indicates the desperate lives of people without employment, shelter, sufficient food, clothing, and health care. This condition has expanded to include the working poor, whose income cannot accommodate the basic needs of their family. So, this should put us in a better position to appreciate the economic disparity between the poor and the wealthy from a global perspective. However, unlike the local homeless issue, millions of impoverished people die each year either, directly or indirectly, as a cause of poverty. I shall not focus on homelessness in this paper but on the larger global plight of some populations and examine the conditions that account for the economic inequality and what, if any, moral duty one has to rectify the injustice among people.

This fundamental question was expressed 42 years ago by Peter Singer's controversial article, "Famine, Affluence and Morality", in which he acknowledges the extreme gap throughout the world between those whose lives are satiated with goods beyond the needs to live a human life and others whose lives are threatened by lack of basically satisfied needs. As he puts it, "There are parts of the world in which people die from malnutrition and lack of food. [Furthermore], that suffering and death from lack of food, shelter and medical care are bad."[①] Most of us familiar with this piece know that Singer invokes the principles of sacrifice, that "if it is in our power to prevent something bad from happening, without sacrificing anything of comparable moral importance, we ought morally do it"[②]. This directs us to prevent comparable bad things but he strengthens this principle by stating we "ought morally prevent bad

---

① Singer, Peter, *Vice and Virtue in Everyday Life*, in Christina Sommers and Fred Sommers (Belmont, CA: Thomson Wadsworth, 2007), p. 368.

② Singer, Peter, *Vice and Virtue in Everyday Life*, in Christina Sommers and Fred Sommers (Belmont, CA: Thomson Wadsworth, 2007), p. 369.

things without sacrificing anything morally significant"①. So, people of developed nations are in a position to alleviate the suffering in the world, and ought to bring about a greater balance of happiness over misery. The critics about that demonstrate the unrealistic expectations this utilitarian framework strikes a balance socio-economically. Despite critics, Singer's emphasis on justice endures and prompts philosophers to care about this injustice and rectify it. In the following, after assessing some of the global agents of economic disparity, I propose a new social contract that would improve the just standing of underdeveloped and developing countries' community. In the argument, the countries referred to are discussed within a collective framework. So, the interactions between institutions and them are considered at a collective level, not as individual citizens that comprise them. Although citizens are affected by the failed government practices, in the majority of instances, their interests are decided upon at the national level. This is due to the policies and practices proposed and designed to meet needs the underdeveloped country leaders prioritize. These proposals for financial assistance are for the assumed benefits of the respective countries which citizens either reject or may not know about.

Before going further, it is important to give a profile of facts that reflect the severity of need among people in poor countries. This issue is in the numbers that would give us pause to why priorities of poverty eradication aren't persuasive. Nearly one-sixth of all humans live below $1/day. Persons need only $560 annually to count as nonpoor in the United States, or $140 annually in a typical poor country. ②Thomas Pogge points out that severe poverty has grave consequences: some 850 million human beings lack access to safe water, and 1,037 million lack basic sanitation (UNDP 2005, 24, 44,

---

① Singer, Peter, *Vice and Virtue in Everyday Life*, in Christina Sommers and Fred Sommers (Belmont, CA: Thomson Wadsworth, 2007), p. 369.
② Pogge, Thomas, "Priorities of Global Justice," *Metaphilosophy* 32, No. 1 - 2 (January 2001): 712.

49), more than 2,000 million lack access to essential drugs, 1,000 million are without adequate shelter, and 2,000 million without electricity (UNDP 1998, 49)①. One hundred seventy-nine million children under 18 are involved in the worst forms of child labor including hazardous work in agriculture, construction, textile, or carpet production as well as "slavery, trafficking, debt bondage, and other forms of forced labor, forced recruitment of children for use in armed conflict, prostitution, pornography, and illicit activities"②. (ILO 2002, 9, 11, 18) "Roughly, one third of all human deaths, some 50,000 daily, are due to poverty-related causes and thus avoidable insofar as poverty is avoidable."③ The deaths resulting from violence of volatile countries over the past 15 years, among them Iraq, Bosnia, Kosovo, Somalia, and Rwanda, pale by comparison to deaths caused by starvation or other deaths related to poverty: 300 million! Something has gone terribly wrong if the original aim of some major global institutions was to improve the socioeconomic life of people across the world. The World Trade Organization (WTO), the International Monetary Fund (IMF), and the World Bank, conceived as agents to invigorate trade between all members, wealthy and poor alike, consequently benefit the wealthy nations.

There are 147 developing countries as members in the WTO and because of their numbers their trade prospects are thought to increase and raise their economic value as a result. These are diverse groups with a common interest, but their means to attain this is as diverse as those among wealthy nations. However, it is the expanded and less visible role of the World Bank and the

---

① Pogge, Thomas, "Priorities of Global Justice," *Metaphilosophy* 32, No. 1-2 (January 2001): 712.
② Pogge, Thomas, "Priorities of Global Justice," *Metaphilosophy* 32, No. 1-2 (January 2001): 712.
③ Pogge, Thomas, "Priorities of Global Justice," *Metaphilosophy* 32, No. 1-2 (January 2001): 713.

IMF's lender role to relieve debts of struggling economies that, at the same time, stymies the enrichment among underdeveloped countries. The result of this practice over 50 years has made it more difficult for these countries to work their way out of poverty. The mechanism of providing financial relief to desperate countries through loans is not focused on the human needs of the citizens of those countries but the larger view of the economic expansion and benefits that may accrue from this.

There are in general, three levels of explanation for how institutions that set out to diminish poverty actually exacerbate it. There well may be others but these will suffice for our purposes. The first is individual leaders of corrupt governments. They orchestrate proposals for loans and assistance that reap personal rewards rather than distributing to their citizens. For example, Uganda's Idi Amin and Mugabe of Zimbabwe. In 1999, after a $200 million loan, Mugabe used his army and ties to rebels to protect diamond mines from Ugandan rebels. Punitive measures were shortsighted requiring him to undo the more progressive measure he instituted in his country. Of course, the more common cause of impoverishment in the third world nations was by "borrowing hard currency that was unnecessary, destined for white elephant projects for arms expenditures and importing luxury goods. The banks were guilty of loan pushing; the IMF and World Bank ignored the moral implications of the recipient of the loan"[1]. "The external debt of the world's developing countries could never be paid at higher rates and the IMF in its early function, enforced repayment to Northern banks ... in exchange the IMF gains power over those countries to impose austere macroeconomic policies."[2] The payment of these outstanding debts, with loans for up to 40 years, weighs like

---

[1] Bond, Patrick, *Against Global Apartheid* (Cape Town, South Africa: University of Cape Town Press, 2003), p. 21.

[2] Bond, Patrick, *Against Global Apartheid* (Cape Town, South Africa: University of Cape Town Press, 2003), p. 21.

Sisyphus' struggle. Such reality is generally masked by the optimistic chorus of free trade promoted by the WTO. However, this has brought about socioeconomic injustice. The former director of the WTO exclaimed "the world was once polarized by the Cold War; it is now becoming polarized between wealth and the lack of opportunity"①.

Second, there are political considerations for which countries receive loans from the IMF. The United States has significant weight in determining this since it holds more votes than other member countries. The number of votes permitted is weighted by the contribution of members; the USA gives the most and has greater influence, and despite recent decline remains persuasive.②For example, "the World Bank refused loans to Allende's Chile, Vietnam and Sandinista Nicaragua."③ At the inception of the IMF many members supported a quicker response to countries in financial crisis but this changed at the persuasion of the U.S. to invoke conditionality.

In the early 1980s, in the course of a debt crisis in developing countries triggered by U.S. Federal Reserve interest policies, conditionality took a distinctive form, which pervaded the developing world and has persisted ever since. The IMF and the World Bank imposed "structural adjustment" conditions including fiscal austerity (with consequent reduction of social expenditures), privatization, and liberalization of foreign trade and finance-large scale shifts meant to open a country to what President Reagan described at their 1983 joint meeting, as the magic of the marketplace.④

This appears to work well for developed countries at the expense of underdeveloped and developing countries.

At first glance it may seem that the growth in development of export goods

---

① Moore, Michael, *The Guardian*, 1999, p. 21.
② Richard W. Miller, *Globalizing Justice* (New York: Oxford University Press, 2010).
③ Richard W. Miller, *Globalizing Justice* (New York: Oxford University Press, 2010), p. 136.
④ Richard W. Miller, *Globalizing Justice* (New York: Oxford University Press, 2010), p. 137.

such as coffee, cotton, sugar, and lumber would be beneficial to the exporting country, since it brings in revenue. In fact, it represents a type of exploitation called *unequal exchange*. A country that exports raw or unprocessed materials may gain currency for their sale, but they lose it if they import processed goods. The reason is that processed goods—goods that require additional labor—are more costly. Thus a country that exports lumber but does not have the capacity to process it must then re-import it in the form of finished lumber products, at a cost that is greater than the price it received for the raw product. The country that processes the materials gets added revenue contributed by its laborers. [1]

The focus on the capital flow of goods and services is a crucial feature of globalization. As the trade restrictions were lowered, capital value rather than social humanitarian needs was the mainstay of the free market policy. According to some sources "the political process of this program nearly erased social justice as a concern of international regimes, where they exist, and of the absence of mechanisms of global governance, can go unchecked as ever before"[2]. This increase of financial transactions between countries illustrates this moving from $15 million in 1973 to $1.8 trillion in 1998.[3] Again, the focus of this growth in international trade has little to do with production of goods and services. However well-intended the financial forces to improve the impoverished countries, this improvement has been redirected from human interests. The result is greater economic inequality pushing farther away from the grasp of those most in need, the humanitarian assistance that would provide opportunities for developing human capabilities. Nagel notes that aid "should be directed at the impoverished purely in virtue of their humanity and not in virtue of their special

---

[1] Robbins, Richard, *Global Problems and the Culture of Capitalism* (Boston: Pearson Allyn and Bacon press, 1999), p. 95.
[2] De Vita, Alvaro, "Inequality and Poverty in Global perspective," in Thomas Pogge *Freedom from Poverty Is a Human Right* (New York: Oxford University Press, 2007), p. 114.
[3] Oxfam, 1999, 1.

relation to the donor. Everyone at the bottom deserves help"①.

Third, structural adjustments are notorious for increasing the level of poverty and extending its recovery. In 1998, there were fifty-two countries subject to IMF structural adjustment conditions. "The average Latin America country was subject to six IMF or World Bank adjustment programs in the course of the 1980s while sub-Saharan African countries averaged seven."②

Throughout the Third World there is a pervasive hopelessness about their poverty. There is at first subtle then increasingly recognized control of the internal life of underdeveloped countries by either marketing goods that challenge cultural values or altering landscapes that displace populations and vegetation by constructing dams. Continual need for loans enforces a structural adjustment plan on the indebted country. This removes much of their choice of how to allocate funds locally before they can make their payments to the Bank. Yet, this plan implicitly leads to more loans since the government cannot meet their social demands for education and health, among other things. It is like being in debtor's prison. The cycle cannot be broken as it is set up. Reactions are heard around the globe, criticizing the tactics of the International Monetary Fund, World Bank, and the World Trade Organization. Their policies drive more people into a quality of life without much hope and lacking any respect for autonomy, at least by market demands.

Structural Adjustment has been the most far-flung coordinated project of large-scale policy transformation in human history. It has changed the contract between government and citizens in developing countries from a state commitment to manage development to a state commitment to give the lead to global private enterprise. The role of international trade-capital flow in setting

---

① Nagel, Thomas, "The Problem of Global Justice," *Philosophy and Public Affairs* 33, No. 2 (2005): 117.
② Nagel, Thomas, "The Problem of Global Justice," *Philosophy and Public Affairs* 33, No. 2 (2005): 138.

the pace and shape of economic change has been substantially enhanced. While economic displacement has created extensive needs for help, social expenditures as a proportion of GDP have normally been reduced, often sharply. ①

Africa continues to be stymied by dependence which spirals many of its countries into debt and marginalized from world trade. Many countries in Africa today rely on a narrow range of agricultural and mineral products as they did in the past which leads to decreased export income. So, Africa faces a losing struggle to improve exports to Europe and the United States.

These three levels that explain the deep global poverty wrought by lopsided policies entail an injustice that diminishes humanity. The human toll exacted from weaker economic countries is morally reprehensible. Attribution of moral blame for this condition can be traced to the policies internal to the central global agents, IMF, WTO, and World Bank, but shared by those developing countries that entered into an agreement. For within each their mission and goals are directed to enact policies and procedures that emphasize a free flow of capital that rewards markets, for the most part, that are already successful. The underdeveloped/developing countries compromised their autonomy for what was an opportunity for growth. The latter merely rendering a re-direction of their resources from local needs such as infrastructure, education, and health, to accept loans with conditions that were apart from their own priorities and that served the global agents more than themselves. Although, both parties share the responsibility for not only failing to rectify poverty but to exacerbate it, casting many more people into the throes of severe poverty. Yet, if responsibility entails knowledge, these powerful organizations should shoulder most of the burden since they were in a position to know the greater implications and impact on weaker economic countries.

By insisting that national leaders place the interests of international financial

---

① Miller, R., *Globalizing*, p. 139.

investors above their own citizens, the IMF and the World Bank have short circuited the accountability at the heart of self-governance, thereby corrupting the democratic process. The subordination of social needs to the consensus of financial markets has, in turn, made it more difficult for national governments to ensure that their people receive food, health care, and education—basic rights as defined by the Universal Declaration of Human Rights.[1]

What direction can be taken? As fellow human beings, we should find these conditions deplorable and instill duty in us to eradicate humiliating poverty. "Our failure to make a serious effort toward poverty reduction may constitute not merely a lack of beneficence, but our active impoverishing, starving, and killing millions of innocent people by economic means."[2] Some philosophers, such as Nancy Fraser, calls for a politics of recognition, one that focuses on these sorts of injustices discussed above that disrespect other peoples. She aims for a politic of affirmation. To do so there must be a renegotiation of agreements and to start, the debts ought to be forgiven. It is believed that countries deep in debt, rather than pay loans, can reprioritize their cultural infrastructure and invest in education and health policies for their citizens. But this would leave the already defaulted loans to be paid by other countries that may be making progress and weaken their efforts for overall success. Establish a new social contract that stipulates criteria of successful World Organizations and require a five-year review that includes one index: Are governments making progress? The contract can also include some provisions that frame the role of multinationals who benefit by the reduced taxes and inexpensive labor, perhaps by demonstrating community responsibility by providing education for adults and children. If the concern is global justice, companies that benefit by

---

[1] "How the International Monetary Fund and the World Bank Undermine Democracy and Erode Human Rights." In *Global Exchange*, 2001.
[2] Pogge, T. "Priorities," p. 714.

agreements with underdeveloped countries, companies such as Monsanto, DuPont, Exxon-Mobil, and others, can be instrumental in this effort by providing scholarships for local citizens to study abroad with the condition that they return and contribute to their society's well-being.

The above evaluation conducted by a World Organization functioning as an advocate for global justice between countries could identify abuses of the contract. Any evidence of abuse such that an agreement could worsen than improve quality of life in the recipient nation, channels of recourse should be established. An international court of appeal at The Hague should be the adjudicator, addressing actual rights violations in these agreements. Responsibility for violations can be in the form of reparation to consider repairs or compensation for harms inflicted on weaker and lesser informed nations. Failure to recognize the duty of reparation would be failure to acknowledge equal values of their citizens' lives.

The role of philosophy in public life is without agreement. Peter Singer's encouragement to "put into practice what moral philosophers are so willing to propose as valued ends" has not been followed to the extent that he argued. ①However, it is a worthy ideal of a discipline that focuses on the meaning of "justice" "happiness" and "goodness" among other things to assume an advisory role to analyze, clarify, and underwrite social contracts, preferably through a global body (perhaps the United Nations). Terms of contracts will include a criterion of short-term success within manageable timeframes for poor countries. These terms will also assess a social benefit against any economic shortfalls. Renewable terms would be available with expectations that are within their revised goals. The long-range view of contracts is to sustain steady growth and appreciation of local goods and examine how these local goods are expanded into the global context. Central to this new agreement is

---

① Singer, P. *Vice*, p. 374.

the value to respect freedom of the country's local development and not insert conditions that would compromise this central value. For a contract that preempts or provides a large measure of freedom to be undercut allows this slippery slope of sacrificing more social goods on the assumption that they can achieve a standard of good defined by the wealthier countries. Indeed, this only diminishes the moral integrity and, therefore, the identity of the nations involved. As Rousseau reminds us, "such a compromise is incompatible with man's nature: for to take away all freedom from his will is to take away all morality from his actions and strongly remove any hope of living his notion of the 'good life.'"[①]

[①] Rousseau, J. J. *The Social Contract* (New York: Penguin Press, 1997), p. 15.

On Values of Contemporary China

Jiang Chang*

Abstract: There are three forms of Chinese values that dominate the society in Chinese history: feudal values, the values of despotism and socialist values. Socialist values can be divided into the traditional socialist values and values of socialism with Chinese characteristics. Values of socialism with Chinese characteristics are the contemporary Chinese values. Contemporary Chinese values take national prosperity and revitalization, particularly people's happiness as the ultimate goal. Meanwhile they take prosperity, democracy, civilization, harmony, freedom, equality, justice, rule of law, patriotism, dedication, integrity, as well as kindness as the core values. What's more, under the leadership of the Communist Party, they advocate people's dominant position, releasing and developing social productive forces, promoting the reform and opening up, safeguarding social fairness and justice, propelling common prosperity, and promoting social harmony and peaceful development and taking them as the basic principles of value. Compared with traditional Chinese values and modern Western values, the values of contemporary China is obviously featured with putting people first, equal, community-oriented or collective and moral.

---

* Jiang Chang, "Chang Jiang" Scholar by Ministry of Education, Professor at IAHS, Hubei University.

Key words: contemporary Chinese values; feudalistic values; despotism values; modern capitalist values

论当代中国价值观

江 畅

摘 要：在中国历史上占主导地位的中国价值观主要有三种形态：封建主义价值观，专制主义价值观，社会主义价值观。社会主义价值观又有传统社会主义价值观与中国特色社会主义价值的区别。中国特色社会主义价值观是当代中国价值观。当代中国价值观以国家富强、民族振兴特别是人民幸福为终极价值目标，以富强、民主、文明、和谐、自由、平等、公正、法治、爱国、敬业、诚信、友善为核心价值理念，以人民主体地位、解放和发展社会生产力、推进改革开放、维护社会公平正义、走共同富裕道路、促进社会和谐、和平发展、共产党的领导为基本价值原则。与传统中国价值观、现代西方价值观相比较，当代中国价值观具有人民性、平等性、社群性或集体性和道德性等明显特点。

关键词：当代中国价值观 封建主义价值观 专制主义价值观 现代资本主义价值观

Contemporary Chinese values are Chinese national values since China's reform and opening up has been implemented. Relative to traditional Chinese values, they are different from the values in planned economy before the implementation of reform and opening up. The eighteenth Congress of the Communist Party of China which was held in 2012 made a clear definition of the core of contemporary Chinese values (namely socialist core values) for the first time, and required to cultivate and implement the socialist core values throughout the country. Although the core values of socialism society have not yet been widely recognized, the Chinese party and government are taking political measures to cultivate and practice it. Thus, it's reasonable to put the socialist core values as the core values of contemporary China. Here, I'll give a brief introduction on the development and core content of the contemporary Chinese values as well as some features that differ from the traditional Chinese values and modern Western values.

1. The Evolution of Chinese Values from Tradition to the Present Day

After entering civilization, Chinese began to form values of their own nation and country. In the 5000-year history, the Chinese values have experienced great vicissitudes, and inherited some spirits and content. The evolution of Chinese values is directly linked to the country's political condition. In general, in national unity, there is a dominant national value; while the nation is in disruption or turmoil, the values are various. Throughout its history, China has experienced five stages of values, among which three are relatively stable and unite and two are comparatively tense and turbulent. While the latter are often pregnant with the revolutions of value and new age.

Xia Dynasty (21 B. C.—16 B. C.) put an end to the war of "Five Emperors" period and preliminarily established a unite nation. From Xia Dynasty (21 B. C.—16 B. C.) to Western Zhou Dynasty, the earliest form of Chinese values —patriarchal feudalism had been established. This is the first unified form of Chinese values. After "Three Sovereigns and Five Emperors", Xia Dynasty (21 B. C. —16 B. C.) established a multi-tribal alliance country, or in other words, a complex chiefdom nation. In this stage, primitive tribal abdication system was ended and the hereditary system was set up. Later, this federated social structure was replaced by enfeoffment system. It is feudal system that leads the dukes to set up separatist rule during the Spring and Autumn

Period (770 B. C.—221 B. C.). During this period, the nation's value was featured by the pursuit of safeguarding the nation's long-term stability. Since god worship and ancestor worship is combined, the son of heaven and god is legitimated, and so is the government. In the Xia (21 B. C.—16 B. C.), Shang (1600 B. C.—1046 B. C) and Zhou (11 B. C.—256 B. C) Dynasties, only the emperor had access to the heaven worship. The heaven worship was always with the ancestor worship, and this is what we called "enshrining as foils to heaven". In Zhou Dynasty, this concept developed into "heaven worship, respecting ancestors and protecting people", which converted the ancestor worship into politics and morality one, and thus the external god worship was gradually internalized and moralized.

In Eastern Zhou Dynasty (770 B. C—476 B. C.), dukes set up separationist rule, the countries fell into pieces, and this is so-called the Spring and Autumn Period (770 B. C. —221 B. C). During this period, there was no unified social value. However Confucianism, Taoism, Mohist, Legalism and other philosophers emerged. And it was in this period that a hundred schools of thought contended, and Confucianism was formed. Represented by Confucius and Mencius, Confucian inherited the idea of "heaven worship, respecting ancestors and protecting people" of the Zhou Dynasty and other concepts, and formed a value system. This system, based on the relations between virtue, kinship, patriarchy and ethics, followed the principle of practice and was featured by the good over truth so as to achieve benevolent. Confucianism in Han Dynasty (202 B. C. —220 A. D.) and Neo-Confucianism of the Song (960 A. D. —1297 A. D.) and Ming Dynasty (1368 A. D. —1644 A. D.) further developed the Pre-Qin Confucianism. Thus the Pre-Qin Confucianism had gradually been theorized, systematized. Meanwhile it also differed from the Confucianism in Han, Song and Ming Dynasties in some certain problems. The Confucianism in Han Dynasty and Neo-Confucianism of the Song and Ming Dynasties deviate from the original Pre-Qin Confucianism. However, the traditional Chinese Confucian thoughts share a same basic orientation: "Heaven should serve for the humane value. Dealing the relationship between nature and man, humanity, and heaven, we should take humanity as the main body. Heaven should serve for humanity and virtues. We should uplift human's status and value; one's personality should serve for the spirit. The pursuit of noble personality and spiritual transcendence requires cultivation and practice as well as moral self-discipline, and advocate people's morality; benefit should conform to the social value. We should emphasize on individual's responsibility and obligation to society, pay attention to human relations, attach great importance to virtues and benevolent governance.

After unifying China in 221 B. C., the first emperor of Qin carried out the policies of "rejecting the other schools of thought and respecting only Confucianism". Therefore the second unified Chinese values were formed, and that is the patriarchal despotism. These values took "three principles and five virtues" ("three principles" are namely "ruler guiding subject, father guiding son, and husband guiding wife"; "five virtues" are "benevolence, righteousness, politeness, intelligence and trust") as the core content. During 2000-year authoritarian, although experiencing splitting, the basic despotism in China was not affected. During this time, China was also influenced by external values. The greatest impact came from India Buddhism. After India Buddhism was introduced into China, "three religions into the same flow" (the Confucianism, the Buddhism and Daoism) came into being. But generally speaking, Chinese Confucianism was still the dominant ideology in the era of despotism, and also the main theoretical basis for China's despotism.

Since the Opium War, China became a semi-colonial and semi-feudal nation, with traditional values suffering constant attacks. The traditional values were not eventually replaced until the establishment of the People's Republic of China. A lot of Chinese values sprang up in just 100 years. Differing from the Spring and Autumn Period, this diversity and complexity were not due to the contention among the domestic values, but the debate among different western values were accepted by people. During this period, liberalism, republicanism, Marxism (scientific socialism), Soviet socialism, anarchism and other values poured into China. Meanwhile Chinese traditional values were still working in social life, and some thinkers and politicians still sticked to these values. After the Revolution of 1911, Nationalists promoted Sun Yat-sen's Three People's Principles (Nationalism, Democracy, the people's livelihood), which were a Chinese capitalist values, or in other words, values of social democracy. The Communist Party of China was born to believe in Marxist values which were Sovietized. Later, localized Marxism values represented by Mao Zedong Thought were formed. Since 1930s, democratic values, represented by Sun Yat-sen (although changed a lot in the reign of Chiang Kai-shek), and the Marxist values, represented by Mao Zedong, became two dominant values in their different scopes. While, traditional Chinese values are still popular in the public's daily life.

After the founding of the People's Republic of China, democratic values were completely abandoned. Socialism (Marxism) was established as dominant values. Then the third unified form of Chinese values —socialist values, from then on came into being. In so far sixty years, the socialist values experienced two stages. The first period was before "the Great Cultural Revolution" when socialist values on the basis of planned economy were dominating. Socialist values in this period were also called traditional socialism. The second period started from the reform and opening. During this period, the socialism on the basis of market economy, the values of socialism with Chinese characteristics' was dominating. The main content of traditional socialism is Mao Zedong Thought, while the socialism with Chinese characteristics takes Deng Xiaoping Theory as the core content. Both two values advocate people being the masters of the country, adhering to the socialist road and socialist system, as well as the leadership of the Communist Party, and taking Marxism as the guiding thought. Sharing a same standing point and same opinion and other aspects of the position and views, the two values still have differences in the understanding towards socialism. Traditional socialism takes enhancing dictatorship of the proletariat and preventing the restoration of capitalism as the purpose and main task, so it takes class struggle as the value orientation and guiding principles. This value not only affirms the necessity of economic development, but also insists on "politics in command". Regardless of the real situation and the scientific laws, it is anxious for success, launching "Great Leap Forward", "running into communist". Adhering to these values resulted in constant political campaigns, and eventually Led to the ten-year disaster of "the Great Cultural Revolution". While in the value of socialism with Chinese characteristics, socialism is regarded as the common prosperity of the whole society. Therefore, it takes economic construction as the central task, encourages a part of people to become rich first then brings along the poor. Later it was further interpreted as socialist modernization and rejuvenation of the Chinese nation. So it advocated a comprehensive "five in one" construction, namely economic, political, cultural, social, ecological construction. After recalling the painful experience of bias and serious results in the traditional socialist values, values of socialism with Chinese characteristics are formed and established. Values of socialism with Chinese characteristics are strongly advocated by Chinese communist party and government.

2. The Core Content of the Contemporary Chinese Values

Values of contemporary China are socialist values with Chinese characteristics, of which the core contents are socialist core values. Like other core values of social values, socialist core values can be divided into three aspects: the ultimate value goals, key value ideas and basic value principles.

The ultimate value goal of values of contemporary China is the political report of the 18th CCP's "great rejuvenation of the Chinese nation". Xi Jinping, the General Secretary of CPC Central Committee summed it up as "China Dream" which included national prosperity, national rejuvenation and people happiness.

He pointed out that the 80 years witnessed our national liberation, national prosperity and people's happiness with their unremitting hard work. Sixth Plenary Session of the Sixteenth CPC would take harmonious society as an important guarantee of our national prosperity, national rejuvenation as well as people's happiness. Seen in this light, national liberation and rejuvenation, national prosperity as well as people's happiness are the ultimate value goals of the socialist revolution, building and reform which are led by Communist Party of China and its people. In these three goals, people's happiness has more profound meanings because the target of national liberation and revitalization is to make Chinese people live a better life, and play a role of the master of their country. From this point, people's happiness is the ultimate goal of socialism with Chinese characteristics. This goal is also in line with and targeting at the communism which was put forward by Marx. According to Marx, communism society is a society that based on the principle of full and free development of each individual. Full and free development is the basic meaning of happiness. When everyone gets access to the full and free development, the whole society has entered into an ideal state of universal happiness. Under the present conditions, our country still cannot fully get this ideal state. But because of this, we have to make it our ultimate goal of building socialism with Chinese characteristics. People's happiness is the happiness of all members of the society, so putting the general happiness as the ultimate value goal of socialism with Chinese characteristics will be embraced and supported by all the Chinese people.

Core values of contemporary Chinese values refer to the "three advocates" that were proposed at the 18th CPC Congress: advocating a prosperous, democratic, civilized and harmonious society; advocating freedom, equality, justice as well as the rule of law; advocating patriotism, dedication, integrity and kindness. The author summarized the core values of socialism with Chinese characteristics into ten words before the 18th CPC Congress, namely: prosperity, harmony, justice, rule of law, democracy, freedom, responsibility, virtue, wisdom, and grace. Obviously, such kind of generalization is not only in line with the core values of the political report of the 18th CPC conference, but the expression of it. The expression of democracy, harmony, freedom, justice, the rule of law is exactly the same. "Prosperity" includes wealth and strong, "justice" includes equality, while "responsibility", "virtue," and some other basic principles contain the value of the "patriotic", "dedication", "integrity" and "kindness". "Civilization" is a concentrated expression of all the values that the author advocates. Although the socialist core values statements from the author are not consistent with the 18th CPC Political Report, they help to deepen our understanding on the socialist core values and ideas of the 18th CPC conference. As for the socialist core values and ideas of the 18th CPC conference, we need more time to deepen the research, making it theoretically more complete and mellow. Among the twelve core values of the 18th CPC Congress proposed, five of which are the cores of the cores. They are freedom, equality, justice, democracy and the rule of law. These five values are generally accepted in the contemporary world, and how to highlight its socialist nature and Chinese characteristics is urgent , so we need to give an answer from the theory and practice.

The 18th CPC Political Report noted: "To win the new victory of socialism with Chinese characteristics under the new historical conditions, we must adhere to the following basic requirements, and make them a common belief of the whole Party and people of all ethnic groups. We must stick to the people's power of subject status and insist on releasing and developing social productive forces, furthering the policy of reform and opening up, maintaining social fairness and justice, pursuing common prosperity while promoting social harmony and peaceful development, as well as adhering to leadership of the Communist Party of China." These eight basic requirements can be regarded as a basic principle of values of contemporary China. According to the latest achievement of Marxism, modernization and popularization as well as the basic contents and ideas of socialist core values, the author will summarize the basic value of socialism with Chinese characteristics into the following ten principles: the principle of Marxism, the principle of socialism, the principle of patriotism, the principle of the leadership of CPC, the principle of the rule of law, the principle of putting people first, the principle of scientific development, the principle of reform and innovation, the principle of fairness and justice as well as the principle of awareness on graces and disgraces. Obviously, such ten basic principles are totally consistent with eight the "basic requirements" of the 18th CPC political report. All of the above basic principles, from the spiritual value to the operational level, together with a more specific value principles constitute an interrelated and mutually supportive system of value principles, which maintain, support and propel the socialism with Chinese characteristics. The socialist economic construction, political construction, cultural construction, social development and ecological civilization construction with Chinese characteristics must adhere to the basic principles of values.

3. Characteristics of Contemporary Chinese Values That Differ from Traditional Chinese Values and Modern Western Values

Modern Western values, accompanied by the rise and development of the market economy in the West, are the values of Western capitalism and are based on the theories of the Enlightenment thinkers. In the early 20th century, it had undergone some changes. Overall, the ultimate goal of Western capitalist values is personal happiness. First, these values advocate that happiness belongs to everyone. The individuals are the subjects of happiness, and they shall be responsible for their own, pursuing and achieving their own happiness. In the process of individual pursuing happiness, society can only provide a peaceful and stable environment, making some rules to prevent people get hurt and ensuring such rules be fully implemented. Society does not have the responsibility for providing personal happiness. However, capitalist society added a new function which intends to provide basic living allowances for the members of the society who cannot support themselves. This happiness is identified by the value targets, of which the content has undergone a process of change. Modern Western mainly regards happiness as benefit; they think people will live a happy live by getting benefits, so they encourage people pursue their benefits. Thus, the modern Western egoism of happiness spread fast. After the 20th century, in order to stimulate economic growth and pursue happiness, people in the West were not only encouraged to pursue their own interests, but to shop and enjoy their life. So consumerism and hedonism were getting popular. There are some changes in core philosophy of Western capitalist values, but not too much. Some core values are still changing. There are ten core values that have been widely recognized in the West, namely: interest, market, technology, environmental protection, responsibility, freedom, equality, justice, democracy, the rule of law. The first five concepts are directly associated with the economic life, and the latter five are the pursuit of political life. Capitalist values also contain a series of principles that reflect its ultimate value goal and core values. The following are the ten basic ones: (1) the principle of giving priority to individual; (2) the principle that the self-interest is human nature; (3) the principle of natural rights; (4) the principle that the private property is inviolable; (5) the principle of acting according to their own wishes; (6) the principle of equal personality, opportunity, rights and obligations; (7) the principle of individual sovereignty; (8) the principles of governing the country by law; (9) the principle of separation and balance of powers; (10) the principle of country's appropriate intervention of the economy and society. Modern Western culture may seem as individualism and liberalism, but its fundamental nature is capitalism. Or specifi-cally speaking, it's the starting point and the destination is personal liberation, freedom and happiness. But such values have been changed in the process of liberation and freedom, and finally they are based on the proliferation of capital. Because capital has penetrated its entire structure and function, putting everything under control. As a result, people get access to personal liberation and freedom from tyranny, but the whole society based on this value is contr-olled by capital. Individuals have been slaved by this kind of slavery force which is the capital. And there is no real liberation, freedom and happiness. Because of this, we cannot simply say that it is individualistic values, but capitalist values.

Compared with traditional Chinese values and modern Western values (including Chinese feudal values and despotism values), the contemporary Chinese values that are under construction have the following salient features.

First, people oriented. This is a prominent feature that contemporary Chinese values differ from traditional values and modern Western values. Chinese traditional values regarded a state and a country as the home of an emperor; member of the society are the subjects of a feudal ruler. Master of the state and society is the dynasty, not the people. Modern Western values are individualism, and it is individual-centered. This value is based on opposition to feudalism, which requires the members of society freed from the shackles of tyranny and the church, so that members of the community become independent individuals. It should be admitted that, after a series of revolutionary movements, Westerners have become masters of society and the state. But this "men" refers to the individuals rather than people as a group. Contemporary Chinese values are different from either of these two. It neither regards the dynasty as the masters of society and the state, nor regards members of society as the masters of society. It gives priority to a collection of individuals and groups of members of the community as the master of a national the society. The supreme power of the state should be given to people rather than the government or any citizen. Therefore, contemporary Chinese values advocate making people the master of the country and the society. It is the value that keeps sovereign in people's hands.

Second, equality. This is a prominent feature that contemporary Chinese values differ from traditional values and modern Western values. Western bourgeois liberty and equality were like twin brothers opposed to the feudal system and the Catholic Church. They opposed tyranny with liberty, used equality fight against the hierarchy, and eventually won. However, there are some inherent contradictions and conflicts between freedom and equality: equality may be sacrificed if we emphasize on freedom, vice versa. In the face of this conflict, the West made a freedom-oriented choice. Therefore, the fundamental value of modern Western orientation is freedom. It gives priority to rights, especially the rights of freedom. The state is subordinate to the rights of individuals, whose sole mission is to protect and expand the rights of citizens. In order to protect the rights and freedoms of individuals, it regards the country as the watchman, the government is seen as limited government, all state and government must be authorized by the citizens, or is not legitimate. In the 1930s, with the emergence of the West Roosevelt's New Deal, Keynesian, and Rawls justice, modern laissez-faire had changed, and it had to some extent noticed social equality. However, the basic liberal values had not changed, and such neoliberal equality that tended to equality had been widely criticized. There are some modern Western political theories with liberalism, the most typical being Rousseau, as well as a large number of utopian socialists, Marx and Engels, and so on. But these western theories have not become mainstream ideology and mainstream values. Overall, the mainstream of modern western values is liberalism. Traditional Chinese society is " patriarchal landlords' authoritarian society", of which the mainstream value is both hierarchy and despotism. However, in traditional Chinese non-mainstream culture, especially among the huge group of farmers, egalitarianism was very popular. Contemporary Chinese value belongs to Marxism and socialism, and the basic value of Marxism and socialism is equality, the pursuit of common prosperity as well as free and comprehensive development of each member of society. Therefore, contemporary Chinese values are on the whole based on equality and justice. Of course, it does not mean that contemporary Chinese value denies freedom, but pays more attention to equality.

Third, the community or collectivity. This feature is more of Chinese characteristics, and differs from modern western values. Modern western values takes the individual members as the ultimate entity of society, and the state and other communities belong to the individuals but not entities. Traditional Chinese values put the state as the ultimate entity; the individual is not a social entity, nor even an independent personality, but belongs to the whole part. Therefore, traditional Chinese values are typical holism. Contemporary Chinese values, while having some characteristics of the traditional values of holism, but unlike traditional holism featured with hierarchy and despotism, they take into account the equal and free collectivism. Therefore the members of society are no longer just a part of the country, but a separate personality and rights of individuals. In this respect, the contemporary Chinese values have been positively influenced by the West, especially when the 18th CPC Congress clearly took the "freedom" and "equality" as the core concept of the basic concept of socialism. It has made meaningful progress in the historical process of evolution.

Fourth, the morality. This is of prominent Chinese characteristic in contemporary Chinese values. There are two basic ways when it comes to the measures and mechanisms of the national and social governance, namely the rule of law and virtue. Traditional Chinese values respects rule of virtue, and the rule of law is subordinate to it. Modern western values are not based on rule of virtues; they take rule of law as the only way of social governance, emphasizing the government and state are neutral on ethics. People's moral life won't be intervened no matter what kind of morality they believe in and follow. Although the rule of law has been taken into the contemporary Chinese values as a basic national policy as well as the core values of socialism promoted by the CPC Political Report. However, in our social life, morality has a strong influence. Therefore, the party and the government implement and advocate communist morality as well as socialist morality. What's more, both the party and state leaders have explicitly asked for "the rule of virtue". Seen from the influence of traditional Chinese culture and values of future, Chinese contemporary values cannot completely take the rule of law as people in the West do, but will pay more attention to the social role of morality on the premise of giving rule of law and rule of virtue equal value. Of course, how to handle the relationship between rule of law and rule of virtue requires further exploration.

图书在版编目(CIP)数据

文化发展论丛.世界卷.2014/强以华主编.—北京:社会科学文献出版社,2015.3
ISBN 978-7-5097-7154-9

Ⅰ.①文… Ⅱ.①强… Ⅲ.①文化发展-世界-文集 Ⅳ.①G11-53
中国版本图书馆 CIP 数据核字(2015)第 037878 号

文化发展论丛·世界卷(2014)

主　　编 / 强以华
副 主 编 / 李家莲

出 版 人 / 谢寿光
项目统筹 / 周　琼
责任编辑 / 张建中　周　琼

出　　版 / 社会科学文献出版社·社会政法分社(010)59367156
　　　　　　地址:北京市北三环中路甲29号院华龙大厦　邮编:100029
　　　　　　网址:www.ssap.com.cn
发　　行 / 市场营销中心(010)59367081　59367090
　　　　　　读者服务中心(010)59367028
印　　装 / 三河市尚艺印装有限公司
规　　格 / 开本:787mm×1092mm　1/16
　　　　　　印张:20.5　字数:298千字
版　　次 / 2015年3月第1版　2015年3月第1次印刷
书　　号 / ISBN 978-7-5097-7154-9
定　　价 / 89.00元

本书如有破损、缺页、装订错误,请与本社读者服务中心联系更换

▲ 版权所有 翻印必究